KENT

A SHELL GUIDE

SHELL GUIDES

edited by JOHN BETJEMAN AND JOHN PIPER

CORNWALL
John Betjeman

DORSET
Michael Pitt-Rivers

HEREFORDSHIRE
David Verey

THE ISLE OF WIGHT
Pennethorne Hughes

LINCOLNSHIRE
Henry Thorold and Jack Yates

NORFOLK
Wilhelmine Harrod and the Rev. C. L. S. Linnell

RUTLAND
W. G. Hoskins

SOUTH-WEST WALES
PEMBROKESHIRE and CARMARTHENSHIRE
Vyvyan Rees

SUFFOLK
Norman Scarfe

WORCESTERSHIRE
James Lees-Milne

---

edited by JOHN PIPER

ESSEX
Norman Scarfe

NORTHUMBERLAND
Thomas Sharp

WILTSHIRE
J. H. Cheetham and John Piper

NORTHAMPTONSHIRE
Lady Juliet Smith

THE SHELL PILOT TO THE SOUTH COAST HARBOURS
K. Adlard Coles

Martyrdom in 13th-century stained glass in CANTERBURY Cathedral.

A SHELL GUIDE

KENT

by PENNETHORNE HUGHES

Royal Arms, ACRISE Church.

LONDON: FABER & FABER

First published in 1969
by Faber and Faber Limited
24 Russell Square London WC1
Printed in Great Britain by
W. S. Cowell Ltd, Ipswich
All rights reserved

SBN 571 09091 5

ILLUSTRATIONS

5

FOREWORD AND ACKNOWLEDGMENTS

PENNETHORNE HUGHES died shortly after the first typescript of this book was finished, before he could revise it. He would certainly have amended and added to it had he lived. Subsequently I have made excursions in the county and have described villages which he had so far omitted, and I have not hesitated to make additions that seemed desirable within his context, especially about monuments and stained glass. These are offered in admiration and affection for the author as well as for the county.

Deirdre Wheatley visited Kent with him, typed the original manuscript beautifully, and has given much help and encouragement since in preparing it for publication.

The author would have wanted to thank clergy and owners of houses for their kindness in giving him access and information. He would also have acknowledged books, including some of the volumes of *Archaeologia Cantiana*, and works on the county by Marcus Crouch (Batsford), F. R. Banks (Penguin), Arthur Mee (Hodder & Stoughton), F. W. Jessup (Darwen Finlayson), and the Red Guide (Ward Lock). These should be supplemented by Murray's *Handbook* and Methuen's *Little Guide*, in their various editions; Francis Grayling's two volumes in the *County Churches* series (1913); books on the Cathedral stained glass by Bernard Rackham and the Rev. D. Ingram Hill, and on the Cathedral in general by Canon Shirley and others, as they all helped me in my additions and revisions. So has *Canterbury* by William Townsend (Batsford 1950) which it would be good to see in print again.

I should also like to thank the Rev. Basil Clarke for his list of Victorian churches and restorations, and Dr A. E. M. Hartley for his comments on Royal Arms in Kentish churches.

JOHN PIPER

INTRODUCTION

All counties claim a special beauty and interest. The quality of Kent is so well publicised that it tends to promote automatic and ignorant reaction. For some Kent is still the "Garden of England": for others the garden is disfigured by concrete. The first group, dewy-eyed from the brochures, only want a museum, and try to find one, admiring every 1920 mock Tudor villa as a yeoman's house, and revelling in the "Kentish cherry-blossom" when the cherries are only in the trim gardens of ribbon development. They are simpletons. The second group point to the spread of outer suburbia, the new buildings which pepper the villages, the dirt of Thames-side industry, and the holiday conurbations of the coast, and shudder. They are perhaps over nice. But the beauty is abundantly there, not always conventional, and the contemporary development is not always disfiguring. It is possible to enjoy the remaining natural charm of a remarkably variegated countryside, and the rich evidences of history, without constant disparagement of the present. Meanwhile, to less analytical thousands, Kent is just the quickest way to the coast for a popular holiday, or a lift to the continent. To over $1\frac{1}{2}$ million people, with or without loyalty, it is home.

And there is loyalty. Whilst no one is quite clear which is a Man of Kent or which is a Kentish Man (born east or west of the Medway respectively, say most), men are proud to be one or the other. Rightly indeed. London may sprawl out and swallow huge areas of the north-west, whilst the coast precariously battles with the sea on the south-east: a commuter society brings residents without roots: communications bring visitors without discrimination. But there is still an infinity to wonder at and to enjoy. Kent is a wealthy county, and has been so all through history. But as well as standardized comforts it

has unique evidences of its past, and a depth and historic quality evident to the most transient visitor but which a lifetime cannot satisfy. The initimidating blurbs about "Glorious Kent"— quaint, picturesque, Dickensian, romantic, olde, hop-heavy, mysterious and blossom-blown— may be vulgar in degree. They are also right. But they are only part of the story.

That story, of the land, the people, and the architecture, all derive from the physical placing and composition of the county.

Topography

This is the most south-easterly county of England, projecting into the sea, with on its western borders the London suburbs, Surrey, and the weald of Sussex. Its greatest length is 64 miles, from the North Foreland to London, and its deepest width some 38 miles from the Isle of Sheppey in the north to Dungeness in the south. It has 126 odd miles of coastline. It is still nearly a million acres in area, although much land in the north-west has been swallowed by Greater London. This makes it the ninth largest county in England. It is also the ninth in order of population.

The geological formation is important, and fascinating. England was still part of the continental land mass at the end of the fourth Ice Age, when the Thames was a tributary of the Rhine. Because of this the Kentish geological pattern really stretches through into Normandy, only interrupted by the narrow seas which broke through some 6,000 years ago. The break was not a clean one: the Goodwin Sands were land in historic times, and the whole east coast has gained or receded throughout history—for instance leaving the medieval port of Sandwich $2\frac{1}{2}$ miles inland, or submerging half of Reculver beneath the waves. The battle goes on. Meanwhile the Strait of Dover is only 21 miles wide. Deal and Dover are closer to France than they are to Maidstone.

CANTERBURY Cathedral from the top of the West Gate

The land formation is conventionally and best described as fan-shaped: a series of ridges stretching roughly from the north-west down to the coast. A cross-section almost anywhere across the county shows successively London clay, gravel belts, chalk, gault clay, greensand and Wealden clay. First, and along the northern edge of Kent, are the marshy low-lying lands fringing the Thames estuary. They slope up to the North Downs, the main ridge, which enters Kent from Surrey, to the north of Westerham, and stretch down to the coast to bare itself on the edge as the white cliffs of Dover. South of the Downs runs a narrow strip of gault, known in part as Holmsdale. South again is the lower greensand strip, rising to what is variously called the Greensand Ridge or the Ragstone Hills. South of these lie the vast stretch of the weald— the Low Weald, of clay, and to the south, stretch-

ing through Tunbridge Wells into Sussex, the High Weald, that is both clay and sand. Quite separate from this pattern, which is constant throughout the county, the secret and separate triangle of Romney Marsh, rescued from the sea by the Romans, has its individual character and history. The North Downs are broken by three rivers, all flowing north: the Darent, emerging at Dartford, the Medway, breaking through in the lovely gap at Maidstone, on its way to Rochester, and the Stour, running through the Wye valley to meet the sea eventually on the east coast below Thanet.

Each of these areas has its own qualities: but Kent remains primarily an agricultural area.

RECULVER

The Thames-side belt has seen its chalk exploited for lime, but even here sheep and orchards creep down to the marshes and survive precariously amongst the industrial spilth. To the east the clay, turning to gravel, runs along the coast sometimes in low cliffs to the edge of the chalk outcrop of Thanet, now only an island in name, but once separated from the mainland by a useful shipping channel called the Wantsum.

The northern slopes of the Downs rise fairly gently to the chalk ridge that is the backbone of Kent. This is unassuming country full of small villages and farmsteads, mainly unspoilt. Indeed the great M2 motorway to the coast, a wide metalled utilitarian gash though it is through the county, has the aesthetic advantage that it draws the traffic, leaving many villages by-passed and in comparative peace. The crest of the ridge has many superb views, and then comes a steep escarpment to the south, with grass, beech trees, whitebeams, yews, and villages hidden in the valleys. Over the whole area much of the building is in the flint which glistens in the fields. The gault strip of soft clay, running at the foot of the chalk, meets the sea at Folkestone, in a special luxuriance of flora and fossils.

The next ridge, the Greensand Hills, running across the middle of the county, provides to some people the most delightful country of all. To the south of Maidstone and east of the Medway these are often called the Quarry Hills, and from this area comes the warm-coloured Kentish rag which is distinctive of the old houses and churches of so much of the county. From the Sandstone Ridge—from below the church at Boughton Malherbe, for example, on Ide Hill, or Crockham Hill—the weald lies below, rich, wooded and magnificent. Everywhere is intense cultivation, broken by parklands and splashes of the rhododendrons introduced by the Victorians.

The culture of the Weald may, in its luxuriance and beauty, appear as an infinitely ancient cradle of man. In fact the great Andreadsweald, stretching into Sussex, was virtually uninhabited until the late Middle Ages: because the forest was too thick, and because the clayey roads were impossible for any sort of traffic. There were clearings and "dens", but that was all until the development of the iron industry in the seventeenth century. This and ship-building used up numbers of the oaks. The old buildings here are generally of half-timbering. Now there are still oak trees, but generally there is pastureland, orchards and hops, with rich villages and old market towns that are new shopping centres. To some of the markets still come sheep and cattle from the richest pastureland of all, that in Romney Marsh. This, in spite of resorts along its sometimes sandy beaches, or the power station and concrete at its shingled end, remains the rich low land won from the sea by the Roman wall and its extensions from the twelfth century onwards. The shingle of Dungeness, through a freak of the conflicting tides, still grows out into the sea at the rate of some 18 inches a year.

This is the pattern of the land. What man has made of it is the result of history.

History and people
The political history of Kent is largely that of England, except that in so far as most influences on these islands tend to have come from the continent, they were earliest apparent in the south-east. The Romans described the Celts in Kent as more civilized than those of the hinterland: the Saxons came to Kent first by invitation, and not as conquerors: St Augustine and his missionaries came to a Kent which already had a Christian community and a long Christian tradition: to the Normans the area was already "all Frenchified". Culturally ideas from the continent arrived first at the Kent ports, and were observed in the retinues of the early kings as these passed through between their palaces at London and their possessions on the mainland. Above all, in Canterbury there existed a spiritual head who was also an arm of the Catholic faith in Europe. It is the paradox of the county to

Kentish Landscapes at CHILLENDEN, GRAVENEY and BIDDENDEN

have been at once passionately patriotic and yet more internationally minded than the rest of England. Increasingly London itself became a centre of fashion and ideas, and these flowed easily into the county growing rich on its door-step. Physically, the effects can be observed in the architecture of the county: the normal building style in Kent in the sixteenth or even the eighteenth centuries tends to be years ahead of Northamptonshire or Northumberland. Foreigners, scholars, couriers and trend setters all had to pass through Kent: it learnt today what London, Paris or Rome would learn (weather permitting) tomorrow or next week. The villages might be sleeping and remote. But along the veins of its road system flowed the life blood of civilization.

The roads flowed early. Not of course between the Ice Ages, when remains at Swanscombe suggest human existence there 200,000 years ago. Nor perhaps where the first few families of hunters crossed the swamps of what is now the straits, from the mainland block, or the makers of eoliths operated in the Medway valley. But some kind of trackway system had begun by the time of the megalith builders of say 2,000 BC, who left their memorials at Kits Coty, the Coldrum Stones near Trottiscliffe, or the stones in Addington Park. It was certainly in full use by the ages of bronze and iron, which have left their extensive evidences: as in the hill forts of Bigbury and Oldbury. The main east to west track, leading on to the early centres of civilization in Wessex, ran along under the escarpment of the North Downs, taking advantage of the contours to avoid the gault clay beneath. This ancient way, used by primitive man for thousands of years, is generally and romantically known as the Pilgrims' Way. Some pilgrims may no doubt have used it, although most of those making for Canterbury followed, as did the pilgrims described by Chaucer, the path of the Roman Watling Street. But it is immeasurably older than

The Pilgrims' Way
near KEMSING

this. The label Pilgrims' Way was only invented by an Ordnance Survey Officer just over a hundred years ago.

The agricultural prosperity of Belgic Kent, newly settled by tribes from the mainland, its corn and less significantly its oysters, attracted the Romans. Julius Caesar's reconnaissance expeditions landed at Deal, but conquest and occupation started with the troops of Claudius in AD 43. For 400 years, longer than the time between Elizabeth I and Elizabeth II, Britain became a frontier settlement of the Empire. Kent was the first area to be settled: the last to be vacated. It gave little trouble. On the coast the legions, the administrators and the traders came and left by the then ports of Richborough, Reculver, Dover and Lympne. Inland were the towns of Durovernum and Dubrivae—Canterbury and Rochester. Both lay on the paved street to London, and the straight Roman roads, which still in many places exist, stretched across the county, except for the impenetrable weald. The Rhee Wall was built to make firm and fertile the salty marshlands of Romney Marsh. Villas were built. Many have been excavated, and the most interesting is that extremely well shown at Lullingstone. As the Empire contracted the defence system against the Teutonic pirates was strengthened, and the so-called "Count of the Saxon Shore" had his headquarters at Richborough.

When the Romans had left the Romano-British Celts traditionally invited Hengist and Horsa to serve as mercenaries in their defence against other invaders, and against internal disruption from the so-called Picts and Scots. Whether Hengist and Horsa existed or not (other than as street-names in the Thanet resorts) the mercenaries remained as conquerors. From the landing at Ebbsfleet in 449 they spread across the country, families and tribes from Northern Europe, seizing land from the softer and more sophisticated Celts. Those in East Kent are described as Jutes, rather than Saxons. They perhaps came from Frisia, but were not greatly different from the Saxons who eventually seized Wessex and occupied the land west of the Med-

way—one explanation of the distinction between Men of Kent and Kentish Men. But they introduced the system of Gavelkind—equal inheritance between all of a man's sons, rather than all his property going to the eldest—which was to continue, with importance, as a Kentish custom. Place-names show that the county was in the first wave of occupation, and there are many villages originally ending in "-ingas", indicating a particular family or group of people—those for instance of Eastling, Bobbing or Malling. The "-dens" and "-hursts" of the Weald are centuries later, indicating settlements when at last the forest was being cleared. There are practically no early place-names in the Weald.

Amongst Saxon names Wye means a place for idols, and Woodnesborough Woden's Hill. But the physical remains of the Saxons are largely Christian and the churches of Kent are full of Saxon work, often incorporating Roman bricks. For in 597 came the third historic landing: after Caesar and the Saxons, St Augustine. The acceptance of Christianity meant another link with European civilization, and the establishment of Canterbury as the spiritual headquarters of the British Isles, and so a vital force in its political and social history. In the ninth century Kent suffered from the attacks of the Vikings, who made inroads, burned towns and monasteries, and wintered their long boats off Thanet and Sheppey. But the Danes made no permanent settlements of importance.

The Normans did not first land in Kent. But there were already close ties with Normandy and the people of Kent claimed a special relationship with the Conqueror, who granted them the continuance of their old laws and customs. The Angevins and Plantagenets built their strategic castles, and the Church founded its great religious houses, of which remains exist in such places as the Cistercian monastery at Boxley, or that now wonderfully restored by the Carmelites at Aylesford. Canterbury, always a place of

top: *Between Thames and Medway,*
centre: *Medway valley (the nearly-lost village is WOULDHAM).*
bottom: *Milton Creek, SITTINGBOURNE*

16

pilgrimage, became a shrine of continental importance after the murder of Thomas à Becket in 1170. The Cathedral, profiting from the gifts of the visitors, was built up to its maximum architectural glory. But the Church was a great landlord as well as a centre of the Faith: Canterbury and Rochester owned innumerable manors, not only in Kent but beyond it. As corporations, able to take a long view, they were not bad landlords. But the two great uprisings due to the social discontents after the Black Death both found their leaders in Kent: Wat Tyler, perhaps of Dartford, who led the revolt of 1381, and the more mysterious Jack Cade, whose troops reached London in the insurrection of 1450. Feudalism gave way to Tudor despotism: the monasteries were dissolved: their stones were used to help in the new forts to guard the coast against invasion from France and the Spanish troops in the Netherlands. In the great struggle of the Reformation and Counter-Reformation Christopher Marlowe of Canterbury served perhaps as a political agent, and in 1554 Sir Thomas Wyatt of Allington lost his head for his incautious revolt in favour of Queen Mary. The new Tudor nobility built their great houses, and a stricter centralization contributed to the decline of the power of the Cinque Ports. *See* Deal and elsewhere.

Kent was as passionately split during the Civil Wars of the seventeenth century as the rest of the country and has its innumerable anecdotes. The "Kentish Sir Byngs" were on the whole royalists, but proximity to London, and a wealthy merchant class, kept it fairly secure under Parliamentary control, although the county was never so clearly aligned as was the far west on behalf of the King, or the eastern counties against him. Most families hedged, with adherents to both sides, so that whatever happened property would not be finally alienated. This was not difficult, for two reasons: gavelkind, which already meant that land tended to be distributed into numerous properties of middle size, rather than a few great

RUCKINGE Church and Romney Marsh

p 20 *Orchards at COLLIER STREET*

p 21 *Hop pole stringing near GOUDHURST*

ones, and the Kent habit of intermarriage. For whilst Kent, as a gateway to France, might appear likely to lose its local loyalties and ties, in fact it had these particularly strongly. Because of its long coast-line, and the difficulty of passage through the Weald, the gentlemen of Kent comparatively rarely took their wives from Surrey, Sussex or the rest of England. They married their neighbours. Most of the great Kentish families were and are related, and merged easily into the rising social worlds of lesser gentry and trade.

Politically there was little to differentiate Kent from the pattern of the rest of the country in the nineteenth and twentieth centuries, except perhaps for one rather hushed-up historic episode. The last "Peasant Revolt" of the autumn of 1830, like the first Peasants' Revolt of 1381, started in Kent. It ended in hangings, transportations and a large measure of oblivion.

Economically, agriculture has always been the main industry of the county: fine grain on the downland, sheep in the lush marshes, famous cattle, and nowadays such things as bulbs and sugar-beet. Kent has been "the garden of England" not for its pretty flowers, but for its market produce. As London grew, so did its appetite for soft fruit, sent there, mainly by water, from the Kentish villages. Kent also had the first heavy industry in the country, iron-smelting. The villages of the Weald, on both sides of the Sussex border, still have Furnace Ponds, or Forge Farms to commemorate the fact. Some of the churchyards still have in them the iron tombstones of the early ironmasters, who lived in the rich middle-class timbered buildings of Goudhurst or Tenterden. Hamlets noisy today with traffic were noisy in the seventeenth century with the sound of hammers. Overlapping the iron industry came the cloth trade, when from exporting wool England changed in the sixteenth century to making and exporting cloth, processed through the techniques of the tradesmen specially recruited from Flanders, or

refugees from the religious wars on the continent. The cloth trade moved to the north of England in time to save Kent from the steam, back-to-back houses and general smoke blanket of the industrial revolution. But by now the cherries, apples and nuts were being developed into a hugely profitable and very beautiful market.

Moreover, Kent became, after the early seventeenth century, the county most famous for its hops. They, and brewing, remain pre-eminent today. Like the remaining windmills, the oast-houses are not very old: they mainly date from the early nineteenth century. But they remain as evidences of the annual harvests to make the Englishman's wine, attended for generations by

the East End hop-pickers with Cockney junketings as colourful as the wine harvests of the continent. Now the picking is 90 per cent by machinery, but Kent still grows far more hops than any other English county.

With the nineteenth century came above all the great recreational industry. Already since the seventeenth century the waters of Tunbridge Wells had served to promote a thriving inland spa. At the end of the eighteenth century came sea-bathing. This meant that the fishing villages and even the now sometimes land-locked

SCOTNEY

harbours of the coast became resorts—for the nobility and gentry, if they could attract them, but increasingly also for the new middle classes. The pleasant stucco and columned squares and crescents of Margate, Ramsgate, and Broadstairs are evidences of these days of the Assembly Rooms, the Circulating Library, and the bathing machine. Folkestone, florid and mid-Victorian, developed later. With the coming of the railways also came the day-trippers, to the regret of the genteel but to the prosperity of the tradesmen. The railways also made the market towns of Kent—Sevenoaks or Maidstone—possible homes for wealthy London businessmen. Their sober, expensive, dull Victorian houses still remain, usually greying and converted, near the railway station.

Inevitably the county was becoming increasingly populated by what are now called commuters. The whole north-west was absorbed by London in successive bites, and old and proud places like Eltham, Greenwich or Blackheath became urban. Heavy industry crept along the Thames estuary, making the huge maritime-industrial conurbation of Rochester-Strood-Gillingham. It still spreads, and the latest bite of 1965 has swallowed Bromley and Orpington (although these are included in this gazetteer). The seaside resorts themselves became dormitories. All this process has been enormously increased by electrification. The appalled cry of "subtopia!" is understandable.

Not all the newcomers lived in the expanding towns or along the developing transport arteries. It was long fashionable to sneer at "stockbroker's Tudor", and at the comfortable, rather ugly houses which the wealthy businessmen converted or built for themselves in Kent and Sussex at the beginning of the twentieth century. In perspective it is possible to see that the stockbrokers rescued a number of timbered houses which without them would by now have disappeared, and that the new houses of the businessmen, fifty years on, their garden trees grown, their rhododendrons blooming despite the lack of garden-

Ragstone Towers:
EGERTON and CHARING

pp 26/27   *Unspoiled interiors:*
FORDWICH and BADLESMERE

ers, are not without charm. Occasionally, built by Lutyens or some other architect of merit, they are gracious. More recent building indeed cannot be seen in perspective. The ribbon development between the wars can never be thought beautiful, and much of the contemporary rash of chalets and bungalows is incongruous in colour and feeling. Fortunately their built-in obsolescence will see to it that they cannot trouble more than one or two generations. A few modern estates and individual buildings are planned with care, to blend in spirit if not in material with the older buildings about them and the landscape in which they are built. New building in the bombed cities like Canterbury is usually thoughtful and positive. Pylons sometimes lend perspective to a landscape, rather than destroy it. The Kent coalfields, feared as an eyesore, hardly disturb the orchards and pasture-land round about them.

Architecture

All this history and social development is what you can see spread about you. There are the medieval castles of Deal, Sandown, Walmer and Sandgate, built by Henry VIII for coastal defence. There are others, romantic or picturesque, adapted or altered as private houses now —Allington, Saltwood, Leeds. There are many medieval houses, large and small; Ightham Mote, for instance, and Old Soar, Plaxtol, apart from the well-known show places, which are outstanding, Knole, Penshurst, Hever, and the famous gardens, Sissinghurst and Scotney. And there are churches, Canterbury and Rochester apart, churches better and finer in architecture and detail than might be expected in a county that was without an easily-worked building stone. There were architects at Canterbury always, and the building tradition spread. "Kentish rag" gives a jolly and unusual texture to some church walls. Sandstone was available round Tunbridge Wells and oolitic limestone near Maidstone and in the east. But usually flint was the thing, with stone for quoins and tracery

and mouldings. "Kentish tracery" is not confined to Kent, but is so-called because it was so common here from the fourteenth century. Francis Grayling (*The Churches of Kent*, 1913) described it rather well when he said: "the effect is as if the cusping (of window tracery) formed a natural dentated leaf". There is a lot of thirteenth-century stained glass in the churches (Westwell, Upper Hardres, Nackington and Woodchurch have complete panels), and of course later glass. The Cathedral has more than any other church in England. There are also many brasses: Cobham church alone has nineteen. At Canterbury, again, the monuments of all dates are extraordinary. For atmosphere and character the windswept churches of Romney Marsh are as good as can be.

There are innumerable country houses, often still in private hands, of dignity and interest. There are many Tudor buildings, many eighteenth-century façades, Regency villas, and Victorian hotels. There are pretty nineteenth-century cottages, semi-detached but trim modern villas where once the Romans had noble ones, and contemporary development in all its aspects. There are still wide parklands, and almost an overplus of a modern contribution to landscape planning—golf courses. It is a palimpsest of the history of a rich, populous and pleasant county.

The "Kentish yeoman's house", or "hall house", had established itself as a type by the fifteenth century. It was the house built by freeholders, men who farmed or grew hops independently, and it is a classic in the county because of its consistent and basically unvarying type. You find it in village after village, and between villages, and in all parts of the county. It is of timber and plaster, with a hipped roof of tiles. It had a hall in the middle with a central hearth, open to the roof originally, but a floor has of course been put in at a later date, and the fire moved to one end. The outer sections project a foot or so forwards, and were always of two stories. The grander houses of the kind had a

screen to keep the draught at bay. They are now highly desirable residences, being of convenient size and having "old-world character", and they often appear in the estate-advertisement pages of glossy magazines.

Out of this type grew the later Kentish small farmer's and hop grower's house, sometimes of brick but most commonly of weatherboarding, white or cream-painted. Weatherboarding was used in all the home counties, but probably earlier and certainly with more conviction in Kent than elsewhere. It was used in barns and mills as well as in houses. You could say that the charm of such places as Rolvenden and Smarden depends on it.

Brick was always beautifully laid, and many houses in the villages that have an unpretentious "right" look, well proportioned and well built in their modest way, may be of any date between 1740 and 1840, without much difference or development of style. There is often a well-carpentered central porch of painted wood, especially towards the Sussex border and the Weald. Well-laid brick, incidentally, "makes" some of the bigger houses too, houses such as the handsome "Finchcocks" by Goudhurst. Near Sussex tile hanging is common and is a positive pleasure in the Tunbridge Wells area. Tiled roofs in Kent are everywhere attractive; they often undulate picturesquely and vary the skyline beautifully in such places as Tenterden and Cranbrook.

For those to whom literary allusion adds piquancy, Tunbridge Wells is Thackeray, Watling Street is Chaucer, the little shop world of outer London is H. G. Wells, and pretty well the whole of the Thames estuary and Thanet is identifiable Dickens. He provides, from Jingle, the hackneyed and inevitable quotation: "Kent, sir—everybody knows Kent—apples, cherries, hops and women". But there is a great deal more than that. Above all there is the countryside itself, in all its variety.

The first topographical book about any English county was William Lambarde's *Perambulation of Kent* of 1570. Since then the stream of description and appreciation has never ended.

Romney Marsh churches: BROOKLAND,
FAIRFIELD in the floods of 1960,
and SNARGATE

Tiles at TENTERDEN and (above) *BIDDENDEN*

There are profound works, pieces of subjective journalism, learned monographs or antiquarian crankeries about every aspect of the county's history. The archaeological and historical field has been worked over in detail and societies are informed and diligent. Almost everywhere a visitor who expresses interest will find ready and kindly help, and information to be regarded perhaps with discretion, but certainly with gratitude. To know one parish in detail is perhaps the work of a lifetime: to know a whole county is impossible. But in Kent it is fun to try.

GAZETTEER

The numbers after each entry refer to the square on the map where the place is to be found.

Acol (it means "oak-wood") 12 is still an entity, but the parish is being drawn into Birchington, two miles to the north, and to the residential resort strip of north Thanet, and increasingly loses identity. Near by, on the top of a rise, is an old chalk-pit where tradition had it that an exciseman lost his life pursuing a smuggler in the fog. This became Barham's story of "The Smuggler's Leap" in the *Ingoldsby Legends*. There is a markedly modest Victorian mission church of 1876. Flint and stone, with bellcote.

Acrise 4 is in wooded downland country behind Folkestone, reached by hilly lanes. It has a little flint church amongst trees. Nave, chancel and short spire. Thirteenth and eighteenth century, but the furnishings all renewed. Poor stained glass. Nice west gallery with rare Royal Arms of 1698. Wall tablets to Papillon family. Acrise Place is an Elizabethan manor house of stone-dressed brick, with a double-bowed east front added in the late eighteenth century. With its gardens it is sometimes shown to the public. It was first lived in by the present owners, the Papillon family, in 1666.

Addington 5 lies just north of the A20 and is not entirely unaffected by it. But it is in beautiful park country and the church stands down a tree-skirted lane on an ancient mound. The church is thirteenth century, enlarged and with a tower added in the fifteenth century. It has a painted ceiling and brasses. The mound is probably natural, but there is learned doubt, because the area is one of much pre-historic activity. To the north, through Addington Park, are several groups of Sarsen stones, and monoliths, remains of a series of long barrows.

Adisham 14. A widespread village in pleasant wooded country south-east of Canterbury, with a restored thirteenth/fourteenth-century church standing finely above the road and its mainly modern houses. This is cruciform with a central tower with a shingled pyramid on top, stone bench tables along the walls of the

ALLINGTON Castle

nave, and thirteenth-century painted woodwork which came from the reredos of Canterbury Cathedral. Interior white, but part of the tower arch has been scraped, with an untidy effect.

Aldington 17. Aldington Knoll, where there was a Roman beacon, is a spur of the Quarry Hills. It stands beside the Hythe-Tenterden road, with enormous views over Romney Marsh to the south and Forest and rolling farmlands to the north. The village itself has some pleasant cottages and scattered farms, and the Parsonage nominally housed two famous rectors: Thomas Linacre, the physician and humanist, and Erasmus. A third Tudor member of the parish was the crazy servant-girl Elizabeth Barton, the "Holy Maid of Kent". She prophesied, saw visions, was inspired to denounce Protestantism, and, after unjustly involving Sir Thomas More and other notables, confessed to fraud and was hanged at Tyburn in

1534. There are ruins of a chapel for her, once a scene of pilgrimage, at the hamlet of *Court-at-Street*, on the main road. At Aldington Corner itself are many little houses, new but neat.

The church has a striking sixteenth-century tower, visible for miles, with earlier work elsewhere. There was much renewal in 1875. Nice Jacobean carved oak, and misericords.

Alkham 14 is a pretty village in spite of widened roads and new houses, lying in the valley of the Dour in quiet country a mile or so back from the coast between Dover and Folkestone. It is surrounded by chalk hills and elm trees. The flint church with its red tiles stands up well above the road, and has a good thirteenth-century north chapel. Otherwise overfurnished, and with few attractions. But there is the tomb-slab of an abbot of St Radegund's. The ruins of *St Radegund's Abbey* itself are by a farm, on private property at

the top of a downland track: a tower, now a gatehouse, with traces of the moat in the fields. It was founded in 1190 for the Premonstratensian canons, but decayed early, although the abbey barn remains intact. The content of the soil here turns flowers unnaturally blue, and there are brilliant hydrangeas, and a nursery garden.

Allhallows 3. A village just inland from the north-east tip of the Hoo peninsular. It is bare and industrialized: has an over-restored church and down on the coast an attempt at seaside gaiety, with caravans. To the east are marshes; to the south swampy inlands and the sandbank known as Stoke Ooze; to the north the mouth of the Thames. Like all this district it is dominated by the towering installations of the Kent Oil Refinery on the Isle of Grain.

Allington 6. The castle is best and most conventionally observed from

the outside by walking down the tow-path from Maidstone. Actually to go there from the London road you turn off at the Tudor Garage down a lane which is unmarked, although it also leads to Allington Marina. At the bottom, past quarries, is a dim little church with a shingled spire, St Lawrence, modernized in 1895, and now looking forgotten. Opposite are the gates of the Castle.

The small but ancient parish is in fact on both sides of the Medway, here at its most beautiful. For at this point the river ceases to be tidal, and the electrical sluice gates control the water for the whole Medway valley. The lock buildings are in Kentish rag and there is a popular waterside inn, the Malta, on the poplar-grown bank. Great barges go by from Maidstone to London.

The castle itself, surrounded by its moat and proud with its battlements, looks perfect. This is largely due to its successful restoration between 1906 and 1932 by the mountaineer Lord Conway. Before this it had been largely derelict. It has a full history. It was founded at this strategic curve in the river in early Norman times, and rebuilt in the late thirteenth century by the then Warden of the Cinque Ports, Sir Stephen de Penchester. Of this building the outer wall and its towers, a machicolated gatehouse and part of the great hall remain. The Wyatts made further alterations when they became owners in 1493. Sir Thomas Wyatt (1503–42) credited with the introduction of the sonnet, was born here, and his son also, the Sir Thomas who led the rebellion of 1554 against Queen Mary. It is now a retreat house for Carmelite Fathers, who sometimes open it to the public.

Appledore 16 has a wide street for a village, with houses of all dates, few individually remarkable but collectively satisfying and cheerful. Although on the edge of Romney Marsh, with wide views all round, it is less a marsh village than a rich medieval weavers' one, described as the eastern point of the Andredsweald, and it is not chance that it

ASHFORD churchyard

looks like a scaled-down Tenterden. It was once the head of the northern channel round Oxney Island, and fleets sailed up to it, until a storm altered the course of the Rother in 1287. It had an annual fair till 1899. The church, perched above the canal, is of several periods, mostly fifteenth-century, but was severely restored in the nineteenth century. It has three continuous tiled gables which compose well from the Marsh behind the canal-bank trees, and a low tower. Not much of interest inside; but a large Royal Arms and some bits of old glass.

At *Horne's Place*, to the north, is a fourteenth-century domestic chapel, now in the care of the Ministry of Public Building and Works, but well looked after by the owners of the house—great gardeners. Just outside the village, south-west, is a handsome beef-coloured Victorian house with Dutch gables, on the slope above the canal, with a sloping garden with mixed planting.

Ash (near Sandwich) 15. A scattered village lying three miles inland from Sandwich, on high ground which means that the tall leaded spire of St Nicholas church is a landmark at sea as well as over much of east Kent. The church has fine proportions inside, monuments and brasses, and no redundant furnishings. The monuments include several recumbent effigies of the fourteenth century and two sets of kneeling figures of the seventeenth. Among the brasses, two big late ones are specially fine. A few timbered houses and inns, but also many new dormitory bungalows. Richborough Castle (q.v.) is with the parish.

Ash (near Wrotham) 5 is expanding, but remains a pleasant village in beautiful unintruded downland. Off the main road is an outstandingly attractive small manor house of 1637. It stands, with farm buildings, grouped with the church, which has a thirteenth-century nave and a fifteenth-century tower and roof. There are chestnuts, hawthorn, and vast comfortable trees ringed round the cricket pitch opposite.

Secreted on higher ground, even more wooded, and reached by steep lanes is *Ridley*, two miles away. It has a tiny white-turreted church

which must always have been large for its inhabitants, who have never numbered much more than a hundred. A pleasant eighteenth-century house, and a farm next to it.

Ashford 13 is a nodal point where the two principal streams of the Great Stour meet in the wooded country south of the North Downs. It has always been a market centre, especially for the cattle from the lush pastures of Romney Marsh. It still is, as is especially evident on Tuesdays, market day. When the locomotive and carriage workshops were established in 1847 it rapidly developed into Victorian industrial ugliness. Now the motor-car has succeeded the steam-engine, and brought its own by-pass architecture. Altogether the town, with 28,000 inhabitants, is crowded, rushed, overbuilt and flourishing.

Amongst all this there are a few Tudor houses with timbering and some good eighteenth-century town façades, particularly in the High Street. These are on the ground floor, colourfully disfigured by advertisements for the shops, flashing behind the traffic flow. The church stands in a kind of close, pedestrianized, and with the houses all facing inwards, i.e., towards the church. They include an interesting but disconsolate red brick Grammar School of 1630, founded by Sir Norton Knatchbull. The church is fine and large, with an imposing central tower that has high corner turrets with pinnacles. It was built between 1350 and 1475 and has some good details. Wooden galleries to the nave.

Industrial and dormitory development lies thickest to the south: to the north and west are trees and parkland.

Ashurst 5 is a small place on a hill, on the Sussex border. It has an over-restored little fourteenth-century church with white weatherboarded bellcote and a wagon roof, at the top of the steep main street, an inn at the bottom, and the station, which did not bring much new building. *Chafford Park* lies to the north, and the Chafford bridge is the first over the Medway when it has entered Kent, a young river, unpolluted, here very beautiful and much visited by fishermen.

39

Aylesford 6 has great charm and historical interest. It is incessantly visited, most successfully by the towpath along the Medway from Maidstone, leaving on the right *Cobtree Manor*, with the zoo started here by the late Sir Gerard Tyrwhitt-Drake, and identified with the Dingley Dell of Pickwick Papers.

This approach provides the well-known view of the church and the red-tiled roofs beyond the river and stone bridge. This is fourteenth century, although the middle span was enlarged a hundred years ago. This approach avoids most of the industrial development, and the commuter homes round the railway station. These exist, and Aylesford is a vigorous and busy contemporary community, not just a show piece. Indeed individually there are few buildings of importance, although a few pleasant examples of Tudor work and other façades are seen from the towpath downstream. The general effect of the rooftops is most striking from the churchyard, up steps from the High Street. The church itself stands high amongst elm trees. It was restored in 1848, but has two fine tombs: one to a Colepepper (Sir Thomas, died 1604, with two reclining figures) and the other of baroque ostentation to John Banks, 1696, an enormous monument with three figures. The building is somewhat over-furnished.

Just beyond the village, and catering for visitors in motor coaches, as well as more conventional pilgrims, is the *Friary*. Lord Richard Grey, of Northumberland, who had been entertained by the friars of Mount Carmel when on a crusade, persuaded a number of them to come to England in about 1240, settling some on his northern estate and some here. At the Dissolution the Friary was broken up, and passed into lay hands. The Restoration wit Sir Charles Sedley was born here in 1639. In 1949, after nearly three hundred years, the Carmelites returned, and have with their own hands restored and extended the buildings, damaged by fire in 1930. The piazza outside the Sanctuary, and much of the new design, is striking: the whole group of buildings, marrying the early and contemporary work, is to most tastes moving and effective.

On the Chatham road an almshouse of 1607, restored in 1842, is noteworthy. There are also sandpits, and further on a village, *Eccles*, that is almost entirely industrialized.

Aylesford's early importance was due to its position as the lowest ford on the Medway, and on an ancient trackway. The invading, if legendary, Jutes, under Hengist, defeated the British here, led by Vortigern, in 455, and this must have been the crossing place of most pilgrims on their way to Canterbury.

Kits Coty House is in the parish, north towards Chatham. It is in a field on the high ground south-west of Bluebell Hill, best reached by a path leading up from the Pilgrims' Way, lower down. It is the most famous prehistoric monument in Kent, magnificently placed here on the hillside looking out over the Medway valley. It consists of three upright stones, seven to eight foot high, with a capstone 13 feet long on top. It was formerly enclosed in a barrow, to which it was perhaps a false entrance. The name probably derives from the Celtic "Kid Coit", the tomb in the wood. It is much visited, and for this reason now sadly surrounded by iron fencing.

Aylesham 14. A gloomy brick mining village of estates and avenues in the coalfields of east Kent, with rows of semi-detached houses, a few shops and a cinema already looking forlorn. Better than northern colliery aggregations of the nineteenth century, and it has lovely country and hopfields all round, with a windmill on the skyline. But a sad shock for those who mistake it for Aylesford.

Badlesmere 13 lies with *Leaveland* 13 (which see) which has a fine green, on either side of the road south from Faversham to Ashford. It is a pleasant district of farms, cottages and one or two individual large houses of character, but the interest lies in the minute church of Badlesmere, down a lane to the east. It is an extremely plain building, stuccoed outside, originally medieval, but the interior has survived as an example of Georgian church furnishing, almost untouched by the Victorians: an aisleless building, softly lighted, with

box pews listening to a big double-decker pulpit.

Bapchild. *See* Sittingbourne.

Barfreston 15 (locally "Barson"). The most admired Norman church in England is on a hill in a pretty and remote village. It was built about 1080 of Caen stone, and remarkably well restored in 1840. It is small, with only a nave and chancel, but with sumptuous carvings, a magnificent south doorway, very like that of the west doorway of Rochester Cathedral, and a "wheel" window through the chancel arch. The only post-Norman feature is a fifteenth-century window in the west wall. And of course there was a good deal of Victorian touching up. There is a string course running round the outside of the church, half way up, with another, incorporating openings, above it. It is one of the outstanding examples of Norman architecture in England, deserving its place in all the textbooks, and pleasant to look at for anybody.

Barham 14 and **Derringstone** 14, its extension to the south, are now very much on the main road. But the road is beside the river in a valley with the downs and prehistoric earthworks above, and the country is attractive with beech trees. The church has a green copper spire, and a fine roof. It is a big-boned fourteenth-century church, which has been somewhat ruthlessly dealt with in Victorian times and later. Attractive outside, it lacks atmosphere. Brasses. There is a striking classical monument with four urns at the corners of a marble pyramid, and a fifth at the apex, misplaced at the west end of the south aisle. The best churchyard stones have sadly been removed and placed round the walls (to facilitate mowing). Many of them are double-parked. But at least it is good to see them not destroyed. An attractive, basically Queen Anne house, *Anne Court*, is north of the church. It has a pediment on its main front, and is in fact a house of various dates. There are several nice brick houses in the village and about the parish.

On Barham Downs great armies assembled throughout history, with a vast camp of troops here during the Napoleonic wars, to match the

AYLESFORD

French one across the Channel, behind Boulogne.

Barming. *See* East Farleigh.

Bearsted 6 is becoming a dormitory suburb for Maidstone, but of the better sort. The green, its historic pride, where Alfred Mynn played cricket and Wat Tyler's men assembled in 1381, is splendid and unspoilt. Round it are many well made, well restored, well-kept houses, Tudor, eighteenth-century and decent nineteenth-century Kentish-style build-

ings. The restored fifteenth-century church of the Holy Cross is up a lane, with a good tower and sculptured lions at three angles of the battlements. To the north the slopes of the downs show up wide and wooded.

Beckenham 1. Even when Cobbett wrote in 1830 he said "when you get to Beckenham, which is the last parish in Kent, the country begins to assume a cockney-like appearance". A hundred years later it was a suburban town. Now it is a postal address for nearly 78,000 people, part of the

sprawl of outer London. On the map and the main road it merges without distinction into Penge on the west, Bromley on the east, and the artisan suburbs of Lewisham and Catford to the north.

In fact it retains some character, and round the church, on a hill, is a suburban town with a shopping centre in its own right: stores, schools, banks and offices. Here are the better-class houses of the Victorian residential development, and outside, the new ring of housing estates, factories, villas and concrete.

41

Some streets have the ugly individual comfort of North Oxford, others are mock Tudor, mock Georgian, or undisguised middle-class Victorian. There are miles of modern bungalows. The overall effect is relieved by the breathing space of two golf courses, once the parks of large houses: Langley Park to the south and to the north Beckenham Place Park. This is wide, green and attractive. The stables and principal lodges are those of the house built in Portland stone by John Cator of Bromley, who bought the estate in 1773. He was a friend of Dr Johnson, who advised him on the shrubs and plants for the gardens, and Fanny Burney was a frequent guest in the house. What is left, with an Ionic portico, is now the Golf House.

The church is a restoration of 1885–7, with a tower of 1903, some memorials from the older church inside, and a restored but still basically thirteenth-century lych-gate. South of the High Street is a large Roman Catholic church with an imposing tower, and at the entrance to Beckenham Place Park a modern brick church which looks to some tastes like a consecrated launching-pad.

Bekesbourne 14 has modern buildings near the station, but lying back are a delightful group of eighteenth-century houses, and the church, reached by a path over the brook and through exotic trees, perched high in a field. It is much rebuilt, and the tower is modern. Flint, which shows internally too where the walls have been scraped. Nave, chancel, west tower and south chapel. In this chapel (now vestry) and under the tower are wall tablets: one good one, with a kneeling figure, seventeenth century. Dr Beke, the African explorer, lived and died here, and there are scanty remains of a Tudor palace razed in the Civil Wars.

Belvedere 2 is an industrial strip to the north of Bexleyheath. Two main arteries sweep through it east and west, and to the north are works and marshland. There are huge new blocks of flats, and a shopping precinct on the main road. St Augustine is a church of 1916, built by Temple Moore from designs by C. Hodgson Fowler.

To the west, green and pleasant, is

Abbey Woods. On a sloping bank here, looking down to the coast road and a row of mean houses, and out to the Erith marshes, chimneys, cranes, refineries and the river, are the ruins of *Lesnes Abbey.* This was an Augustinian house founded in 1178 by Richard de Lucy, chief justiciary of England. It was suppressed by Wolsey, decayed, and was excavated by the local archaeological society from 1909 onwards. The complex of buildings only rises a few feet from the ground in most places, but is beautifully kept and displayed. A fine mass of trees behind, and beyond the woods a desolation of buildings, and signs to the Dartford Tunnel.

Benenden 9. A long village four miles from Cranbrook with twentyish and later development not spoiling a large and splendid green famous for cricket. This is dominated by a Perpendicular sandstone church emphatically restored into Victorian Gothic inside, by the first Earl of Cranbrook. There is a wall monument with a bust by Peter Scheemakers, and a fine George III Royal Arms. A building beside the green was put up as a grammar school in James I's reign by one of the Gibbon family, forbears of the historian. They lived nearby at Rolvenden. Black and white façades, weatherboarding, red roofs, and many chestnuts.

Lying back north from the road to Cranbrook is a fine park, with a point at 370 feet which is the highest in the Weald, and in it Benenden School for girls. The large rose-coloured house is basically Elizabethan, but extensively enlarged and modernized.

Bethersden 13 is a village famous for its paludina marble. This consists of the condensed fossilized shells of a fresh-water snail, found in the Wealden clay. It polishes up into glittering blues and browns. As well as being exploited locally for numerous medieval churches it appears in the cathedrals of Rochester and Canterbury. The village itself is now mainly of little new housing units without distinctive character. The fifteenth-century ragstone church stands well on a rise off the main road. Its interior has been rather poorly Victorianized. It is spacious

and symmetrical, but has few distinguished features. In the churchyard is one of the few "oven" graves—a sort of eighteenth-century barrow, with three graves in one. Great ladies coming to church here used in the eighteenth century to have their coaches drawn by teams of oxen: Bethersden had a reputation, when all Wealden roads were boggy and ghastly, for the worst roads in Kent.

Betteshanger 15. Victorian-Jacobean house in a park. Norman-Revival church. Fine carved Stuart Royal Arms.

Bexley 2 was carved away from Kent to form a new London Borough in 1965, and with Bexleyheath involves administratively 89,000 souls. Vestiges of the old Kentish village survive, with narrow streets and one or two tired Georgian façades, one a nursing home, and a manor house, which was once the home of Camden the antiquary. It has a Tudor hall. The Norman church was over-restored in 1883, but has a tower with an odd spire, a clock, and six bells. There is Danson Park, with a lake, Bexley Park Wood, brick-girt to the south, and two golf courses. Danson Hill House, of about 1770, was designed by Sir Robert Taylor: an individual villa on a rusticated basement standing beautifully on the rather flat landscape.

The rest is suburb and industry, except for *Hall Place,* to the east, on the River Cray. This is an estate of 62 acres, acquired by the Bexley Council as a pleasure park, and the House itself is now a school. It faces the road, a Tudor building put up on an earlier site in 1537, for a Lord Mayor of London, Sir Justinian Champneys. It stands below the road level behind fine wrought-iron gate and railings, a building with great dignity and symmetry, in alternating white stone and flint, giving a light and cheerful effect, which is not spoilt by the large seventeenth-century additions in red brick. The fine interior is not normally open to visitors, but the exterior of the house and the delightful gardens justify the publicity as a beauty spot, even though the ghost of the Black Prince is unreliable.

BARFRESTON Church from the south and detail of the south door

The Red House, BEXLEYHEATH

Bexleyheath 2 has, of course, nice spots. But the label means the gigantic conurbation grown out from East London which has swallowed the little town of Bexley itself, over-run the villages which lived on providing London from their market gardens, pushed up in concrete and brick to the Erith marshes, stretched east to Crayford, and now merges across the Cray itself with unbroken lines of building into the fringes of Dartford. Some of it is tolerable residential suburban, some commercial, some industrial. The centre has a long hideous High Street with a clock tower at one end, and is rich with multiple stores, cinemas, neon, mock Tudor, genuine chrome and evident vitality. All about are rows and avenues of featureless houses, mainly of the twentieth century at its less considered.

A marked exception is at *Upton*, east of Danson Park, where there is the *Red House* which Philip Webb designed for William Morris, who elected to live here when there was still much open heath, and this was the country. The date was 1859, in the heyday of the over-ornamented Victorian villa. This instead is plain

brick and tile, remarkable for its period.

Christ Church, built in 1877 to the design of T. Knight, is a stately and effective Victorian Gothic church, with a stone roof of banded slate.

Bicknor 6 is a hamlet on the top of the North Downs, peacefully hidden down winding lanes of beech trees. There are a fruit-packing station, a farm, and one or two nondescript houses. The church, down a further lane, is curious in that it is built of chalk blocks, renewed after a frost disaster in 1861. The interior has splendid proportions and is full of atmosphere. High nave and chancel, narrow nave aisles, with square transitional piers. Forest of oil lamps, some on brass poles. Painted chancel ceiling and reredos and restrained glass in high-up east window—all a model of Victorian taste. Good Royal Arms of George III.

Hucking church nearby, but even more impenetrable, which goes with Bicknor, has a tiled bellcote and an unattractive cement-coloured interior, with a "stock" Clayton and Bell east window. The country is delightful, and the lane from Hucking

emerges after a cheerful inn on to the Pilgrims' Way at *Broad Street*, with some pleasant houses.

Bidborough 5. Off the road half way between Tonbridge and Tunbridge Wells, and inevitably a suburb although still a village. It remains pretty and delightful, high up, with landscapes down to the Sussex border. Spires at Tunbridge Wells shoot up into the sky, and housing creeps across the landscape. Small thirteenth-century church, dull and darkish, but pleasant enough. An inn at the other end of the street. Little villas, bungalows, and occasionally older cottages set back amongst well-kept gardens and trees. Lawns and rhododendrons. The new has not taken away from the old, and the effect, particularly in summer, is gay.

Biddenden 9 is saddled with the folk-lore anecdote of the "Maids of Biddenden", Siamese twins called Eliza and Mary Chalkhurst, born about 1500 (or 1600), and joined at the shoulder and hips for thirty-four years. They are said to have been benefactors of the village, and a dole

44

of food, with cakes embossed with their figures, is distributed every year on Easter Monday, to the available poor. No trace of their burial appears in the church itself.

The village is delightful: brick, board and tile-hung houses, some notable timbered ones, and the wide main street flanked by pavements made of slabs of Bethersden marble. There is a green at one end of the High Street and at the other the fine Kentish ragstone church, with a Jacobean pulpit and good brasses. All these evidences of wealth date from the prosperity of the cloth trade hereabout centred on Cranbrook in the fifteenth century. The timbered Cloth Weavers' hall still stands. The village survived beneath a sky path for enemy bombers during the last war. Twenty-six aircraft were shot down in the parish. The invaders now have cameras. The numerous new council estates do not spoil the centre of the village.

Biggin Hill 4 is a large suburban area, streaming north past its airfield into *Leaves Green*, and seeping south into the outskirts of Tatsfield. The wide main road is planted with trees, the shops and villas lie back from the street, and it is busy and clean. The latest development is more orderly than that of the twenties, and throughout the area occasional farms and old houses show that man lived here before the twentieth century poured its brick and concrete. On the main road is a modern yellow brick church designed by Sir Giles Gilbert Scott, and dedicated in 1957. It is built from materials salvaged from the Church of All Saints in North East Peckham.

Bilsington 16. One of the string of parishes on the Hythe-Tenterden road along the crest of the high land overlooking Romney Marsh. The little thirteenth-century church, back from the cross-roads and approached through a farm yard, has a low tower with a wooden belfry, and tremendous Marsh views beyond the Military Canal running at its foot. Old Royal Arms (correctly placed) over chancel arch. Commandment boards (incorrectly) on west wall. Oval text boards, as in other Romney Marsh churches. Bell hung under low gable

in churchyard. On a mound just opposite, amongst sheep, is an obelisk: a monument to Sir William Conway, who owned the old Priory and the land here, and was killed by a fall from a stage-coach in 1835. It is a landmark for miles. *The Priory* contained the ruins of a house of the Austin Canons founded here in 1253, when the spot was only two miles from the sea. Now it is four.

Birchington 12. Arriving along the coast road from the west it superficially presents just the "First-in, Last-out" effect of the seaside conurbation of North Thanet. In fact the town escapes the indiscriminate embrace of Margate, of which it is administratively a part, and is a comparatively quiet resort, with a

large retired population. Its fine coast has three bays: *Epple Bay* on the east, *Grenham Bay*, under a grassy cliff-top, and *Minn's Bay*, open to the west. Farther west again are the marshes to Reculver, and Plumpudding Island. In the foreground lie sand, bungalows and guest-houses. There is also an old Birchington. The main road from Margate to Canterbury runs through its Square, but there are a few mellowing houses, and a striking little Methodist chapel of 1830, standing back from the street, with a white tower and battlements. The much restored Parish Church has its shingled spire unusually placed at the east end of the south aisle. Inside the thirteenth-century chancel is a painted screen and a triptych of the Last

BICKNOR. The interior of 1861

BONNINGTON

beautifully planted, with the Little Stour running through it. The house, built in 1701, has an aristocratic yet comfortable symmetry and dignity. Unmistakably Kentish, it is of brick, pedimented in the centre, with stone porch and white paint. The village is hidden from the road by lines of pines and beeches, has a stream, some delightful houses, and has had residents of distinction. Richard Hooker ("the Judicious Hooker"), the Elizabethan theologian, was rector here and was buried in the church when he died in 1600; so was Bancroft Reade, the God-fearing pioneer scientist, who died when rector in 1870. A white farmhouse beside the church, the present rectory, was, as "Oswalds", the home of Joseph Conrad from 1919 until his death in 1924.

The church has a fine presence outside. Spacious interior, with a big Clayton and Bell east window. Burne-Jones west window, 1874, of Faith, Hope and Charity. Much sixteenth-century glass, some of it foreign. Fourteenth-century fragments (tracery lights in chancel). There is old woodwork, with poppyheads in stalls, and one very well composed wall tablet of 1603, with a bust and cherubs. Later ones, too. But all is dominated by Victorian over-attention and love.

A brick house at the north end of Bourne Park, now called *Bridgehill House* (and near Bridge church), is related in style and material to the main house.

Blackmanstone 17. An old parish and lost village on Romney Marsh.

Blean 14 is a scatter of mainly suburban houses just out of Canterbury on the way to Whitstable, in what was and in parts remains rough tangled country. The Forest of Blean was a royal one, once noted for smugglers. Now part is preserved as a nature reserve, and has public paths through the woodland and undergrowth.

Blean church is some way off the road. It was ruthlessly restored in

Supper by Westlake. In the south aisle is a memorial window to Dante Gabriel Rossetti: "Honoured . . . among painters as a painter, and among poets as a poet". He died at Birchington in 1882, and his grave is marked by an Irish cross and inscription, not far from the south door. There are also memorials to members of the Quex family, and *Quex Park* lies about half a mile to the south. William III often stayed here. The house was rebuilt in 1808, and amongst trees in the grounds is the Waterloo Tower of 1819. It has an odd lattice spire, a peal of 12 bells, one of them from a Burmese temple, and the mausoleum of the Powell-Cotton family. There is a museum of the late Major Powell-Cotton's exotic collection of zoological, ethnological and other bits, and of local archeological finds.

Birling 6 and its neighbour *Ryarsh* are both straggling villages perhaps happy to have little history or outstanding distinction. They lie north and just escape the by-pass development of the A20 out of Maidstone, without retaining or perhaps losing any special character, and with decent unimportant old churches. The tower of Birling church stands up picturesquely by the road side. The fabric is largely rebuilt, but has Nevill arms and hatchments, and a large and unusual Royal Arms of William III. Very steeply to the north of them, up tremendous lanes, lie megaliths, the Pilgrims' Way, and the line of woods above it.

Bishopsbourne 14 is an enchanting place, green and peaceful below the Canterbury to Dover road, lying beside the splendour of Bourne Park,

The Royal Military Canal at BONNINGTON

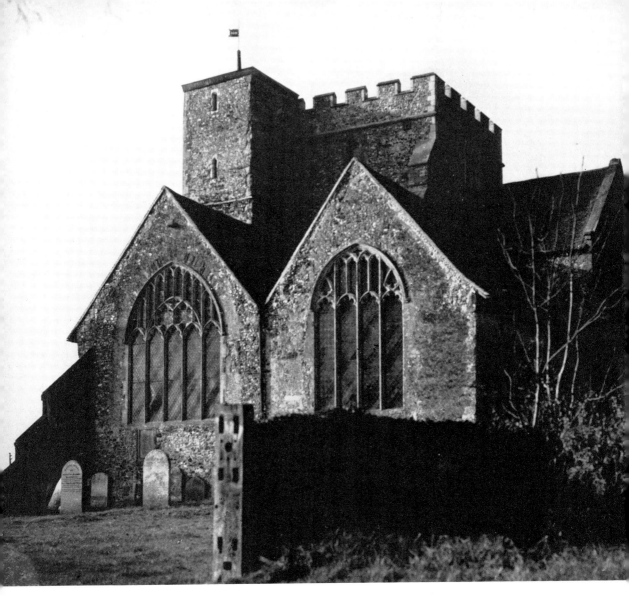

BOUGHTON ALUPH

1866. It is dedicated to SS Cosmos and Damian, the patron saints of physicians, and has one handsome wall monument in marble of 1717, and tiny medieval glass fragments.

Bobbing 10 is in orchard country, and has outliers with intimate names like Cold Harbour, Howt Green and Upper Toes. It is, however, on the Sheppey Way, from Maidstone to Kingsferry, and has bungalows and pylons. Also a small church, much Victorianized, but with two charming seventeenth-century wall monuments with busts (two each), a

carved medieval figure and fine brasses. There are vistas from the churchyard of the marshes down to the Swale, and the Isle of Sheppey beyond it. The "Execrable" Titus Oates was for a time vicar here.

Bonnington 16. A straggling parish some miles west of Hythe on the verge of Romney Marsh, with the Military Canal at its foot and rolling forested country behind it to the north. It has a little plain grey church, curiously dedicated to St Rumwold, Prince of Northumbria. It is mostly thirteenth century, but of

Norman origin. Royal Arms and Commandment boards, and a good eighteenth-century pulpit.

Borden 13 has a full complement of estates for workers from Sittingbourne, but retains a core of old houses, from Tudor to Regency, farms and pleasant rooftops. The church has a squat Norman tower (top later), a carved oak roof of about 1500 in the south chapel, and the monument of Dr Robert Plot, the historian, naturalist, and first custodian of the Ashmolean Museum at Oxford, who died in 1696. *Borden*

Hall, north of the church, is an 1896 restoration of a Tudor building. There are fine orchards all round, but even at *Hearts Delight*, down the road, not much else.

Boughton ("Bawton") Aluph 13 is surprising and delightful. Up a lane off the Canterbury road out of Ashford is a classically grouped church and manor, Boughton Court. The present house is recent, but it has Tudor and earlier parts, and a fourteenth-century crypt: a dovecote in the garden. The church is mellow flint with rose brick edging, and the inside mainly fourteenth-century work with some contemporary glass. It is airy, spacious, well-cared for and gains enormously from the expulsion of the Victorian pews. There is an early thirteenth-century screen. The seventeenth-century monument to Amye Clarke, who died in childbirth, has an attractive recumbent figure. There is a medieval Trinity painting. Most of the houses are down by the large green at what is called *Boughton Lees*, where there is a Chapel of Ease and the cricket pitch.

Boughton Malherbe 13. From the steps of the church here on the Greensand Ridge is one of the finest views in Kent, across the Weald. Below is the flat valley of the Beult river, and in the distance the steeple of Tenterden church and the far away Fairlight Hills over Hastings. The manor belonged to the Wottons, of whom the most famous is the witty Elizabethan poet and diplomat Sir Henry. The house still lies behind the church, but the panelling from it was sold to America in 1922. The church itself is over-restored. There are monuments—not very grand—to the Wottons and to another famous Kentish family, the Akers-Douglases. There is utilitarian modern development at *Grafty Green*, smothering an old hamlet in this rich and fertile valley.

Boughton Monchelsea 6 is the name of the parish surrounding Boughton Place. Most of the inhabitants now live in a modern spread called *Boughton Green*, north towards Maidstone. The church is half way down a heavily wooded hill. It stands up from the lane, approached through a medieval lych-gate, a show-piece.

The church is medieval, with an unusual low central tower, but was ruinously over-restored and enlarged in 1876. It is scraped inside, and pointed in dark grey cement. There is a splendid Scheemakers monument (Powell). The churchyard is thickly planted with roses, and has a vast unimpeded panorama of the Weald down to the hills east of Hastings. In the foreground is the park of *Boughton Place*, itself, with fallow deer. The house is a grey stone, battlemented, originally Elizabethan building. With its landscaped grounds (and their views) it is sometimes open to the public.

Boughton Street 14 is a large village which used to be called Boughton-under-Blean. This because Kent has several Boughtons (all pronounced "Bawton"), and because it does in fact lie below and climb up to the heights that were Blean Forest, on the hills west of Canterbury. But "Street" is expressive and true. There are excellent Tudor and eighteenth-century façades up the long hill, and the paths each side of the through traffic stand above green banks. The church has a fine monument by Epiphanius Evesham to Sir John Hawkins and his wife, 1587, very handsome, with two reclining effigies in stone. There are sixteenth-century brasses, but the fabric—Early English to Perpendicular—is sadly and harshly Victorianized.

Higher up on the crest of the road is *Dunkirk* with a church of 1840. From here pilgrims traditionally obtained

BOUGHTON STREET. The monument by Evesham

their first view of Canterbury Cathedral below them—now a more difficult feat.

Boxley 6. A very pretty village, although only two miles from industrial Maidstone. It is at the foot of steep wooded downland, with a belt of ilex trees to the north. Tennyson stayed at Park House in 1842, made long walks down the Pilgrims' road, and wrote about it. The church stands back on a little green facing an inn. The approach to it is attractive, and the fabric promising, but the interior is an anticlimax, through its double entrance. There is little of interest but some wall tablets and fragments of late glass from Rochester Cathedral. The parish serves 30,000, although only about 100 people live in Boxley. It is likely to remain untruded, as the land is agriculturally outstanding, and the village is in the North Down Conservation Area. *Boxley Abbey* is to the west, above *Sandling*, now a suburb of Maidstone. The modern building incorporates bits of a Cistercian house founded here in 1146. Its fourteenth-century guest house remains as a barn. The abbey was famous for a holy hoax— a "bowing rood", or miraculous crucifix with moving parts which brought pilgrims to Boxley and profit to the monks. In 1539 it was seized by Henry VIII's Commissioners, who declared it to be contrived of "certain engines of old wire, with old rotten sticks at the back". It was publicly destroyed at St Paul's Cross in London, and provided much-quoted propaganda. Boxley provided much of the fuller's earth which was an important factor in the Kentish cloth industry and the early prosperity of Maidstone. A fulling mill, now visible as the *Old Turkey Mill* on the main road, was converted into a paper mill by James Whatman in 1739, and "Whatman" and "Turkey Mill" are now trade names for high-class hand-made papers.

Brabourne 14. A pleasant hamlet, in a tangle of lanes at the foot of the high chalk downs south-east of Wye, with the Pilgrims' Way running along to the north. It is little more than one

street of cottages, with a pub at one end and the church at the other. The church, with a sturdy tower supported by a large buttress, was restored by Sir Gilbert Scott, but remains a palimpsest of styles, from Norman onwards, with some rich details. In Norman days it must have resembled Barfreston. The chancel arch is wide and high, and the chancel was clearly vaulted. There is a stump of a Norman tower, and Norman glass in one window. Later features include a strange seventeenth-century altar table with crestings and carvings, including shields in front. There are fine brasses.

Brasted 4, under the North Downs, has a long main street of generally pleasant houses on the main road from Sevenoaks to Westerham. In the middle of a tiny green with a village pump and a chestnut tree in front of tile-hung cottages: one or two small late Georgian buildings, and no eyesores, but too much traffic. The *White Hart* inn has a Battle of Britain memorial, having been much used by the pilots from Biggin Hill during the second World War.
The church lies north, beside a farmhouse and a big yew tree: a Victorian re-building with a partly thirteenth-century tower. Its most attractive feature is the large buttress in the centre of the tower west wall, with the groined entrance to the church *through* it, at ground level. There is a good deal of over-discreet modern glass. An impressive black and tawny marble monument of 1642 (Heath) has recumbent effigies. Between the village and Sundridge, to its east, is *Brasted Place*, in a large park. It was built of local stone by Robert Adam for John Turton, physician to George III, and the façade is fine and typical, but the building was greatly extended in the nineteenth century. Napoleon III lived here in 1840, before his unsuccessful attempt to land at Boulogne and seize the throne of France, and he used to walk the village with his tame but symbolic eagle.

Bredgar 13 has a village pond and war memorial, and is comparatively peaceful. There is a concrete housing estate: but some good mellower buildings, and in the parish an out-

standing Kentish yeoman's house, *Bexon*. The fifteenth-century church was originally a collegiate one, and part of the college building remains, altered and adapted with care and imagination. The church has a pleasing, light interior, with no incongruities. Old timbers in roof. Good fifteenth-century glass. Norman west doorway.

Bredhurst 6. A little village on the slope of the North Downs, and practically on the M2 motorway, but by-passed by it so completely that it is hard to reach. It is quiet, agreeable and unspectacular, with, down a long lane, a bellcote church much rebuilt in 1872, though there is thirteenth-century work in chancel and south chapel. Much Victorian glass (not very good).

Brenchley 6. A large and most attractive Wealden village. High, hopgirt, and with excellent black and white timbered buildings, including a town house of size with a central porch, and a much restored block called the Old Palace, now including the Post Office. Also a Georgian House of some distinction, and on another side of the little shady square the church, approached through an avenue of yew trees. It is very much restored, and has a pre-Raphaelite-influenced east window. Airy and light. From the churchyard are splendid views.
To the south, down lanes, is *Brattles Grange*, a half-timbered house of 1500, once the home of the Elizabethan antiquary William Lambarde, whose *Perambulation of Kent* was the first real county topographical history. Nelson's brother also owned the house, and the Admiral was a frequent guest. Fine garden.

Brenzett 16 is a tiny hamlet in Romney Marsh. It is a map point on the Rhee Wall and the road from New Romney to Appledore: a cross with an inn, a few cottages, outlying farms and a church, fiercely restored by the Victorians, that has a seventeenth-century monument to two male Roundheads of the name of Fagge. Also a nice eighteenth-century reredos now in the north aisle and a well weathered exterior with a shingled spire on a wooden tower held up by vast timbers.

Bridge 14 is an old and large village extended on the Folkestone road outside Canterbury. The traffic hurtles through ceaselessly, but the High Street retains a cheerful dignity, and is lined with agreeable although not outstanding houses, mainly Georgian. The church is a fascinating study in mid-nineteenth-century restoration (1859) or rather rebuilding (architect apparently unknown). The style of restoration is Norman-and-Early English. Really rather little of the original remains. The arcades, and other mouldings, avoid pure imitation. The glass (Gibbs) is colourful and good in detail—some highly-coloured patterned windows, one well preserved, and well worth preservation. (*See also* Bishopsbourne).

Broadstairs 12 is smaller than Ramsgate or Margate, and very consciously less dedicated to the greatest happiness of the greatest number. It merges indeed into both resorts, but retains the qualities which made it a successful watering place and seaside home for the middle classes until the 1930s. It has the required paraphernalia for a resort, and the range of those who enjoy it has widened, but there is a sense of intimacy, of not entirely faded distinction, and of gaiety, not mass-produced.

In early times it never was much more than a village, although it fitted out some ships for the cod fishing off Greenland and Iceland. This trade was badly hit by the destruction of the pier in 1792. Salvation from mere smuggling came soon, however, with the discovery of the seaside for health and recreation. The resort faced east, had several little bays (Viking Bay is the main one) with excellent sands, pleasant public gardens and chalk cliffs for "bracing" walks. At once it became more fashionable than Ramsgate, and less intruded from London.

The old part of the town, with wandering streets and some early Victorian houses, is of this period. The present pier is basically that of 1808, with extensions, and there is a cheerful little harbour, used by yachts and light vessels. Over it, dark and less cheerfully, stands out the crenellated Bleak House. This is not the setting of Dickens' novel, but he did live here in 1850, when it was smaller and called Fort House. It had

belonged to Wilkie Collins. There Dickens wrote *David Copperfield*. He was fond of the town, and came back almost every summer from 1837 till 1851. He stayed first at what is now No 31 in the High Street, working on *Pickwick Papers*. Then at a building now absorbed into the Albion Hotel, where he finished *Nicholas Nickleby* in 1839, and then at Archway House, off Harbour Street. Dickens House, at the north end of Victoria Parade, is claimed as the setting of the home of Miss Betsy Trotwood. Compulsive Dickensians attend a Festival every October to visit these and other sites.

The steep Harbour Street has a flint arch over it called York Gate, built about 1540, during the invasion scare, to secure the gap in the cliff from potential landing parties. Both Eastern and Western Esplanades have some charming houses, and in Albion Street is the former Chapel of St Mary, rebuilt in 1601. It is the Parish Room of Holy Trinity Church, itself rebuilt in mock Renaissance style in 1925.

St Peters, a separate parish a mile-and-a-quarter inland, is now civically and physically part of Broadstairs, although it has its own history. It possesses the mother church, which preserves part of the original building of 1070, and has a sixteenth-century tower, used as a signal station during the Napoleonic Wars. In the High Street are some very early Victorian Almshouses. At Pierrepont Hall Queen Victoria spent some of her childhood. "We can't do better than good old Broadstairs", said Mr Pooter, discussing holidays. Many devoted families still agree with him. *North Foreland* Lighthouse is a mile-and-a-half north of Broadstairs, along a coast road of seaside villas. It stands on the most easterly part of Kent, over prominent white cliffs, and its light is visible for 22 miles. The site was known to the Romans, and there was probably a beacon here from the earliest times, although documentary evidence only dates from 1505. Out to sea here, in 1666, General Monck defeated the Dutch admiral De Ruyter, after a four-day battle.

The tower of the lighthouse is clean, white, functional and 85 feet high, and can be visited.

Bromley ("The glade among the broom") 1. The kindest view is still perhaps from the train: buildings climbing and surmounting a hill, obviously in a completely built-up area, but from this perspective still with trees and some sense of dominating from its gravel ridge the country round it. On foot this ancient market town, on the outskirts of London and enduring the main roads to Sevenoaks and Hastings, is a contemporary mess. It has always had historical importance. It was a favourite home of the bishops of Rochester, an important market centre, and visited by the famous down to the eighteenth century. Although in 1851 the population was still only 4,000, in 1858 the railway came and by 1900 the population was 27,000. Today, as part of Greater London, it is over 68,000. Apart from one or two old buildings the houses tell the story: residences for prosperous Victorian merchants and the churches for their worship, shops increasingly flashy and standardized, jazzed-up façades and streamlined new ones, amenity buildings, offices, and above all traffic. Bromley is, however, a town, not an aggregation of mean streets: its newer buildings are better than those of its recent past: it has an active repertory company and vigorous societies: its future no doubt continues prosperous.

At the London entrance to the town is Bromley College, an almshouse founded in 1666 by John Warner, Bishop of Rochester, for twenty widows of orthodox and loyal clergymen. It is a pleasant block of Restoration brickwork: two quadrangles with cloisters, not improved by a Gothic chapel of 1865. The central porch, seen from the road, has attractive coloured arms on it, warm and mellowed. Fine wrought iron gates.

In the complex of roads at the Market Place is the Parish Church of St Peter & St Paul. It was destroyed by a German bomb in 1941, except for the tower, which is marvellously restored and married to a new functional body designed by J. Harold Gibbons. Dr Johnson's wife Tetty, who died in 1752, whom he always mourned, was buried here. *St John the Evangelist* is a "development" church: uncompromisingly Victorian

BROOK: inside and outside

Gothic of 1880 by G. Truefitt.

In a park amongst a maze of streets also off the Market Place is a handsome Georgian building of 1775, enlarged and used as a training college for teachers. It was once Bromley Palace, the residence of the Bishops of Rochester.

Bromley Common, with its bracken, still exists to the south, and to the north Sundridge Park has its golf course on the grounds once laid out by Repton round the house classically designed by Nash in 1799.

Brook 14, being only about five miles north-east of Ashford, is very much built up as a dormitory. It is a long straggling village, with one or two pleasant old cottages, in beautiful country framed by trees on the escarpment of the broad downs. The Norman church restored in 1896,

stands remote. "One of the best examples of an unaltered church representing what the majority of larger Kent churches were like before aisles were added" (Francis Grayling). Completely Norman, with impressive proportions. Restored, but keeps its "bone-structure". The quoins are of oolitic limestone from the Isle of Wight. There are wall-paintings which before the colour had faded richly illustrated the Bible story for the medieval illiterate, and a good Tudor pulpit.

Wye students cut the Wye's Crown on the downs to the west, to mark Queen Victoria's Jubilee, and use a fine old barn in the village for a museum of agricultural implements.

Brookland 16. An inland Romney Marsh village, which seems self-contained and remote although on a

bend in the main Folkestone–Rye road. It has a pleasant inn. Beside the church is a curious detached bell-tower. This campanile has tremendous timbers, said to come from nearby wrecks, to carry the weight of the bells, and is tiered like a wooden crinoline and covered with shingles, formerly weather-boards. It never stood, nor was intended to stand, on top of the church.

The church itself, red-tiled and beside a little rhine, is airy and attractive, with box-pews, king post roofs and a twelfth-century font of lead, showing the Signs of the Zodiac and the Occupations of the Months.

Broomfield. *See* Leeds.

Burham 6 is an unattractive village of modern and nineteenth-century brick stretching along a road with

Mercery Lane, CANTERBURY

with a fifteenth-century tower, and a few nondescript houses. The inland cliffs climbing to Lympne Castle make a dramatic backcloth.

Canterbury 14 is the cradle of English Christianity, and its Archbishops are historically the Primates of All England. It is also a county borough of over 30,000 inhabitants, and a busy shopping and market centre, on what has always been the main road from London to the south-east. It is packed with visitors who have come to see it and the people who use it: yet its main incident and interest lie within the area enclosed by what remains of the medieval walls—a good deal—about half a mile from east to west, and slightly more from north to south. The best impression of it can be gained very early before breakfast or on a wet Sunday, when it can be resolved into its main ingredients: the medieval buildings and dominating Cathedral, which pilgrims come to visit: the county town of variegated architecture which reflects the normal development of a prosperous city into the twentieth century: and finally, post-blitz utilitarian development.

Canterbury straddles the River Stour, and was a natural spot for a settlement from the earliest times. Whilst its history is mainly that of the Cathedral, the results of bomb clearance and excavation for new building have exposed much that was not known earlier of the Roman Durovernum (the city of the marsh) which was set up here on a site already used in Neolithic times, when Bigbury to the north was probably a tribal capital. There was a Roman theatre, the largest so far discovered in Britain, public baths, barrack facilities, and what was necessary for a small but key centre for local administration. The hypocaust and tesselated pavement of a Roman town house are preserved and on show under a block of new buildings in Longmarket. For four hundred years the legions marched through the city, for it was the junction of the roads which led from London to the ports of Ritupiae (Richborough), Dubris (Dover) and Lemanis (Lympne), and so to the heart of Empire.

Bridge Wood and the downs magnificent above it, and the industrial Medway to the west below. The cruciform Gothic-revival church dates the village's Victorian redevelopment here, when between 1861 and 1881 the population doubled with the coming of the cement industry. The old village and manor were west, down by the river. The manor itself and a few scattered buildings still remain, together with the old flint and stone church, which is charming but almost disused, though well repaired. It has clear glass. A Roman

temple to Mithras was found hollowed in the sandbank when the lime works were first built here. All this gives a certain sad charm, in spite of the factories across the river at Snodland and the traffic through the village above.

Burmarsh 17. A typical flat Romney Marsh parish extending to the coast. The village is only five miles from Hythe, but seems remote, down twisting lanes bordered with bulbs and sheep. Scattered farms beside a dyke, a plain grey church, locked,

The Crypt,
CANTERBURY Cathedral

STAY GENTLE READER PASS NOT SLIGHTLY BY
THIS TOMBE IS SACRED TO ... THE MEMORY
OF ... THORNEHVRST WHAT HE WAS & WHO
THESE FEW LINES ENOUGH IN ME TO SHEW
NOBLING BRAVE & STOUT AT LENGTH I EXPLAINE
BOTH GERMANYES, THE NEW FOUND WORLD & SPAINE
OSTENDS LONG BRIDGE & NEWPORT BATTLE TRYD
HIS WORTH, AT LAST WARRING WITH FRANCE HE DYD
THE BLOOD-REALD ... LAST CONQVEST FOR BLACKE FAIR
GAVE HIM AT ONCE A DEATH AND VICTORIE ...
HIS DEATH AS WELL AS LIFE VICTORIOUS WAS
YEARING ... LEAST FEE (AS MIGHT BE BROVGHT TO PASS)
BY OTHERS MIGHT BE LOST ... IN TYME TO COME
HE TOOKE POSSESSION TILL THE DAY OF DOOME

The Saxons took over the city, and it became Cantwarabyrig: the "stronghold of the people of Kent". By 560 it was the capital of Ethelbert, the fourth Saxon king of Kent. His Frankish wife, Bertha, was a Christian convert, and Christianity had a tradition here since Roman times, for a hoard of Roman silver, some with the Christian monogram, was discovered by workmen making the new Rheims Way into the city in 1962. At all events the missionary expedition of St Augustine, when it arrived in 597, was obviously welcome. Ethelbert granted Augustine the church of St Martin, already in use for Christian services, and was himself baptized. Augustine established a Benedictine monastery. Then in 602, after a visit to Rome, he founded a second monastery on the site of the Roman basilica. This church grew under the Normans into the first and great Cathedral. The struggle of its archbishops with the secular power of the kings, internationalism versus nationalism, is the central theme of English and indeed European history throughout the Middle Ages. The dramatic highlight was the murder of Thomas à Becket, who had been appointed Archbishop eight years before, in 1170. He was canonized in 1172, and the pilgrims already accustomed to visit Canterbury became a river of devotion that swelled from the twelfth to the sixteenth centuries. Christ Church Priory was also the greatest landlord in southern England, owning tens of thousands of acres, with twenty manors in Kent alone. Something of the story of the shrine at its peak emerges, with the licence of a poet and the dispassion of a civil servant, in the *Canterbury Tales*. Chaucer compiled these between 1373 and his death in 1400. Pilgrims, and contributions at the shrine of St Thomas, were declining by Tudor times, so that the social and moral shock of the Dissolution did not cripple Canterbury. In 1538 the great monastery was suppressed, the rich shrine itself plundered, and there were martyrs of both sides in the religious struggles. But Elizabeth I gave shelter here to French and

Walloon refugees, and their descendants still have their chapel in the Cathedral crypt. Further immigrants in the seventeenth century improved again methods of the silk weaving, which exists as an industry today. Cromwell's soldiers breached the city walls and desecrated the Cathedral, but Canterbury became a fairly peaceful market town by the eighteenth century, still dominated by its Cathedral, still busy on the main road, famous but undisturbed. In 1830 the Canterbury and Whitstable railway line was opened—the second in England. By high Victorian times there was bustle and some development, with the city increasingly a social as well as a clerical centre, for it was also a garrison town, the Headquarters of the Buffs, the Royal East Kent Regiment. Its cricket week, with the marquees, flowers, flags and Kent often top of the county championship, made a gay turn to the century.

In the last war Canterbury suffered the "Baedeker" raids from German aircraft in May and June 1942, and although the Cathedral itself survived, a large area in the middle of the city was destroyed. The modern buildings that have grown up round this end of the main thoroughfare,

CANTERBURY Cathedral: the Black Prince

CANTERBURY Cathedral:
Lady Margaret Holland with
Sir Thomas Thornhurst beyond.

and the bus station there have aroused bitter controversy, and some are perhaps unimaginative. But it was not a medieval city that was bombed: it was a cross-section of urban architecture round a treasured medieval centre. In the middle of the area, at the top of St George's Street, many old buildings are gone, including that in which Marlowe was born. So has the church of St George, in which he was baptized in 1564, except for the tower, preserved and surrounded by modern shops. More new buildings will come. In the meantime the spaces wantonly opened by bombing make car-parks.

The A2 from London sweeps down a fine new approach which shows well the Cathedral standing back above the rooftops. Then it syphons off the through traffic, going round roughly the line where once were the south-west walls of the city. The direct road from London, for legionaries, pilgrims, and now motorists, passes *St Dunstans Church* before reaching the *West Gate*. Here William the Conqueror traditionally confirmed the ancient privileges of the Men of Kent, Henry II walked in penitence to be scourged at the shrine of St Thomas in 1174, and more recently those committed to gaol in the city were lodged till 1829. It is now a museum, and there is an orientating view from its roof. The present gate with massive twin towers was built by Archbishop Simon of Sudbury in 1380. He also built the *Holy Cross Church*, much restored, lying just to the south.

Inside Westgate the old Watling Street stops being called St Dunstan's Street and the main thoroughfare becomes successively *St Peter's Street*, *High Street*, *Parade* and *St George's Street*. The shops, pubs and municipal buildings at the western end of all this are the normal variegated façades of any old town that has kept up with modern commercial display. The general effect and roof level is agreeable enough. At the eastern end, where bomb destruction was worst, the buildings have stark new lines and are on the whole higher, although gigantic disfiguring blocks have been tolerably resisted. Peppered along, of deep or lesser interest, are older buildings which include, from east to west:

On the left, *St Peter's Church*, an unremarkable fourteenth-century building with earlier work in the Norman arcade and elsewhere, and later work of 1882. Then *The Kings Bridge*, and on its left the *Weavers' Houses*. These were built about 1500, but the half-timbered row hanging above the river has been much restored. It remains photogenic. The Huguenot weavers who settled in Canterbury after the Revocation of the Edict of Nantes (1685) set up some of their looms here. Opposite, the *Hospital of St Thomas*, or Eastbridge Hospital, founded as a hostel for poor pilgrims in the twelfth century. It is still an almshouse, administered under a sixteenth-century statute. Over the crypt, probably the original dormitory, is a hall and a thirteenth-century chapel. The wing jutting over the river is mellow seventeenth-century.

Further on are the *Library and Museum*, elaborate Victorian Tudor, and opposite it the refurbished *County Hotel*. Then a Tudor restaurant, *Queen Elizabeth's Guest Chamber*, re-done, but with an interesting plaster ceiling.

After this *Mercery Lane* and *Butchery Lane*, occupational names, lead off left to the Cathedral precincts. At the corner of Mercery Lane, where the pilgrims bought their souvenirs at the stalls and booths, is medieval "jettying": a remnant of the great pilgrim inn "The Chequers of the Hope". Medieval vaulted undercrofts extend from here towards the Cathedral, under the present shops. Both roads lead into *Burgate Street*, which has fascinating houses of many styles and centuries, including attractive Georgian ones. Straight on are the new buildings and the main road goes out between the eastern walls of the old city.

North of the thoroughfare the northwest segment of the city, with *St Radigunds Street* and *Pound Lane* following the line of the wall, has several pleasant individual houses, several charming bits of river, a cinema, drill hall and *St Alpheges' Church*, another of the eight churches which once stood in the northern part of the city alone. Those that remain repay the interest of the enthusiast, but are hardly to be included in the same experience as the Cathedral.

Nearby, backing on to the Stour, are remains of the priory of the Dominicans, the *Black Friars*, who founded it in 1326. The buildings, which include the refectory, beautifully placed in a garden, and very well kept, have been used as a Christian Science church since 1942.

The south-west segment, on the left bank of the Stour, is much of it unexacting to the visitor. *Stour Street*, however, has, standing prettily over the river, the dorter of the *Grey Friars*, the first Franciscan friary in England, put up here in 1267, and later for a time the home of the poet Richard ("stone walls") Lovelace. Also the *Poor Priest's Hospital*, mainly fourteenth-century, and another of these numerous hostels, *Maynard's Hospital*, now mainly early eighteenth-century and modern. At the perimeter of *Castle Street*, is what is left of the *Castle* itself—a gloomy lump of masonry which is the shorn-off keep. It was once 80 feet high, and has its history, but is dim and unimpressive. A passage opposite to it leads into the south-east segment of the city, and the *Dane John Gardens*. These form a grassy space within the medieval walls, here in fine repair, with four semicircular bastions, and provide a pleasant walk above what was the moat and is now the busy ring road that hugs the perimeter of the old city. The walls indeed run all the way round from here to the north in one of the most impressive stretches of medieval town fortification in the country, including, by postern leading into the close, a bastion which has been made into a beautiful memorial chapel. Some of the foundations of the walls are Roman, but the main work is fourteenth-century, with the bastions rather later.

In the Dane John Gardens is a vast conical lump, probably prehistoric, an inexplicable urban Silbury variously and romantically explained. Perhaps it did indeed serve at some time as a keep or "donjon" to give the gardens their name. It was heightened in the eighteenth century to make it a viewpoint, and a pillar stuck on top. There is a Marlowe monument, and at the east end of the

CANTERBURY Cathedral: The south nave arcade

58

gardens, where the road arrived from Dover, George Stephenson's locomotive No. 12, the *Invicta*. It was made in 1830, plied, not very happily, on the Canterbury and Whitstable railway.

Outside the walls to the east, facing them across the trim *Lady Wotton's Green* is the great gate of *St Augustine's Abbey*, which was built in 1300, but elevated and embellished in the fifteenth century. Rescued from service as a brewhouse, it is now the entrance to *St Augustine's College*. This is a grey and institutional, but by no means unworthy 1848 Gothic building by Butterfield, including parts of the ruins of the original monastic cloister. The college was founded for training Anglican missionaries, but, after extension in 1952, has now a wider and more ecumenical purpose.

A path by the side of the gate leads to the ruins of the main part of the old abbey—the site Ethelbert had given to Augustine in 597, and which grew, with the fame and splendour of Canterbury, to become the greatest Benedictine house in England, and a rival to Monte Cassino itself. Henry VIII grabbed it as a royal palace after the Dissolution, and royalty used it occasionally up to the time of Charles II. Then it declined and by 1836 was a brewery. It was rescued, excavated, and is now the property of the Ministry of Works. The whole ground plan can be traced, but few of the walls are more than a few feet high. It is peaceful, with a playing field on one side, remains of a windmill on the horizon, and on the north the expanding modern buildings of the Christ Church College of Education. Still going east down *Longport Street*, past the prison and on the right a row of little seventeenth-century almshouses (*Smith's Hospital*), a road turns up to the left to *St Martin's Church*, very much the most important in Canterbury, and perhaps the earliest place of Christian worship extant in England. It stands up steps off the narrow road, like a quiet village church, made of simple Kentish ragstone with a squat fourteenth-century tower. Here St Au-

CANTERBURY Cathedral:
The south aisle

gustine is supposed to have baptized Ethelbert in 597. The Foundations are Roman, and there is Roman work throughout the walls. The chancel is perhaps the Saxon one built for Ethelbert's Queen Bertha, extended eastwards in the twelfth century. There is much else.

The Cathedral

The main and proper entrance to the precincts is through the ornate *Christ Church Gate*, at the end of Burgate Street, and facing the Butter Market. This was built at the beginning of the sixteenth century, but the doors are seventeenth century. The front was restored and magnificently repainted just before the last war. Inside is space, discreet provision for the needs and guidance of visitors, and the first close view of the building which majestically dominates the whole city. It is not the largest cathedral in England: several cover a wider area, and the biggest medieval cathedral is the Minster at York. In interior length Canterbury is, at 517 feet, fourth. The great tower is 235 feet high. But its glory is not size: rather, and quite apart from sentiment, its blending of styles and components.

The first Romano-British church of St Augustine was rebuilt in 950, with the monastery, by Archbishop Odo. It was sacked by the Danes and destroyed by fire in 1067 immediately after the Conquest. This provided the opportunity for a magnificent new Norman cathedral at once started by Archbishop Lanfranc, and continued under St Aldhelm. Prior Conrad extended the building to almost double its previous size, and this new building was consecrated in 1130. Part remains, but the choir was burned down in another fire of 1174. This accident was again timed providentially; for the cult of St Thomas was now at its peak, and gifts from pilgrims provided funds for reconstruction on the most lavish scale. Rebuilding was begun by the French architect William of Sens in 1175, with stone from Caen in Normandy, landed down river at Fordwich. After he had suffered a crippling fall from the scaffolding the work was finished by William "the Englishman", who built the Trinity chapel and the Corona at the east end, with the crypt beneath them. In 1220 the remains of

CANTERBURY Cathedral:
p 62   *The choir*
p 63   *The nave*

Becket were translated to the great new shrine in the Chapel. The next major building operation was in 1378, when the prolific Archbishop Simon of Sudbury pulled down much of the remaining Norman work, and began a new nave and transept, designed by the master-mason Henry Yevele. Building continued, chapels were added, and the final glory of the great central tower, the Bell Harry, also called the Angel Steeple, was finished by John Wastell in 1498. So that (forgetting one of the western towers, rebuilt in 1831) there is massive early Norman work, the more delicate late Norman choir of William of Sens, and the Gothic spendour of Yevele's nave, and finally and crowning it, the Tudor great tower. The general plan emerging from all this is that of a double cross with two western towers, a huge crypt or undercroft, and at the east end the circular chapel of the "Corona", or "Becket's Crown".

The wonder of the interior is a matter of individual reaction. The most casual visitor will be struck by the sweep of the building from the west end of the nave to the choir, on a higher level, behind the thirteenth-century screen, and on to the Trinity Chapel, raised again, behind the altar at the east end. But from the east end the full majesty of the building is perhaps best seen, owing to the commanding height. The crypt beneath is in two parts. The western part is the earlier, of about 1100, and has carved capitals; the eastern part is higher and bigger, and about 80 years later in date. In St Anselm's chapel here is one of the masterpieces of Romanesque painting, St Paul and the Viper. There are also paintings of twelfth-century date in St Gabriel's chapel, of scenes in his life.

The scene of Becket's martyrdom is altered from its twelfth-century setting, and the stone indicated as the spot is directly below a rather complacent monument to Alexander Chapman of Norfolk, 1629, outside the Lady Chapel. Some will be more moved by the incomparable rich colour of the early medieval glass. Others by the *tombs*. The oldest tomb

61

in the Cathedral is of a Crusader, Archbishop Walter, who died in 1205. The most thrilling of the medieval monuments is that in the Trinity chapel, where Becket's shrine was, to the Black Prince, 1376, eldest son of Edward III, hero of Crecy and Poitiers and ravager of Limoges. He is recumbent, in golden plate armour (gilt latten), with the arms of England and France blazoned across his body's front under his praying hands. The head is clearly a portrait—he was 46 when he died. A wooden canopy hangs above him, and replicas of his surcoat, gauntlets, shield and scabbard, the originals of which are preserved under glass nearby, below the Pilgrim's steps. In the bay next to the Black Prince is the tomb of Archbishop Courtney, 1396; and across the chapel is Henry IV with Joan of Navarre, his wife—a composition of immense style and grandeur, with double effigies. Next to this is the Renaissance tomb—nearly two hundred years later in date—of Dean Nicholas Wotton, 1567, a fine work, imaginative and touching, its classicism marrying easily with the earlier Gothic tombs and glass in its neighbourhood. Between choir and High Altar, on the north side of the Presbytery, is an immensely decorated and much restored monument of Archbishop Chichele, 1443, supporter of Henry V and founder of All Souls College, which is zealous in maintaining and re-decorating it. He is on a table tomb, lying in prayer, with a sculptured corpse as *memento mori* visible through the table's arched supports. On the other side of the Presbytery, Archbishop Strafford has a fine canopied effigy, 1348. These are the highlights at the east end of the cathedral.

In St Michael's chapel—the "Warrior's chapel"—are more remarkable monuments. The great central one with three figures is for Lady Margaret Holland and her two husbands, John Beaufort, Earl of Somerset, and Thomas Plantagenet, son of Henry IV. The chapel, which had in it Stephen Langton's tomb, which is now half in and half outside its east wall, was rebuilt by the lady. The big tomb with reclining figures and two dressy soldiers holding back alabaster curtains, is of 1627 to Sir Thomas

Thornhurst. There is a striking marble bust (Sir George Rooke) in the south-west corner. In the Lady Chapel—north of the north choir aisle—is a fine late thirteenth-century black marble tomb of Archbishop Peckham. And here too is the impressive late monument of Dean Rogers sitting in meditation with his elbow on a table; while not far away, outside the Lady Chapel in the north transept and opposite the Martyrdom is Archbishop William Warham, 1532, under a tremendous canopy against the wall. In the nave the most rewarding are the "Maces monument" with a relief carving of a ship, 1596; Dean Boys, reclining on his side, 1612 (these on the north side); a Rysbrack (Sympson), 1759; and a Weekes (Sir George Gipps), 1849 (on the south).

The splendid font is of seventeenth-century black and white marble, the wooden cover supported by a wrought-iron construction with a cresting supporting the Stuart Royal Arms. The pulpit is by Bodley.

The imaginative will wish to recreate the interior as it was in its prime, decorated, curtained, filled with chapels and colour. But this needs solitude, which is improbable, though there is, in fact, much more, and richer, colour here than usual. The stained glass at Canterbury is wonderful. Walk in the Close along the south flank of the church and see the lustreless but beautiful greys of the glass in the windows outside, pitted with age and varied with subtle changes of tone. It has a *patina* that is wholly agreeable with the weathered stone that frames it. Then go inside, and see these aged greys coruscate into intense and virile colour. The required shock of delight that early glass can give is more positive at Canterbury than anywhere else in England. Chartres, Bourges, Le Mans, Sens, Auxerre— all have a mass of early glass. In this country only Lincoln otherwise has much of its original coloured glazing left, and Canterbury has infinitely more than Lincoln. Walking round, past the base of the windows, the lower panels being often on eye-level, what strikes us is the apparent disorder and casualness—the tangled skein look—of the leading at close range, and then the rigid geometrical

order of the panels themselves in the whole window. The appeal of all this to our twentieth-century eyes, conditioned as we are by the contrasting tones, bright colours and ordered disorder of much modern art, is as great as it can ever have been since the windows were new.

Some of the glass is late twelfth-century—after the fire that destroyed the choir in 1174; more is thirteenth-century. Among the oldest are the "genealogical" windows, which were intended to show the descent of Christ from Adam (Luke, 3). The ones that remain are not together, but can be seen (some of them high in clerestory lights) in the transepts, the Trinity Chapel and the west window of the nave. This last has glass of different dates, a lot of it moved here in the eighteenth century. The genealogical figures including (centre) the famous picture of Adam delving, dressed in a sheepskin, are near the base. The mass of thirteenth-century glass—and it is this that impresses us as we enter— is the "biblio pauperum", the strip cartoons used for instruction and sermons on the Bible, and on lives of saints and martyrs including, of course, Becket (Trinity Chapel aisle, north side. Restored, and not all of original design).

The Precincts, remains of the conventual buildings of the cathedral, are full of charm. The Great Cloister was built largely by Prior Chillenden at the beginning of the fifteenth century, but includes some of Lanfranc's cloister. The heraldic decoration has recently been repainted with skill and remarkable effect. The Chapter House was also completed by Chillenden, but also incorporates earlier work. It is much used for entertainments during the festivals of the Friends of the Cathedral, and Eliot's *Murder in the Cathedral* was first staged here. The Library is new, made of Kentish flint, and harmonises well with the older buildings. Near it, with Norman piers and arches, is the water-tower which supplied the Priory. Beyond a passage divides, leading one way to what is left of the Infirmary, and the other through the

CANTERBURY Cathedral: Stained Glass figure in the clerestory

CAPEL LE FERNE Church

Sir William Holford and Partners whose work included the campus two colleges and another building Farmer and Dark designed the next college, and are at present planning consultants for the whole complex.

Cape 15, near Tonbridge, has a small church of nave and chancel with fourteenth-century wall paintings and a rather attractive interior. Creed, Commandments and Royal Arms have all been placed on the west wall.

Capel le Ferne 18 (or Capel Street) is a mass of development on the highest part of the Downs, along the coast road from Folkestone, two miles out towards Dover. It is ugly enough, but has magnificent views across the channel. It is named from the fact of the hamlet being originally a chapelry of Alkham, and retains, remote from the road, a tiny church with a fourteenth-century stone rood screen, three-arched, with another arch over for the rood. Well-carved churchyard stones.

Chalk 3. On the map is a prong of suburban development at the eastern tip of Gravesend. The church, a place of pilgrimage to Dickensians, lies half a mile farther on, off the Rochester road. Here there are farms, one or two cottages, and on a mound the church of medieval dark flint and stone which Dickens used when he spent his honeymoon in Chalk. There are grotesques over the porch door which he enjoyed: a laughing figure with a jug, and a merryandrew. Between them an empty niche made for a statue of the Virgin Mary, to whom the church is dedicated. To the north, marshes, the river, and, according to the light, marine activity or a sense of *Great Expectations*.

Challock Lees. *See* Eastwell.

Charing 13 is by-passed by the main road but much visited as a "show village". Considering this, and a fringe of concrete cottages, it is remarkably unspoilt. The High Street climbs up the steep slope of the Downs. It has pretty timbered and eighteenth-century houses and the tiny square in front of the church is charming, with on one side of it the

Dark Entry, the haunt of Nell Cook in the *Ingoldsby Legends*, into the courts of the *King's School*. This, although perhaps the oldest school in the country, having been started as a monastic foundation in the seventh century, was re-founded and named for Henry VIII in 1541, as a grammar school for 50 scholars. As well as Christopher Marlowe its old boys have included William Harvey, the discoverer of the circulation of the blood, the great Lord Chancellor Thurlow, and such disparate moderns as Walter Pater, Sir Hugh Walpole and Somerset Maugham. It has a new assembly hall by Darcy Braddell and a main block of creditable nineteenth-century buildings, but also the grey beauty of medieval ones, and the roofed Norman external staircase

to the Hall which is famous and understandably over-photographed. Outside the King's School, and so the precincts, lies Palace Street, with the infinitely beamy school tuckshop and much else to wonder at.

Amongst many other buildings and vantage points there lies at the opposite and east side of the precincts a beautiful garden, once belonging to the Dean and Chapter but now the Kent County War Memorial, designed by Sir Herbert Baker. From it the cathedral and the Great Tower are seen rising in majesty. Behind it lies the city wall, and underneath this, where the moat flowed, is a car park.

The University of Kent is still being developed on its fine site overlooking the city. The original architects were ruins, now part of a farm, of one of the chief palaces of the Archbishops of Canterbury. Henry VII and Henry VIII both stayed here as guests, with enormous retinues, and it ranked as a town of minor consequence.

The church is impressive: mainly a rebuilding after a fire of 1590, but with a fine west tower in Kentish Perpendicular style, a nave roof (1590) of Wealden oak, carved, and a well-proportioned interior, with modern screen and other fittings.

Chartham 14 is ugly but clean: industrialized but has history. It is in fact pleasantly placed in a valley beside the Stour, below the Ashford to Canterbury road with the traffic upon it and the hop-fields behind. It has an open green with the church on its south side, and some agreeable old houses as the core of the village. A large modern paper factory, spreading across the river, forms the rest of it. But paper-making has been going on here for centuries.

The church is fourteenth century and impressive, with a fine use of flint. The restored interior has a splendid roof of vaulted oak beams. The chancel has famous fourteenth-century "Kentish" traceried windows. There is enough old glass in these to have allowed a complete (and quite sensitive) replacement of what had been destroyed. There is an outstanding brass effigy of Sir Robert de Septuans, who died in 1306, and a monument of 1788 by Rysbrack with two near life-sized figures. The churchyard has been very much tidied up, and the stones set round the perimeter, like naughty, or infectious, children. On the river just north of the village are two tiny hamlets with medieval but unimportant churches, *Horton* and *Milton*, and on the heights to its east a huge hospital.

Chart Sutton 6 has an 1820-ish church, gothic, with a lot of poor later glass and a squat stone tower. There are medieval traces.

Chartwell. *See* Crockham Hill.

Chatham 3 is at once a chapter of British Naval history and part of the long busy unbroken urban strip that

CHEVENING: The 'Keyhole'

starts at Strood and stretches through to beyond Gillingham: centuries of nautical history, lines of multiple stores, three miles of naval dockyard, some Dickens relics, nearly 50,000 inhabitants and very few memorable buildings.

It is the dockyards which give it individual character. Henry VIII started using the fishing village here for defence purposes. Queen Elizabeth, in the crash defence programme against the threat of the Armada, founded the giant dockyard and the arsenal. This was enlarged by the Stuarts to become the main naval station in the kingdom. When it was surprised and humiliated in 1667, as Van Ghent sailed the Dutch fleet up the Medway, a series of forts were built along the banks of the river, and in 1758 the fortifications known

as the Chatham Lanes were begun to the north-east. All this was further strengthened during the Napoleonic wars. Meanwhile a dockyard and garrison town had developed with all the colour and heartbreak of these places everywhere, and some of this emerges in Dickens. He came to the town as a child in 1816, his father in the Navy Pay Office. They lived at No. 2 Ordnance Terrace until 1821, and then in other houses now destroyed. Some of the picture is included, in caricature, in *Pickwick Papers* and the *Sketches by Boz*. For most of the nineteenth century Chatham Dockyards constituted the largest industrial centre in Kent, and prosperity was swelled by cement, engineering and until 1946 flying boats. Nothing could prevent proximity to London, raw materials, and

the available waterways making the whole strip a cluster of dedicated and prosperous ugliness.

The cheerful and crowded *High Street* has no old houses of distinction, except perhaps the *Sun Inn*, although they are better than the gimcrack ones in *Military Street* which crosses it, and leads down to the *Town Hall*, a piece of proud municipal architecture of 1899. But down a few steps on the north side of the High Street is *Sir John Hawkins Hospital*, founded by the great navigator and slaver in 1592 for "poor decayed mariners and shipwrights": an odd little group of houses and a chapel round a tiny square, with further steps down to the Medway. It was restored in the last century. Opposite is *St Bartholomew's Chapel*, originally part of a leper hospital founded by Bishop Gundulph of Rochester in 1078. The huge modern hospital which dominates this side of the street claims continuity from it. There is some riverside incident down by the *Sun Pier*, up in the *Victoria Gardens* behind the Town Hall is space, and a fine view across the Medway. *Fort Pitt*, near by, was built in 1803, and after vicissitudes is now a girls' Technical School. Round about it are one or two depressed Regency houses.

Churches: *St John*, by Sir Robert Smirke, 1821, and unhappily restored, 1869; *Christ Church*, E. R. Robson, 1884, and, most imposing, *St Mary's*. This is on a rise leaving the town towards the Dockyard entrance. The site is Saxon, bits are Norman, but the building as it stands is the work of Sir Arthur Blomfield, who effectively completed in 1908 a rebuilding of the Georgian church of Dickens' time. The tower is particularly striking.

The Dockyard, beyond, has an imposing gateway, and occupies some 500 acres of stern institutional buildings. It still builds ships, repairs them, and is a Naval headquarters. Beyond the gates the next bit is historically called *Brompton*, and was once a separate village. It became residential for the officers of the dockyard, and a restored eighteenth-century tavern remains in Mansion Row. But the main road continues with the vast *Barracks* of the Royal Engineers and the *School of Military*

CHILHAM

Engineering, with a statue of General Gordon on a camel, by E. Onslow Ford, and inside the Royal Engineers Museum. On again are the *Royal Naval Barracks*, with 15 windows by Hugh Easton in the Garrison Church chancel.

Interest in Chatham is historical and specialized. But it is there, although the tide of traffic sweeps more urgently than that of the Estuary.

Chelsfield 2 is bifurcated by the Orpington by-pass. It is high up on the chalk hills, still surrounded by country, and with views of the Orpington valley. On the east side of the road is a weatherboard inn and some old cottages, trying to preserve dignity. On the west, very dignified indeed, lie back the church and the fine Court House. The church, fairly large with a tower and shingled spire, is mainly thirteenth century, but restored, and has some fifteenth-century brasses.

Dignity is lost at *Pratt's Bottom*, on the other main road to the south: it is built-up and unrepentant.

Chevening 5. Less than a hamlet—a clump of model estate houses and a church outside the gates of a great park, with a backcloth of heavily wooded hills. The church is much restored thirteenth century, with a fifteenth-century tower, and modern windows. In the south chapel are alabaster monuments to the Lennards, and a fine marble effigy by Chantrey of Lady Frederica Stanhope, who died in 1823.

The Lennards and then the Stanhopes lived at Chevening, and the house has been in its time attributed to Inigo Jones. The third Earl of Stanhope, a modernizer, about 1790 covered the main block of the building with yellow tiles of his own design, clamping them to the old brickwork, and his the roof with a high parapet. Later improvements have been more skilful. The park is magnificently landscaped, and, with the gardens, full of roses and herbaceous borders, sometimes open to the public. Lady Hester Stanhope was born here in 1776.

Chiddingstone 5 is named by folk etymology from a solitary but unremarkable outcrop of sandstone in the parish, by this explanation called the 'chiding-stone", became used as a seat of judgment. The village was in fact the "tun" of some Saxon

CHILHAM

Ceddun, and his "ing" or family. It is acclaimed as the "prettiest in Kent". The popular spectacle is the unspoiled row of sixteenth- and seventeenth-century houses facing the church. The half-timbered inn and shop are fine, and the whole group is in the care of the National Trust. The church is fourteenth century with a lofty tower with octagonal turrets and crocketed pinnacles. Much of the inside work is of 1625, when restoration followed a fire. There has been more restoration since, and the walls are partly scraped. There are also memorials to the Streatfield family: not remarkable.

The Streatfields, a great Kentish name, owned, from 1500 till 1936, what is still called *Chiddingstone Castle*. In 1679 Henry Streatfield built himself a fine new red brick Carolean house on the site of an older manor. Parts of it remain inside the pseudo-Gothic building his great grandson, another Henry, finished in 1830. This he refaced in sombre sandstone, towered and embattled by the architect Henry Kendall. At the same time the High Street of the village was diverted to its present position, to make way for a lake of nearly three acres. The building, after doing service as a school, is now used by its present owner as a museum, largely of oriental objects. Tucked away disconsolately at the back is a little orangery. There is a pleasant wildish garden, with fishing.

The early Streatfields were Wealden ironmasters, and some lie under iron grave slabs in the churchyard. This is lovely wooded country with great oaks, thriving on the Wealden clay.

Chiddingstone Causeway 5 has a green lying beside the embankment, and the village street runs along the railway line which misleadingly stops here at "Penshurst station". The church of St Luke, a solid Victorian Gothic building of Bath stone, was finished in 1898. It is an effective and unassuming village church designed by J. F. Bentley, the architect of Westminster Cathedral.

Chilham 14 has the misfortune to be labelled a "beauty spot" and is infested in summer, particularly as it lies, visibly delightful, on the downs just above the main road from Maidstone to Canterbury. Nevertheless, it remains neither too artificially preserved nor self-consciously renovated. A little square has the church at one end and the gates of the castle at the other. The cottages are all pretty and, particularly down the road from the Woolpack Inn, heavily timbered. Behind the church the red brick Queen Anne rectory sits charmingly contrasting with the black-and-white work of most of the village. The general effect is of mellow prosperity without feverish exploitation.

The restored church is beautiful and interesting. It has an embattled tower chequered in flint and stone. The interior is spacious, with colourful Victorian glass. There are good monuments. One of 1610 has delicate engraved decoration on the columns. A splendid Nicholas Stone composition has verve, with a tall marble column with four life-sized allegorical girls at its corners. There is a Chantrey of 1822 and a monument by Munro of 1858. The sarcophagus of Purbeck marble, long hoped to be that of St Augustine, was found to be empty when opened in 1948.

Chilham Castle is Jacobean, built in 1616 for Sir Dudley Digges, Master of the Rolls. Roman remains discovered in the grounds suggest a settlement here. There are traces of the twelfth-century keep of an earlier castle, and a fourteenth-century curtain wall. But the interest of the park, which is sometimes opened to the public, are the terraced and topiary gardens, with mulberry and wisteria (here first grown in England): the mile-long avenue of Spanish chestnuts, and the heronry.

Above the Stour valley, to the southeast, are *Julieberri Downs*, with rich views. The mound here was the burial place of a tribune of Julius Caesar's armies called traditionally Laberius, and Julieberri is inaccurately offered as a fanciful contraction of the two names. It is in fact a neolithic long barrow.

Chillenden 15 is a small village with a small much restored church, visually undisturbed by the adjacent collieries, in a wooded country, formerly of several large estates. On the downs above it to the north is a white post-windmill whose sails are a landmark for miles. It has been repaired, and is open for inspection. To the south-east is *Knowlton Park*, with its own rather secret little grey church among the trees, very dark inside, with a three-decker Jacobean pulpit, later box pews and two eighteenth-century monuments (urns, cherubs, bust on marble table tombs) one with a relief carving of a ship commanded by the deceased Admiral. The brick Queen Anne house has been much rebuilt and added to. There is a pretty brick built dovecote. The family name was Narborough.

Chislehurst 1 is essentially a suburb, and historically, with Orpington, one of the earlier and more "select" ones in the outward sweep of London following the railway extension into Kent of 1865. As part of Greater London it embraces administratively some 87,000 people.

It retains a centre with character, and is helped by its splendid common of 150 acres of birches and woodland. Just off the crossroads and the traffic is a little group of village houses with shops and an inn with a good painted sign, all lying back from the road behind grass verges with trees on them. Above this is the parish church of *St Nicholas*, a fifteenth-century building, with a south aisle added in a creditable restoration of 1849, a Norman font of Bethersden marble, and some box pews. Catering for the Victorian expansion, *Christ Church* was built in 1872, and the *Annunciation* in 1873, designed by J. Brooks with a tower by E. J. May.

To the west of Chislehurst Common and its silver birch trees are the caves, famous but of early industrial not romantic origin, and the golf course. This uses as its club house the large brick mansion of Camden Place, built by the antiquary William Camden in 1609. He died here in 1623. Napoleon III lived gloomily in the same house, in exile with the Empress Eugenie, from after the collapse of the Second Empire until his death in 1873.

Chislet 11 is a village scattered and abstracted in marshy country south of the bare strip of north Kent coast between Herne Bay and Margate. Farms, cottages, and a Norman

CHILLENDEN Mill

70

church tower with a curious and more recent wooden top looking like a water tank. (The spire was never finished.) The church is Norman and Early English, of nave, chancel and aisles, symmetrical. The high Early English chancel is striking in its proportions, and has much not unattractive Victorian glass. There are several elaborate wall tablets in variegated marbles, and hatchments and square text canvasses (dated 1848, and signed by a coach-painter at Grays). To the north-east, an attractive dyke-bordered road with swans and willows leads past *Marshside* towards Reculver. One of the marshes is called *Dog-Whippers*, because its rent paid for the man who whipped the dogs out of church. Down the road at *Hersden* is Chislet Colliery and a plantation of miners' houses.

Cliffe 3. An extensive built-up village on the north-west corner of the Hoo peninsular, on a chalk escarpment. It has a large Early English church strikingly banded in flint and ragstone, with inside a medieval rood beam, and some old glass, including a good Virgin and Child. Royal Arms of 1661. There are fine views out across the marshes: but old quarries and industry to the west. Altogether, somewhat reserved and colourless.

Cliftonville. *See* Margate.

Cobham 3. A charming and interesting village, not spoilt by its popular adulation, in lovely country south of Gravesend, on the unspoilt side of the M2. The outstanding point is the church, standing back beside the road. Inside it has ornate sedilia and piscina, and the finest set of monumental brasses in England. An altar tomb of Lord Cobham and his wife, who died in 1558, in life-size alabaster, fills the east end of the chancel. It is ostentatious and remarkable. There is a splendid spacious chancel, with thirteenth-century windows—the east one of three lancets filled with rich Victorian glass, predominantly blue—the whole slightly marred by the scraping of the plaster off the window splays. The great Cobham monument is in the

COOLING Castle

centre. The brasses spread across the floor on their array of slabs. They are also to the Cobhams, and are beautifully and precisely engraved, with tremendous detail, though they were refixed and somewhat restored in 1841. There are 19 in all, covering a period of two hundred years.

Sir John de Cobham, who died in 1365, enlarged the church, and is shown with it in his hands. He also founded the college which forms the basis of the building on the south side of the churchyard. Much of the work dates from 1597, when it was re-established as an almshouse, but the hall and kitchens are original. It is a fine high building, still used for old people to live in.

Opposite the church, across the narrow street, is a half-timbered inn, *The Leathern Bottle*, used by Dickens as an important setting for *Pickwick Papers*. There are other attractive buildings, including the *Darley Arms*, with a Georgian façade, and *Meadow House*, of 1771, but the most important is at the far end of the road, *Owletts*. This is a warm red-brick Charles II building, not grand, but nearly perfect, with a peaceful garden and magnolias. It belonged to Sir Herbert Baker, who gave it to the National Trust. He also presented it with a Kentish yeoman's house at *Sole Street* nearby.

Standing in its large park behind trees south of Watling Street and down a long drive, is *Cobham Hall*. It is now a school, but is sometimes shown during the holidays: a very large brick building, originally Elizabethan, but with Jacobean additions, and some Adam interiors. It has domed towers, clusters of Tudor chimneys, and a picture gallery 130 feet long. The classic mausoleum in the park is one of the earliest works of James Wyatt, who later also Gothicized the entrance hall and staircase. The landscape gardening was by Humphrey and George Repton, and George Repton designed the fanciful *Thong Lodge* at one of the park entrances. Besides this, there are ash trees, a lime avenue, and a famous chestnut called Four Sisters.

Coldred. *See* Shepherdswell.

COBHAM Hall

Collier Street 6, has a Victorian church, among orchards, by P. C. Hardwick, 1848.

Cooling 3 is in the Hoo peninsula, with Cooling marshes stretching flat and desolate to the north, much as described at the beginning of Dickens' *Great Expectations*. The church has an Early English font and nave, some old oak benches, rows of stone stalls on each side of the chancel, and thirteen children's gravestones near the church porch which are tradition-ally identified with those of Pip's little brothers.

The village itself is negligible, but down the road is Cooling Castle. This was built by Lord John Cob-ham in 1381, to defend the Thames from French raiders who had plun-dered the coast the previous year. The castle and the title later passed to Sir John Oldcastle, who died in 1417, was a supporter of the Lollards, and is supposed by some to be the original of Falstaff. The castle was attacked by Sir Thomas Wyatt during his rebellion of 1544 against the Spanish Marriage of Queen Mary, and was much damaged.

It remains striking. There are frag-ments of two wards, which had mas-sive walls, corner towers, and a moat. The outer ward is approached through the fine fifteenth-century gatehouse, intact, which stands on the road, with heavy machicolated towers. It has a curious copper plate let in to the easternmost tower, pro-claiming the builder's intent, and that the castle was "mad in help of the cuntre". An unrelated private house sits cheerfully inside the gates.

Cowden 4, on the Sussex border, has a number of half-timbered build-ings and excellent white weather-boarded ones: a specially fine group round the old Crown Inn. The church is fifteenth century, restored by the Victorians, but has a tower with pro-digious oak beams inside it, restored well in recent times. The shingles climb from the walls up the tower and cover the spire without interruption by eaves. It is suggested that the nave and chancel were also originally both shingled. The shingles, originally oak, are now cedar, and were put up in 1947 as cheaper and, it is hoped, more durable. There is a Jacobean pulpit with sounding board, and an

unusual hour-glass stand. At the north of the churchyard are some eighteenth-century iron grave slabs, underlining that this was the middle of the Wealden iron industry. There is still a forge today, busy just beside the church gates.

Cranbrook 9. A delightful market town and shopping centre, rivalling Tenterden as the capital of the Weald. It has not Tenterden's long wide main street, but a fine one none the less, which turns an L-shape in the middle, with the church set back above the bend. There are houses of all periods, and Victorian buildings merge with the weatherboarding and timber façades without spoiling the general effect. Modern buildings are on the whole bright and appropriate, and the whole sense is of historical continuity into vigorous contem-porary life.

Cranbrook had no castle or major religious foundation, and is the only considerable old centre in Kent which grew up entirely through trade. In the early Middle Ages it was a headquarters of the iron-smelting of the Weald forests. But real prosperity came with cloth. The trade started in the thirteenth century and was enor-mously boosted in the fourteenth by Edward III's introduction of Flem-ish weavers. Wool from Kentish flocks was less productive than from some sheep elsewhere, but there were streams and fuller's earth readily available. By the sixteenth century Cranbrook was doing extremely well, and had a population of 3,000 when Maidstone only had 2,000. Simon Lynch had founded his "free and perpetual grammar school", which has greatly helped the town although its modern red buildings on the hill at the entrance to it are un-prepossessing.

After the sixteenth century the cloth trade declined, going to the north and the west country. But Cranbrook remained busy and beautiful, largely undesecrated by subsequent in-dustrial development.

The church is dedicated to the Kentish St Dunstan. It dates from the high tide of prosperity, the late fifteenth century, and is of weathered Wealden sandstone. Inside it is light, with piers of clustered shafts in the nave. It has a curious baptistry, built in 1710, for the total immersion of

adults, a parvis, and various monu-ments, hatchments and memorials, notably to the Roberts of *Glassenbury* whose seventeenth-century moated house and garden still exist, some-times open to the public, a mile or so west towards Goudhurst. Outside, above the vaulted fourteenth-century porch, is a splendidly ornate clock, paid for out of the profits of the parish farm, with the figure of Father Time.

The Union Mill, dominating the town, is the largest working windmill in England, the tallest in Kent, and the most photographed anywhere. A splendid functional building, the climax of wind-activated machinery. It was put up in 1814 for Henry Dobell, brother of the poet Sidney Dobell. The work was done by a local millwright, called Humphries, for £3,500. It stands 70 feet high to the top of its cap, and the frame is the original one. The sweeps are not, having been renewed several times, the current ones having been set up by experts specially acquired from Holland. The fantail, which turns the sails to the wind, was added in 1840. Most of the smock windmills of Kent, built in the nineteenth century, are decaying or coyly converted, but this, admirably restored, stands white and proud above the red roofs.

Cray. *See* St Mary Cray.

Crayford 2. An industrialized area where Watling Street passes over the northern end of the River Cray just before this joins the Darent and flows into the Thames. It claims pre-historic remains, woolly rhinoceros and cave lion, a Roman camp, whilst according to the Anglo-Saxon Chro-nicle, Hengist defeated the Celtic Vortigern here, killing 4,000 men. Now it has a busy main street with a modern centre and multiple stores, a stadium, a modern town-hall and neat unexceptional homes for 32,000 people.

The church, dedicated to St Paulinus, stands aloof on a hill to the north. It is fifteenth century, with some Norman walling, of flint and stone, with an array of beautiful white limestone tombstones in the church-yard, well carved and in their original positions. In the church, a central

COWDEN Church

74

arcade bisects the nave and ends with a half arch over the apex of the chancel arch—an unusual arrangement. There is a splendid monument to William Draper and wife, 1652, with life-sized effigies, baulked by the organ. Another—very pretty—monument in the south transept is to Elizabeth Shovel, 1659, and has florid angels holding curtains aside. There are other wall tablets.

Crockham Hill 4, has a Victorian Gothic church of 1842, and houses which suggest comfortable retirement. Also one of the finest views in Kent. It stands on a spur of the Greensand Ridge, and looks out over the Weald, with landmarks that can be picked out right down to Ashdown Forest. Appropriately there is a cenotaph to Octavia Hill, who did so much to found the National Trust, and her grave is under a yew tree in the churchyard. One of the many Trust properties in this part of Kent is amongst the woodland here, which is almost too leafy for the view in

high summer, but particularly beautiful with bluebells in the springtime. By a lane to the east the main road is reached beside which stands *Chartwell*. This is a Tudor House, beautifully placed above a lake in the trees of a rich estate. Architecturally it is not a showpiece, but a small Elizabethan manor comfortably enlarged and converted for modern use. It was the home of Sir Winston Churchill for more than thirty years, and was presented to the National Trust in 1946. Since Sir Winston's death it has become a place of pilgrimage and a museum. It is visited essentially for its personal associations, but is attractive also for its gardens and its view.

Crundale 14. A village of farms and cottages hidden in a beautiful valley under the downs, and reached through narrow and precipitous lanes. The church, isolated high up above it, is remarkable only for its attractive position, and an incised slab to a fifteenth-century vicar.

Norman origin. Very over-restored.

Cudham 4. A leafy hilltop village, reached up lanes hung with trees and surrounded by orchards, built up with Victorian houses and modern bungalows, but still very much in the country, although only about 20 miles from London. The heavily restored church is pleasantly placed, but has little of interest other than two gnarled and gigantic yew trees in the churchyard. There is a large Convalescent Home.

Cuxton 3 is an industrial place on a ridge over the west bank of the Medway, and as such untidy-looking and strained. It has recently become a dormitory, however, for the Strood-Rochester-Chatham-Gillingham conurbation, and the bright creditable new houses climb well up the hills to the north. There is moreover a magnificent view from here of the great new Medway bridge carrying the M2 on a mile of arches and slim concrete pillars. Behind them lie Rochester

Castle and the factories. To the right the North Downs bastions with whitebeam and yew. The church, on the steep eastward slope above the main road, is on a Roman site. It is medieval, but much restored. The site is splendid.

Darenth 2. Named from the River Darent. The largest part of it is a huge area of new development from Dartford, climbing up the hillside to the north of the main road. The old village still remains one, and has a little green and a church of Saxon origin, and with a Saxon look down its chestnut avenue from the north, with Roman bricks in it, no doubt from the nearby Roman villa, now overgrown, which was excavated in 1894–6. The sanctuary is Norman and vaulted, stepped high up above the nave and the later (thirteenth century) part of the chancel. The Norman font has carvings in arcading including the Baptism, and monsters.
South Darenth has paper mills and is urbanized. It has a little modern church with a brick steeple and across the road the huge arch of the railway, with trees under it: an imposing piece of engineering.

Dartford 2 is only 17 miles from London, has nearly 50,000 inhabitants and is wholly industrial. It is not, however, a mere part of an industrial belt. It retains character in its centre. It developed its own industries, even if they are not beautiful ones. It is a busy contemporary centre, but retains a sense of its long and even royal history.
The history is in the books and some of it in the brave little museum: not much in the streets. The town stands at an important point: where the Darent is crossed by Watling Street and only a mile or so above where the river joins the Thames. The Romans were here, and the Saxons, and Watling Street itself is some four feet below the line of the High Street. The place naturally became an important market town, and grew in importance when Edward III founded a Dominican nunnery here in 1349. This covered some 32 acres. After the Dissolution the building became royal property and was lived in successively by Henry VIII, Anne of Cleves, who died here in 1557, and Elizabeth I.

What is left of it (now called the Priory) is offices and has a few evidences, well cared for, in Victoria Road and Kingsfield Terrace. The proletarian rebel Wat Tyler, said to have been born in Dartford, started the insurrection against the poll tax here in 1381.
The High Street is traffic and shopfronts and has practically no buildings of interest or distinction except, at the London end, on the south side the *Bull Hotel*, with a galleried Georgian yard, roofed over. A medieval building near the church, where one or two older houses remain, claims to be Tyler's birthplace. *The Wat Tyler* inn, across Bullace Lane, is also an early building. Round about are wharfs, barges, cranes, factories and offices and the mainly nineteenth- and twentieth-century homes of those who work in them. The main industries are flour and paper mills, chemical works, shipbuilding and the cement which clouds and profits the whole area. The paper industry boomed first in 1860, with the abolition of the excise duty on paper, and again at the turn of the century with the introduction of the halfpenny newspaper. Pulp arrives conveniently from the Baltic and Canada by water, for the finished product to go to London. The industry started here when the first mill was put up by Sir John Spielman in 1617. Similarly, the use of volley-mills for sheet-iron was started in Dartford in 1590. The Cornishman Trevithick had workshops here for his experiments with steel.
The large medieval church of Holy Trinity retains some thirteenth- and fourteenth-century work and has commanding presence at a turn of the main street. It was vigorously restored in 1863 and 1877. It has an odd plan: aisles to both chancel and nave, and a tower between the north aisles of the nave and the chancel. There are good brasses and a painted alabaster and marble tomb of 1607 for Spielman himself, with an inscription in German. Unfortunately, scholarship no longer agrees that the name for "foolscap" paper came from the figure of a jester, the German "spielman", which was used both as part of his arms and as a watermark. Colourful Victorian east window attractive. An enormous painting of

St George and the Dragon dominates the south transept, and a vast Royal Arms (1751) the north transept.

Deal 15 is always under the threat of development. Meanwhile it remains, with Walmer (q.v.), one of the more delightful of the Kentish seaside resorts: visitors, golfers and sea-anglers, but a fairly unselfconscious preoccupation with its maritime and business life.
There is a long promenade, with a 1957 pier, the only post-war one in Great Britain, stretching above a single beach busy with boats and tackle. To the north lie the perfunctory remains of Sandown Castle, and at the southern end Victorian houses and Deal Castle. The houses all along the sea front between here have seventeenth- to nineteenth-century façades, sometimes with warnings against opening the door in a high wind. They are individually unimportant, but collectively coherent and attractive.
Small alleys lead back from the front into two streets running more or less parallel with it, and carrying the shopping and institutional incident. High Street, the more important, has St George's Church, a nice brick building of 1715. Higher, and further inland now than in its heyday, lies Upper Deal. Its parish church of St Leonard is basically twelfth century, but was largely rebuilt in 1684. It has a distinctive cupola, long maintained by Trinity House as a landmark for shipping, and a splendid Pilots Gallery of 1658 over the West Door. To the north of Deal, beyond the coastguard station, in the sands where legend says that medieval criminals were buried alive, lie along the coast the links of the Royal Cinque Ports Golf Club. South, towards Walmer, are the extensive barracks of the Royal Marine Depot, settled here in 1861. Retired Marine officers swell the residents in the newer little houses round about.
Historically, Deal is claimed as the landing place for Julius Caesar's exploratory invasions in strength in 55 and 54 BC. The exact site is a matter for brisk antiquarian controversy, local fishermen intervening. But in any case the coast has altered. As a port, the Romans preferred Richborough, and the Saxons Sandwich, and it was under Sandwich that

Deal was adopted as a member of the Cinque Ports. When Sandwich silted up, Deal flourished accordingly. It practised trade, fishing and piracy, and was a supply centre for the fleets that rode at anchor in the Downs, offshore. In the seventeenth century it was a naval base, and the dockyard only closed in 1863, by which time the town was becoming a discreet resort. Meanwhile in 1682 William Penn had sailed from Deal on his first voyage to America, and Elizabeth Carter, who was to translate Epictetus and hobnob with Dr Johnson, had been born in a house in South Street in 1717.

Deal Castle stands at the south of Victoria Parade, on the way to Walmer, and is now relieved of the William IV Captain's residence, which received a direct bomb hit in 1941. The castle is, for practical rather than symbolic reasons, the shape of a Tudor rose: a three-storey central tower, surrounded by two-storey lobes, inside a round platform with one-storey bastions. It stands low in its moat, and the crenellation of the battlements is "modern", put there because castles should have this. In fact Deal Castle was never really a castle in the medieval sense at all. It was a fortified gun emplacement, which never had a complement of more than about 150 men. The coast here was obviously highly sensitive to invasion, and Henry VIII's officials took strong action in 1540, when this seemed threatened from the Continent. They commissioned a string of strongpoints, geared to the new cannon warfare. Three were round Deal: Sandgate, now a concrete base at the end of the promenade, Deal Castle itself, and, to the south, Walmer. The last two remain as comparatively intact examples of sixteenth-century scientific fortification. Some of the stone used was from the newly destroyed Kentish monasteries like that of St Radegund.

The Goodwin Sands lie, a brown streak four miles out and parallel to the coast, stretching about ten miles from north to south, between Ramsgate and Deal. They are some two miles wide, and landings can be made in low water and good weather. Traditionally they formed part of the territories of Earl Goodwin, father of King Harold, and they do seem to be a remnant of land rather than an accumulation of sand. Hard in fair weather, they become soft when the water rises, and can swallow whole vessels. The lightships which prick the horizon at night from the Deal coastline are to prevent this. The sands are a legend and an historic menace to shipping. But they serve as a natural breakwater for the channel between them and the coast. This stretch of water is the *Downs*.

Denton 14. A cheerful hamlet on the road from Canterbury to Folkestone, with its church in the beeches and clean air of the park of Denton Court. It is tied to *Wootton*, which lies back from the main road amongst lanes and trees in glorious country. Here the thirteenth-century church is small: a yew tree outside, enormous. Just north of Denton is *Broome Park*, the estate once owned by Lord Kitchener. The fine house is now an hotel. It belonged previously to the famous East Kent family of Oxendens. South, off the road but visible from it, is *Tappington Hall*, the timbered home of the Barhams, which figures as Tappington Everard in the *Ingoldsby Legends*. It is now a farmhouse.

Detling 6 preserves traces of when it was a sheltered hamlet on the Pilgrims' Way, although motorroads swish by above and below it, and its long hill is almost entirely lined by new houses and estates. At the top of this, cornering the Way itself, is an old inn, with a black and white timbered cottage opposite, and other Tudor survivals near by. Half way down the hill, behind trees, is the church, much of it Norman, with a broach spire. It is very much restored and refurnished inside. It has a remarkable lectern, a piece of fourteenth-century craftsmanship of great ingenuity, with a double-sided head which swivels, and is carved with symbolic grotesques.

Ditton 6 is a spread of garages and development along the London road just out of Maidstone. Behind these are echoes of an old village round the church, which stands back amongst yew trees with some dignity. There is a green, and a lane, sometimes flooded, with one or two Tudor houses. To the north is the heavily industrialized area of *New Hythe*, where paper works were started by Reeds in the early 1920s, expanded enormously, and now give wide employment over the area.

Doddington 13 is a small village in pleasant wooded country. There are ugly houses as you come in from the west, but these improve until a sharp turn to the left, where the church and vicarage are conventionally grouped up a steep lane. Both are excellent. The vicarage is an eighteenth-century building with sensitive nineteenth-century additions. The church lost its tower through lightning in the seventeenth century, and has now a weatherboarded one, with weatherboarded battlements, of about 1800. The inside is light and graceful, and has a complete roundel of thirteenth-century stained glass (Flight into Egypt). The church backs on to the park of *Doddington Place*, which has gardens sometimes open to the public.

Dover 15 is a vital sea-port and commercial centre which has somehow survived appalling shell-fire and bombing from the Continent in two successive wars. It was "Hell Fire Corner". Much that is busy, dingy and makeshift must be forgiven. The buildings of the front door to Europe, on the Parade and Esplanade, are various: nostalgic Victorian marine architecture, like the *White Cliffs Hotel*, stretching into blocks of modern flats. The docks are exciting with movement, but without charm, the shopping centre is a muddle of unrelated buildings of different periods, and behind and up the London road are rows of little brick houses. Individual buildings catch the eye, like a Unitarian chapel of 1806: but the general effect is bleak and messy. It is none the less a resort, and re-visited.
A number of places are worth seeing. Obvious ones are the old *Maison Dieu Hall* in the High Street, a hostel for pilgrims in 1203, restored by the Corporation in 1860, full of armour and history and with windows by Sir Edward Poynter, and *Maison Dieu House*, behind the War Memorial, which is now the library and was built in 1665. *Dover College* includes bits of the old Benedictine

DOVER Castle

Priory of St Martin, and the Refectory, used as the College Hall, is one of the largest Norman secular buildings in the country. *St Mary's* Church in Cannon Street has a distinctive Norman tower. The sea front shows memorials to individuals who first crossed the Straits of Dover here: Captain Webb, who swam it in 1875, or the Hon. C. S. Rolls, of Rolls Royce, who made the first return aeroplane flight in 1910. A granite aeroplane in Northfall meadows is a memorial to M. Blériot, who made the first of all flights across the Channel, and landed here in 1909.

Dover is, of course, "The Gateway of England", and its Castle "the lock and key to the Kingdom". Bits of Shakespeare Cliff are sent overseas as souvenirs.

Dover Castle stands magnificently, strategically a stronghold, dominating the town and harbour. It makes a proud skyline from the sea and the streets below.

Approached, it is less conventionally romantic, largely due to its having been a working defence position almost until today. The tops of all the curtain walls were cropped to make artillery posts at the time of the Napoleonic invasion scare of 1803. The whole site had been functionally converted into a "modern" fortress in the eighteenth century, and Army occupation was continuous until 1958. It was only in 1963 that the castle was taken over by the Ministry of Works. The atmosphere still remains somewhat that of a garrison headquarters on an open day.

But all history is there, and the Ministry provide an excellent guidebook, with a short bibliography for the technical-minded. It explains that the site represents an Iron Age castle, taken over and exploited by the Romans, who set up two lighthouses here about 50 AD (calling it Dubris) to light their vessels round the South Foreland to Richborough. There may have been a stone castle here before 1066, but the remaining medieval curtain wall and keep were largely the work of Henry II. He and his successors, their carts and troops constantly passing from Dover to Calais, spent huge fortunes on the castle and harbour. So, later, did the Tudors.

The Keep, great tower, or donjon, is the central residential building. It was built by Henry II in the 1180's, of Kentish ragstone and ashlar dressings from Normandy. It has skilful engineering devices, a 250-feet well with twelfth-century piping system, and many wonders, particularly two Norman chapels. St John's Chapel, particularly, is elaborate and superb. Children enjoy the underground passages. These are basically medieval, but were extended as defence works during the Napoleonic wars, and proved invaluable as air-raid shelters in the last one.

Slightly south from the depressing, impressive grimness of the keep is the *Roman "pharos"*. The top nineteen feet are fifteenth-century reconstruction, but the bottom tiers of the telescope-like building are the weathered base of the Roman octagonal building. In later Saxon times it was used as a free bell-tower for the church already built next to it.

This is the weird *St Mary-in-Castro*. It is a tenth-century cruciform building with an aisleless nave and a central tower. It has deep interest, although Scott restored the main body in 1862, and Butterfield the tower in 1888, before adding alarming mosaic work to the nave. Bits of Roman tile show up incongruously.

A 12-pounder brass Basilisk, cast in Utrecht in 1544, and called Queen Elizabeth's pocket pistol, stands just above the entrance to the Castle. It was not an ornament, but saw service in the Civil Wars, and threw shot seven miles. It has pleasant Renaissance ornamentation.

The delights of Dover Castle are panoramic and historical rather than aesthetic. But it is worth the climb.

Downe 4, although only 16 miles from St Paul's Cathedral is a village in the country and not a suburb. There are lanes, not roads, real trees, not just garden ones, and comparatively little traffic. There are of course

new houses, but it is a quiet spot without a main through road, having a vestigial green and surrounded by woods and fine and unspoilt scenery. The small country church is restored thirteenth century with a typical shingled spire.

Here on the chalk plateau on the 500-feet contour Charles Darwin lived for forty years until his death in 1882. *Downe House* is a quarter of a mile from the church. Here he did most of his scientific research and wrote *The Origin of Species*. "House ugly," wrote Darwin, "looks neither old or new—walls two feet thick—windows rather small—lower storey rather low." He extended and improved it, but it is not beautiful: an eighteenth-century building on an older site, with Victorian additions and a nice garden. It is now in the hands of the Royal College of Surgeons, and open to the public, with displays of Darwiniana and the naturalist's study and books as he used them, and a version of Stubbs' *Horses frightened by a Lion*.

At *High Elms*, to the north-east, lived Lord Avebury (Sir John Lubbock) who died in 1913: Darwin's friend, scientific writer, sociologist, and begetter of "Lubbock's Day", the national Bank Holiday. The grounds are now a public park. Some of the trees may have been gifts from the first Lord Chatham, who forested the property of many of his landowning neighbours from Hayes Place, nearby.

Dungeness. *See* Lydd.

Dunkirk. *See* Broughton Street.

Dymchurch 17 was a fishing village and capital of Romney Marsh. It has a church, built of Kentish ragstone, basically twelfth century and with a pyramid cap to its belfry, but extended and spoilt in the nineteenth century. The *New Hall*, nearby, is the Court House of the Bailiffs and Lords of the Marsh, charged with the protection of this dramatic triangle of land won from the sea.

Much of contemporary Dymchurch is dedicated to "Happy Holidays" and is visually disconcerting. The *Dymchurch Wall*, three miles long, the principal barrier against the sea,

is a vast concave of concrete, with groynes jutting out to break the waves. Behind it lie the road, and holiday camps and chalets, indistinguishable and undistinguished. Neglected fortifications put up against German invasion and Martello towers against that of Bonaparte, punctuate the regiments of bungalows.

Excavations have revealed traces of the Roman work here in the early days of reclamation, and Dymchurch has contemporary fame as the home of the detective Dr Syn, written about by Mr Russell Thorndike. But there is little in its visual present to remind the visitor of its historic significance.

Eastbridge. A lost parish of Romney Marsh.

Eastchurch 10. A parish on fairly high ground in the middle of the Isle of Sheppey, and the only real agricultural village in this area of industry, mass recreation and marsh. It is developed but not unattractive, with a much renewed but comparatively unspoiled fifteenth-century church, with a rood screen. Northwards a fine stone wall marks the site of what was once *Shurland*, the great house of Sir Thomas Cheyney. Nearby was the first British airfield, in the pioneer days of Lord Brabazon, and isolated to the south, on what was an Air Force camp, is *Her Majesty's Prison*, an experimental open penal settlement.

East Langdon 15, although near *Martin Hill* station, is like *West Langdon* a largely undisturbed if undistinguished village of flint and tile, enjoying the downland country lying back from the coast behind the South Foreland. The little church has Norman features and a red velvet cope-hood of the fifteenth century with beautiful embroidery. It has a tower with tiled pyramid. *West Langdon* church was rebuilt in 1867, burnt in 1906 and restored after.

Eastling. *See* Newnham.

East Malling. *See* Malling.

Eastry 15. King Ethelbert murdered some cousins here, Thomas à Becket hid himself before his secret flight to the Continent, and down the road at

Heronden there is a Queen Anne house where Nelson stayed with Emma Hamilton. It is a pleasant village, with a large church, Early English, with a Norman tower sitting off the main road. It is somewhat gloomy and Victorianized inside, but it has good wall monuments—one with an elaborate sculptured battle scene and two built, strangely, into the soffits of arches, above the capitals, in the south arcade. The village is on a rising slope of main road two miles south of Sandwich.

East Sutton. *See* Sutton Valence.

Eastwell 13. The Park, in which the whole parish lies, presents an ornate mock Tudor gateway to face travellers leaving Ashford for Faversham. Inside it is the imitation Tudor house and splendid park, one of the largest in the country. Tucked away at the back of it was Eastwell church, a fifteenth-century building much admired by ecclesiologists. This suffered bomb damage during the last war, and is now a lakeside ruin amongst the trees and the passing game birds, sombre and attractive. An unnamed tomb is credited as that of Richard Plantagenet, the son of Richard III, who escaped from the Battle of Bosworth and ended his days here as a carpenter on the estate.

Challock Lees, a hamlet round a large green, farther north, also has a church in Eastwell Park. It too was damaged, but at the end of a fine lane some way from the village, it now stands, bravely restored in 1950.

Edenbridge 4. A little old town with a long main street in the plain of the River Eden, almost on the Sussex border: tanneries, flour mills, and a sense of leisurely agricultural continuity. There are several Tudor houses, and an old Crown inn with a signboard across the street. The "13th-century Restaurant" is more likely fifteenth-century, but certainly old, with another timbered house opposite. The church is early, although heavily restored by the Victorians, and has huge buttresses to the tower, which shows golden lights in the ragstone, and a shingled broach tower. Inside it is wide and airy, with a Jacobean pulpit and like so many churches hereabouts, an east end window by Burne Jones.

The Edenbridge and Oxted Agricultural Show is an annual event of importance on August Bank Holiday, and much is traditionally made of Bonfire Night. The main street is now too narrow for the traffic, but the place retains much character.

Marlpit Heath, to the north, is light industry, grown up round one of the two railway stations.

Egerton church 13 can be seen from miles round. It stands on the edge of the escarpment of the Greensand Hills. The fifteenth-century ragstone tower stands magnificently, and there are gargoyles grimacing on the porch. Inside are modern wood carved altar rails, and everything is very much renewed. Carved font fifteenth century, and glass fragments. There is development going on round the church, but the older part of the village, in the valley behind, is unspoilt, with some Kentish yeomen's houses and outlying farmsteads. One of the best of them is *Links Farm*.

Elham 14 is pronounced "Eel-am". It remains an attractive village, in spite of new buildings and the main street forming part of the road from Canterbury to the coast. It has several good buildings and one outstanding one—a Tudor house in the High Street with good carving both inside and out.

The beautiful flint church stands back from the road, and is more than just "the capital church of the Elham Valley". The tower is massive, with a spire on top, and eight bells. The carved modern woodwork is remarkable; and a Flemish alabaster reredos is unusual. There are good corbels, old tiles, and other details. Altogether it is rich, remarkable, and effective. The excellent modern restoration is by the late F. C. Eden. There is glass by him, and other modern, and some fifteenth-century glass.

Elmsted 14 is a well-hidden village on pleasant heights off the road from Hythe to Canterbury. A delightful church behind trees and a grass verge, with a flint tower having an overhanging storey of shingle, topped by a steeple. Inside it is airy and light,

mostly decorated, with an old font and monuments to the Honeywood family, one by Scheemakers, with bust. Beside it are farm buildings with good typical red roofs, and the general effect, in a country of twisting lanes, is both remote and spacious.

Elmstone. *See* Preston.

Erith 2, is crowded, busy and industrial. Once it was one of the great shipyards of the Thames, and it built the largest vessel of its time in the world, the Great Harry, which took Henry VIII to the magnificence of the Field of the Cloth of Gold. There was rich grazing in the marshes. After centuries of decline, expansion came with development of the river-traffic, then the railways, and especially the setting up of the Maxim Nordenfelt Gun and Ammunition Factory in 1889, subsequently taken over by Vickers. Population doubled with the armaments activity of the 1914–18 war, and more recently came works for cables and electrical equipment. There are brick-fields in the marshes to the east, and the scars from the excavation of loam and sand to provide ballast for ships for the Port of London. Visually Erith is indistinguishable from most industrial development along the south bank of the Thames. The main street is dingy, with Victorian shops amongst the modern ones, and the restored church of St John the Baptist dark on a corner with lorries thundering round three sides of it.

A brave attempt has been made to turn the little High Street, on the edge of the river, into a sort of pleasaunce. There is a certain wharf-side charm: a green, with seats on it, near by a few older houses, an inn, a tiny parade with a chart of the flags of all nations, and a view of some of them, on vessels plying up and down the waterway. There is even, farther on, a little pier, jutting out into the Thames with cranes on it, and past a cement works the way to the yacht club, which holds an annual regatta.

Eynsford ("Ains-ford") 2 is to be pitied. It has been so much cried up as a typical Kent beauty spot that it has become one: a village endowed with a lovely setting and some old things of true if conventional beauty,

intruded by new buildings, commuters whose lives are expended elsewhere, and cheerful hordes on a day's outing. Because of its accessibility to London, and because it takes the main traffic through the Darent valley, when the weather is at its best, intrusion is at its worst.

There is enough to show how pretty it must have been, and on occasions can still be today. There is a fine group of half-timbered cottages, and the little hump-backed bridge over the ford which has been there for 500 years, with a photogenic but quite genuine Tudor house behind it. Also the stream itself, in which visitors paddle. The church on the other side of the road, has a slim broach spire. The thirteenth-century tower has a contemporary Galilee, and there is a twelfth-century doorway.

Opposite the Castle Inn is the entrance to the ruin of a Norman *castle*, now cared for by the Ministry of Public Building and Works. It was the property in the twelfth century of a William de Eynsford who became embroiled with Archbishop Thomas à Becket. The story that popular fury drove him out after the martyrdom, and that the castle thenceforth decayed, is disproved by archaeology: it was inhabited much later. All that now remains, however, is a curtain wall of flint and the parts of the main hall.

Over the bridge a pretty lane, passing under the railway arch, goes on to Lullingstone Roman villa, and the countryside, away from the main roads, is delightful everywhere.

Eythorne ("Ay-thorne") 15 is in the Kentish coalfields, and so of mixed character. Upper Eythorne is far from being the nineteenth-century colliery development of South Wales or Yorkshire: it is neither gritty nor hard-featured. But there are more new houses than old ones, although there is a trim seventeenth-century Baptist Chapel on a hillside. The village serves Tilmanstone Colliery, which also has its own newer housing extension up the road at *Elvington*.

Lower Eythorne, to the east, remains an old Kentish village, with several pleasant cottages and a plain church with one of the three leaden fonts in the county, but nothing else of interest.

FAIRFIELD Church

Fairfield 16. There is no village at Fairfield, a district of scattered farms and marshland, two miles south of Appledore. Amongst the dykes and the sheep is a small plain building of timber and plaster with brick walls. This is the church of St Thomas of Canterbury. There is fourteenth-century work, altered in the eighteenth century, and finally restored with care and affection in 1912–13, by W. D. Caröe. It has the original roof timbers and an eighteenth-

century interior of text-boards, white-and-black painted box pews, three-decker pulpit, altar rails round three sides of the altar and reredos.

East Farleigh 6 is a village in the lush country just west of Maidstone. It is too near the capital to be "unspoilt", and is now sadly nondescript, but has a few old cottages and boat yards, as well as bungalows and caravan parks. Its bridge, 180 yards long, and with five arches, is

perhaps the best of the medieval stone bridges crossing the Medway. Over it, in 1648, General Fairfax marched to capture Maidstone from the Royalists. The church, heavily restored in 1891, is all oak and tiles and "proper" stained glass. All about are parks, hops and orchards. Impressive Victorian Gothic parsonage on the churchyard edge.

Another crossing of the river, midway between East and West Farleigh, is at Kettle Bridge, narrow and

EAST FARLEIGH Bridge

wooden, down a lane. Off to the left, over the bridge, a turning leads to the old church of *Barming*, with a shingled spire amongst the orchards, and inside a group of Flemish choir-stalls. The rest of Barming, farther north, is absorbed into Maidstone.

West Farleigh 6. Another of the lovely Medway villages west of Maidstone. It is a district of big houses—Charlton, Farleigh Hall, Court Lodge—but no real village and no real eyesore. The church, with the early nineteenth-century house beside it, lies by the river below the main road, where there used to be a bridge but is not. It is amongst trees, survey-ing one of the beautiful Kentish village cricket grounds, with the hops and the sweep of parkland behind the river as a backcloth.

Farnborough 1. The main road is an extension of the urban and suburban explosion of Bromley and Orpington, hideous with factories, villas, estates, garages, shops and cafés, which lead into an excelsis of roadside develop-ment at *Green Street Green*, with a stockbrokery retreat up *Worlds End Lane*. A few older façades shrink south to where, in trees at the top of a steep lane, is the church of St Giles. This was considerably rebuilt in the seventeenth century, but has a four-teenth-century font and stands well amongst trees. For its old yew there is an actual date: 1640. North is all London, but south, wooded lanes, parkland, and very soon the real country.

Farningham 2 is now by-passed by the main road, but remains at the centre of a loose knot of highways. It manages to retain both beauty and charm. The Darent runs through the village in front of the attractive Lion Hotel, and under a bridge to one of the best water flour mills in the county, in white painted weather-board, with a rich miller's house be-side it. There is a warm eighteenth-century manor house and several other early but large village houses, like the White House of 1743. Also Tudor beams, weatherboarding, and harmonizing modern buildings like the village hall. There are high barns, chestnuts, and an air of pride. The thirteenth-fifteenth-century church, behind yew trees, has a Kentish tower and is spacious. It has a Seven Sacraments octagonal font, fifteenth century, and a mausoleum, perhaps erected by John Nash, to his father Thomas Nash, who died in 1778.

Faversham 13. A delightful market town and small port, obviously con-scious of its historical and archi-tectural heritage, but busy and con-temporary. It has no showpiece to indulge mass gogglers, but any number of pleasant buildings. It is greatly helped by being by-passed to the south by the motorway from London to the Thanet resorts, and all the people appear to be there on purpose. As well as being a shopping centre it has various industries: grain and flour, oysters, bricks, can-ning and packing works for the fruit and vegetables from the country roundabout, and a pleasant and occasional smell of brewing.

There is also a small shipyard, where once was a considerable port, and the town has fought hard to retain the evidences of its long important gunpowder industry. But its first significance grew from its position on Watling Street, from Canterbury to Rochester, where the route crossed the navigable inlet of the Swale. The creek still comes up into the heart of the town. There are Romano-British and Jutish remains, and King Stephen founded a Benedictine Abbey here in 1147. After the Dissolution the property was bought by a local businessman, Richard Arden, who became mayor. His wife and her lover murdered him in 1551, and the fame of this inspired the play "Arden of Faversham", which is only in recent years credited to neither Shakespeare nor Marlowe. Only bits of the abbey remain, although some foundations were discovered in 1965. But Arden lived at 80 Abbey Street, which also has, obscured by later work, some of the old gatehouse. Abbey Street is a continuation of Court Street. Both are wide, with excellent façades, almost all old and gracious, on both sides. Many have been well and recently restored. At the Market Place end of Court Street is the *Guildhall*. This was built in 1574. The top-hamper of cream and brown was built on in 1814, providentially without filling in the open timber arches which support it. Inside is a heavy Flemish overmantel from the house of Henry Hatch, a merchant adventurer who died in 1533 and owned several properties still standing nearby.

The *church*, St Mary of Charity, stands hidden off Abbey Street down a lane by a brewery, although its tower and lantern steeple are widely visible from farther away. They were put up in 1797, the steeple a copy of Wren's St Dunstans in the East. The nave was rebuilt in 1754 by George Dance, and the best things inside are the misericords, and one or two seventeenth-century monuments, one with a recumbent figure.

To the north is a timbered *masonic hall* of 1587, which was the Old Grammar School. The *Ship Hotel*, in the Market Place, is eighteenth

century, with some Tudor beams and plaster inside. From it West Street leads to *Davington*, where there is a Victorianized Norman church restored by Thomas Willement, who lived here, which once belonged to a small Benedictine nunnery. It has a carved (Flemish) pulpit. There are traces of the nunnery in the adjoining house known as the Priory, now belonging to the Church Assembly. The suburb of *Preston*, beyond the station to the south, has an early church, much restored by the Victorians, beside another brewery. Faversham has irredeemably ugly bits. But some of the newer buildings are responsible and appropriate.

Fawkham Green 2. A straggling

The Guildhall, FAVERSHAM

expanding parish off the main road seven miles south of Gravesend. The church has a little wooden tower and an ancient wooden porch, and is basically Norman. It is on the edge of the creeping industrial area to the north, and the skyline has pylons as well as treetops.

Folkestone 17. A seaside resort of 45,000 people which yet retains style. The North Downs reach the sea here with a beautiful dip into the chalk cliffs, dropping to the shore from a plateau sometimes 170 feet high.

A decayed Kentish fishing village, existing largely on smuggling and the provision of herring and seasonal mackerel for the London market, Folkestone began to develop as a

resort at the beginning of the eighteenth century. Its real boost came with the railway in 1843, and the cross-channel service to Boulogne, 26 miles away. From then onwards it flourished—never as garish and popular as Margate, or as earthily vulgar as Victorian Brighton, but prosperous and gracious: at times even modish. It had no great architect, but its crescents and rows of hotels and boarding-houses, ornate and solid, are still bright and charming.

The Leas is a promenade about 1½ miles long, with the regulation bandstand, Pavilion and gardens, and one of the finest in the country. Beneath it, through winding paths with gazebos and tamarisks, is an Undercliff. Behind are the shops, wide streets, and public gardens of a modern seaside town.

Near the east end of the Leas is the *parish church* of SS Mary and Eanswith. It was founded in 1135, but largely rebuilt in 1216, after being burned by one of the endemic raiding parties from France. The chancel chapels are fifteenth century, and the nave (partly destroyed by a storm in 1705) was rebuilt in Victorian prosperity between 1856 and 1874. A west window by Kempe was presented by the medical profession in memory of William Harvey, who was born in Folkestone.

Round the church are isolated trees of the old fishing town, and from it you drop through narrow streets which suffered much from bomb damage, to the Harbour, with its lighthouse, small fishing fleet, Fish Market, and cross-channel traffic.

The back of Folkestone, beneath the viaducts, is less depressing than the equivalent in most seaside resorts, and leads quickly into the glory of the Kentish countryside. From the front the view stretches west to Dymchurch; east, past the Warren, three Martello towers, and a spot where they discovered Roman remains in 1924, to Shakespeare Cliff and Dover: outwards, over the pier and the sands, to the coast of France.

Fordcombe 5. Church of 1847, in a pretty hill-slope hamlet. Bellcote.

Fordwich 14 vibrates threateningly, for it is less than three miles from Canterbury and there is heavy traffic.

It survives as a small place of great charm, with a bridge, many pleasant houses and a splendid group of buildings round the church and on the river. It was for centuries the port of Canterbury, and medieval boats could sail to the wharves here by the then much deeper Stour. Caen stone was landed here for the building of the Cathedral. Now there are only pleasure boats and the skiffs of the King's School. The town was a "limit" of the Cinque Ports and had a mayor and corporation until 1886. It retains, with its back to the river, a little red-roofed half-timbered Town Hall of the fifteenth century with, inside, the old court house and antiquarian tit-bits. The George and Dragon is a good inn which sells tickets for fishing, and in the little square lie also the village shop (but Fordwich was once a town) and the church of St Mary. This has perhaps Saxon traces, but it is largely fourteenth century, and has good stained glass, original, in quatre foils at the head of nave windows, eighteenth-century box pews, a tympanum with the arms of William III, now hung above the chancel arch for which it was made, and an unusual twelfth-century tomb, once optimistically believed to have been the sarcophagus of St Augustine, with a gabled top and carved arcading.

The village is, especially because of the river, much visited: but not as yet hopelessly exploited.

Frinsbury. *See* Rochester (Strood).

Frinsted 13 lies in splendidly wooded country off the main roads south of Sittingbourne, approached by narrow, twisting and hilly lanes. It is a hamlet of an inn, one or two old cottages and a few new ones, together with a dark little church, over-restored by Gilbert Scott in 1868, and over-glazed and over-painted inside at the same time. It is a prototype of the age. Attractive outside. Over-enthusiastic inside.

Frittenden 6. A large village, enjoying comparative isolation on high ground between the two heads of the River Beult. There are hop-fields, orchards, views, and a Victorian church, with a stone spire. (The base of the tower is old.) Scattered farmsteads, and a pleasant central group

of houses with black and white timbering and red tile roofs, punctuated by oast houses.

Gillingham (pronounced Jill-) 3 is a vast area of urban congestion, with homes, shops and amenities for 73,000 people and practically nothing to look at. It is indeed impossible to detect visually where it begins or ends, for along the main road it merges into Chatham on the west and into the built-up suburb of Rainham on the east.

In fact the town is on high ground, and the greater part of it slopes down towards the Medway estuary, where a coast road has off it a little pier, and there is a wistful wharfside atmosphere round the Strand. The road goes on to *Grange*, a suburb which, once Granche, was a limb of the Cinque Ports, attached to Hastings, and now looks out sadly onto the marshes. Above are rows upon rows of little Victorian terraces, with corner shops. There are larger shops, those of any go-ahead provincial town, in Railway Street, and the High Street, and Gillingham Avenue goes on past the large block of the Royal Naval Hospital to the centre of old Gillingham, the Green, which has the Parish Church on its east, on the brow of a hill overlooking the river.

St Mary Magdalene is mainly fifteenth century, with twelfth-century arcades in the chancel, the whole restored by Sir Arthur Blomfield in 1868. There is an old cresset beacon in the fourteenth-century tower, put there to guide ships on the river. Opposite the Star Inn is a stone *tower*, a memorial to William Adams, the Gillingham traveller who lived in Japan from 1600 till 1620, and set up the first English trading station there. Gillingham is a garrison town (it still includes part of the Royal Dockyard) that has become residential and industrial. It obviously has a civic sense, and pains are taken with the new eastern approaches. But architecturally it is a desert. Rising from this, just off the north side of the main road, is *Jezreel's Tower*, a now derelict temple of alarming yellow brick erected but not finished by the

Jezreel's Tower,
GILLINGHAM

Jezreelites, the New and Latter House of Israel.

Godmersham 14 is accented on the second syllable. Lying back from the main road, near the bridge, is a pretty church heavily restored in 1865, but with a Norman tower and thirteenth-century chancel, and a twelfth-century stone bas-relief of St Thomas à Becket. There is a gay east window of 1852 by Gibbs, with lots of pink. The lane continues running through trees and by water past the gates of *Godmersham Park*. This belonged to Edward Knight, whose sister Jane Austen was a frequent visitor here. The house was largely rebuilt in 1935, but is Georgian and attractive, as is the 560-acre park, full of groups of splendid trees.

Goodnestone (by Adisham) 14. This village, like the other Goodnestone, is named from Earl Godwin, father of the Saxon Harold. It has a few late medieval cottages and an almost entirely rebuilt church (old tower) off the main road, with brasses and wall monuments, many of them to the Boys family. The village is actually in the park of *Goodnestone House*, which extends through trees to the south and east. Jane Austen often visited it when staying with her brother Edward Knight, at Rowling House, farther to the east, which he owned as well as Godmersham.

Goodnestone (east of Faversham) 14 is a bright village of cottages and oast houses in orchard and sheep country off the main traffic routes. The church, up a long path to a farm, is of text-book Norman plan, although the detail is later and it is very much restored. The son of a Victorian vicar here grew up to be M. R. James, writer of ghost stories and Provost of Eton.

Goudhurst ("Gowdhurst") 6. A delightful village, with the amenities of a small town, 400 feet up on the crest and slope of a hill, dominating the western part of the Kentish Weald. From a pond the High Street rises to a curve in the road, where the fifteenth-century church has a curious squat tower rebuilt in the seventeenth century. Inside are wooden effigies of Sir Alexander and Lady Culpeper, of 1537, and good monuments to

this family and to the Campions, another local family. Two of these have kneeling figures, and there is a florid, well-carved white marble bust of 1702. The spaciousness, and the light fittings, are attractive.

The *Star & Eagle* has well restored fifteenth-century half-timbering, and there are numbers of old houses of various dates, many weatherboarded, the best preserved by the National Trust. Two fine town houses in brick and tile are set at an angle to the road, and the whole haphazard arrangement of the buildings, on different levels, is natural and effective.

Goudhurst does not appear in Domesday Book, when the Weald here must have been thick forest, and the "hurst" an isolated clearing. Prosperity came from the iron-smelting industry (Forge Farm, Furnace Field and so on still exist) and then for 300 years from broad-cloth, after Flemish weavers were imported in the fourteenth century. By the eighteenth century the Weald was opening up, fruit and hop-growing had come, and the present landscape emerged of orchards, oasts and chestnuts. Modern buildings are generally appropriate.

Grain 10. A village on the extreme dreary tip of the Hoo peninsula. For centuries it was nothing but a few cottages in the desolation of the flats, with a tiny church and the sea-birds. The land, as the name suggests, was good, but flat and windswept. The Isle of Grain was an island. Slowly the Yantlet and Colemouth Creeks silted up, and are now only muddy dips amongst the reeds: Grain is an island no longer. In the 1920s an oil storage plant and refinery were set up. In 1950 this became the basis of the enormous Kent Oil Refinery. Soon an astonishing forest of chimney stacks, plant and storage tanks, smoke and fire grew apparent even from far across the other side of the Medway. Towards this, over the marshes, stretch wires and pipes and the railway line. Beyond the oil installations the old village has new dormitory houses. The little Norman church, neatly restored in Edwardian times, remains, with its tower oddly lower than the rest of the building. Oil refining smells, but its processes

are not conspicuously noisy. The landscape is bare, but the buildings have a sharp functional authority, and you can still hear the water-birds. *Stoke and Lower Stoke*, on the main road to the west of the Isle of Grain, are villages with echoes of agriculture and the sea, but are fast becoming industrial dormitories.

Graveney 14 stands without special distinction on the edge of its marsh, stretching down to the Swale, with the low outline of the Isle of Sheppey on the horizon. The pretty little church of All Saints, Norman and Tudor and 1914, has some fine brasses. Also old tiles and a pulpit with Grinling Gibbons-date carving. This light and charming interior also has oak eighteenth-century box pews. Some Perpendicular bench-ends have in a few cases, been re-used (and respected) by the eighteenth-century carpenters.

Gravesend 2 is a vast knot (51,000 inhabitants and 22 miles from London) in the string of industrial development along the south side of the Thames. It has a rich history and by the river traces of character. It slopes inland, and to the south the residential suburban extensions have wide views, the upper town giving, over the roofs, a survey of some forty miles of the river. The belt in the middle along the main coast road is busy, go-ahead and mainly characterless. This is due not merely to the material dedication of Victorian and twentieth-century developers, but to disastrous fires in the eighteenth century and heavy bombing in the last war. The famous car-ferry has been superseded by the Thames tunnel, and the riverside area seems depressed and grimy. But there is obvious prosperity, particularly towards Northfleet, from paper-mills, cable factories, iron, printing and rubber works, light engineering and various marine activities. It is, moreover, the pilot station of the Port of London: river pilots for ships coming in, deep water ones for those going out, and attendant Customs and medical officers. It is a famous yachting centre. There is always something happening on the river. From the through road narrow ones of older houses lead down to the water-front. The High Street is

GOUDHURST

distinguishable by a Victorian *Town Hall*, but little else. West of it Princes Street leads to the only tourist spot, *St Georges Church*. This, backing shabbily on to a large car-park, is a typical brick and stone Georgian building of 1731 by Charles Sloane. It was rebuilt at this time because of a fire, and it is a magnet for American visitors because in its predecessor was buried the unhappy Red Indian Princess Pocohontas, who played so important a part in the settlement of Virginia by risking her life to save John Smith, the Father of the Colony. She was treacherously seized by the white men, held as a hostage, and told that John Smith was dead. In her grief she married another English-

man, John Rolfe, and came with him to London in the year of Shakespeare's death, 1616. Here, says popular history, she met John Smith, still alive, and died of a broken heart. At all events, on the eve of leaving Gravesend for home she died there (more probably of consumption) on May 2nd, 1617. Famous American families are descended from the son of Pocohontas, and many pay pilgrimage. The church was badly damaged by German bombs during the war.

Another tablet in St George's church commemorates General Gordon, who spent some years supervising the erection of forts at Gravesend, and ministering to the poor boys of

the Ragged School. There is a Gordon Promenade to the east, overlooking the Thames, here half a mile wide and full of traffic where large vessels, shrimpers and yachts can all be seen, active and attractive. Here, too, is the *Royal Terrace Pier*, used by pilots, and the *National Sea Training School* of the Merchant Service.

The church of *Milton* has an eighteenth-century nave and a medieval tower.

To the east Gravesend thins out into marshes, scattered factories and dormitories. To the west into even denser industry and Northfleet. Before it actually reaches Northfleet there is a district still called *Rosherville*, with its own church of high Victorian

GRAVENEY

Gothic. The estate of Jeremiah Rosher was turned into one of the most popular of Victorian pleasure-grounds, and flourished from 1830, when the tone was high and the attraction "terpsichorean lawns", till 1936, when it had become a down-at-heel fun-fair. The name of Rosherville gardens is a reminder however that although Gravesend's obvious history is nautical and industrial, it had a vast social appeal to mid-Victorians, with the cits swarming down river every Sunday. It accounts for what is left, marooned dirtily by the river, and away from the contemporary affluence of the main road, of the then "villas in all the exuberance of the Florid Cockney style", beside the "usual rows of cardboard lodging houses".

Great Chart 13 is an agreeable village just outside Ashford. There are old and new buildings, red brick or tile-hung, and even the serving kiosk of the garage complies without

affectation with the general pattern. The fifteenth-century Kentish-type church crowns the village on higher land up the main road. It has good, lofty proportions inside, but is over-restored and over-furnished. Considerable remains of fifteenth-century glass, and brasses. There are pleasant farms near by, and *Singleton Manor*, to the east of the village, is a timbered house still surrounded by its moat. *Yardhurst* is a newly restored and displayed Kentish Hall House of about 1450, with fine roof-framing. *Little Chart* (q.v.) is some miles to the north-west, the other side of the railway.

Great Mongeham 15 is scattered two miles west-south-west of Deal, and suffers from being a suburb. It is quiet, however, resigned to its gradual decline from medieval days, when it was a market centre. Its embattled church was restored by Butterfield in 1850. The handsome Perpendicular tower shows finely from the downs behind with the sea beyond, and a good Georgian brick country house sits beneath it. *Little*

Mongeham lost its church during Elizabeth I's reign.

Greenhithe 2 constantly appears in the history of the Thames estuary from Tudor times onwards. Today it is part of the industrial belt between Dartford and Gravesend, powdered with cement dust, shabby and inglorious. *Ingress Abbey* on the outskirts, now a nautical training school, was built with the stone of the old London Bridge, pulled down in 1832. What there is of old Greenhithe is downhill from the main road, towards the sea. There is a mean street with high walls cutting it off from works and wharves, and one or two eighteenth-century fronts and Victorian shops. Suddenly at the end is a little green bank with seats and old men on them, looking out at the shipping, with the wooden-walled HMS *Worcester*, black and white and rather fine, in the foreground. Inland stretch miles of housing estates.

Groombridge 8 is on Kent Water, which hereabouts forms the county boundary between Kent and Sussex, before flowing on to join the Medway. The Sussex part is plain, the Kent part, to the north, delightful: the main road coming down from a ridge of trees to the water at the bottom. The church and main grouping of cottages stand by a green on a slope. There are two outstanding rows, one weatherboard and the other tile-hung. On the third side of the triangle thus formed is the entrance to *Groombridge Place*. This is a good medium-sized seventeenth-century manor house of brick with stone dressings rising from a wide moat, classic but not cold, beside a lake and amongst Wellingtonias. Its design is credibly assigned to Wren, and that of the gardens to John Evelyn, who certainly came here. Groombridge church, beside a footpath through the park, is attractive and unusual. It is of brick, built in 1625 by Lord Camfield, to commemorate the safe return to this country of Prince Charles, who had been sent to Spain by his father, James I, to marry the Infanta. He did not pull it off. England rejoiced, and a commemorative inscription in Latin, above the porch, celebrates the occasion. It is darkened by many windows by Kempe. There is also armorial glass of 1625. There is a seated wall-effigy of Philip Packer, showing him with a broken neck, just as he was found in a nearby lake in 1686. This rare Gothic church, much earlier than any "Gothic revival", was a private chapel until 1872.

The Duke of Orleans, father of Louis XII, was kept in honourable confinement at Groombridge for 25 years, after being taken prisoner by Sir Richard Waller, who then owned it, at the battle of Agincourt.

Guston 15 is a small hamlet of mainly flint buildings: remote, although only $2\frac{1}{2}$ miles north of Dover, without special distinction. The church is a little Norman nave and chancel building, much restored. Whitewashed inside, and simple.

On the high ground to the south and west, and visible from all directions, are respectively the Duke of York's Royal Military School and a large radar station.

Hackington (Canterbury) 14. St Stephen's has a picturesque spirelet

on a low square tower, and stands in a north-east suburb. It has a big nave and chancel, Victorianized, with Victorian glass, and a strange late sixteenth-century monument to Sir Roger Manwood, with a bust in an elaborate setting above a life-sized skeleton carved in wood lying on a rush mat. A fine Royal Arms of 1695.

Hadlow 5 is an unexceptional village north-east of Tonbridge on the road to Maidstone, with hops, much traffic, a few weatherboard and older houses, and modern development. The church is a Victorian rebuilding, except for a fourteenth-century tower and spire. But Hadlow is remarkable for another tower, strange, brown and Gothic, 150 feet high, which is a landmark for miles. It is late for a folly, being built in 1835, and is all that remains of an extravagant Beckfordesque castle put up at that time by a wealthy Walter May with a taste for the picturesque. The ruins of most of this were demolished recently, but the crenellated tower itself remains, absurd and rather charming, high above the oast houses. The architect was G. L. Taylor. The legend is that the intention was to be able to view the sea from the top, but that the South Downs intervened. The effect, however, in an unsteepled bit of country, is ornamental and attractive.

Halling 3 church, beside a small ferry, is a rather attractive building with industrial surroundings. The interior, formerly "scraped", has been whitewashed and is quiet and welcoming. There is a Kempe east window and a brass of 1587 with a bedroom scene with a woman in a four-poster. (*See also* Snodland.)

Halstead 5 is in the commuter belt south of Orpington, but still just "in the country", with orchards and trees. The old houses are of flint, and the new villas trim with many flowers. Knockholt station, just to the north, serves it, together with *Badgers Mount*, and the well-to-do houses which scatter the lanes to the remaining farms. The little church was rebuilt in 1881 to serve the early wave of development and escape from London.

Ham Street 16 is a nodal point on the

map, where the road north from Romney Marsh to Ashford crosses the one west from Hythe to Tenterden. There is an agglomeration of new houses round what must have been once just a few cottages and a drinking point. It also has the only railway station for miles. It has no guidebook history, but beautiful surroundings of orchards and rich farming land in all directions.

Ham Street is, in fact, technically in the ancient parish of *Orlestone*, with a small old church with a shingled bellcote and a late Victorian interior, and manor house tucked away from the station up by some cottages to the north. It should not be confused with a tiny place called *Ham*, down obscure lanes two miles south of Sandwich.

Harbledown 14. Beautifully placed on rising ground on the road west out of Canterbury, which unfortunately stretches towards it with deplorable new buildings. These spoil what was a classic view of the city for Chaucer's pilgrims, for whom it was the last halt before going down to the shrine. The switchback road is supposed to be the "Bob-up-and-down" of the poem. Archbishop Lanfranc founded a hospital for lepers here in 1084, now represented by a group of 1840 almshouses on the south side of the road. In its hall are various relics. Opposite is the church of St Nicholas, mainly Norman and thirteenth century, with some very early seating, a fifteenth-century font, nice capitals and traces of wall frescoes.

On the brow of the hill opposite to the south-west, amongst woods, is *Bigbury Camp*. It is of the Iron Age, and possibly the Belgic predecessor of the Roman Canterbury, and the fort stormed by Julius Caesar during his second invasion in 54 BC.

Harrietsham 13 is completely bifurcated by the by-pass to London, along which it extends on both sides, a shambles of cafés, garages and new houses. To the north is the High Street of the old village, with a few pleasant houses. The fifteenth-century Kentish church, unintruded, is on higher land farther back. An enormous wych-elm in the churchyard. The Norman font is of Bethersden

HADLOW Tower with oasts

marble. Interior Victorianized and Edwardianized completely. The most attractive part of Harrietsham is the unspoilt section south of the by-pass, with a variety of Georgian, weatherboard, and tile-hung façades, and some almshouses. There is a small lake, made by damming the River Len, and by it a miniature Greek temple. *Court Lodge* has a handsome brick frontage with a stucco porch.

Hartley and Longfield 2 are bright, hideous, suburban and new: satellites of the prosperity of Gravesend. Their hamlet history is submerged in their present. All roads, pylons, and cultural affiliations lead northwards, to Thames-side. They thrive.

Hartlip 3. The new houses, some of them pleasant enough, outnumber the old, but Hartlip is not absorbed into Gillingham, and sits quietly amongst lovely cherry and apple orchards. A few good black and white timbered buildings. The church is over-restored. In fact everything almost is Victorianized. Dark with glass (east window by Clayton and Bell, another by Kempe). There is a late brass and a nice wall monument,

hidden by the organ. Pleasant view over orchards westward. To the west at *Meresborough* is the site of a Roman villa.

Harty. *See* Leysdown-on-Sea.

Hastingleigh 14 has a remote church beside a farm in a beautiful upland valley. It is of flint, filed, with an old timber west porch. Good proportions, old kingpost roofs. Brass, slabs.

Hawkhurst 9. A large and scattered place in the Weald near the Sussex border, with a few pleasant and typically Kentish façades and much history. It was a centre of the Weald's iron industry, and in the seventeenth century the furnaces belonged to William Penn, the founder of Pennsylvania. Sir John Herschel the astronomer watched the stars from here: there was a notorious gang of smugglers. The church, mainly fifteenth-century, must have looked like that at nearby Benenden, but was gutted by German bombs in the last war. It is now suitably restored.
The expansion on the main road is called *Highgate*, and is a nexus of traffic, breathless and suburban.

Hawkinge 17. A farmland parish standing high on the chalk hills up behind Folkestone, with a little Norman church. Thirteenth-century church with Norman traces, somewhat over-decorated and over-furnished. The busy main road to London racing through at *Uphill*, just to the west.

Hayes 1 in all the older books is a quiet little village, north of its undefiled common, and famous as the home for many years of Lord Chatham. It was indeed to Hayes Place, which he had built conveniently from London, that Chatham was brought to die in 1778. William Pitt the Younger was born here in 1759.
Hayes Place is now a housing estate, and Hayes village has become a vast suburban spread that is part of Greater London, its edges blurred into Bromley and West Wickham. It is clean, prosperous, new and indistinguishable from the other assembly lines of meads, avenues and closes which make for largely middling affluent residence and commutation. Much is semi-detached and semi-Tudor, much is of the '20s and '30s, more of brick, concrete, and today.

All is cherry trees and gay gardens, competitive and largely identical. The church has a Norman tower and is said to be on a Roman site. Certainly there are Roman evidences here, and some 150 neolithic hut circles—depressions with banked edges, some with mounds in the middle—are on the Common. This, gorse and hawthorn and bracken, remains a pleasant open space, gratefully invaded from London, fourteen miles away. *Keston*, farther south, is still suburban, but well-wooded, and on the edge of open country. There are ponds, fed by a well, at what is traditionally Caesar's Camp. There is, to the south again, Holwood Park, where the younger Pitt moved from 1785–1812. The present house is a classical re-building by Decimus Burton of 1825. The church is late Norman enlarged by the Victorians. In the churchyard is the tomb of Mrs D. M. Craik, who wrote the neglected *John Halifax, Gentleman*, and died in 1887.

Headcorn 6 is a large village which gives the appearance of once having been more considerable, on the rich clay of the Beult valley. It was indeed a cloth-making centre in the fifteenth century, and the Cloth Hall is one of numerous fine black-and-white timbered buildings. Many show the influence of the Flemish weavers who were settled here. The fifteenth-century church stands squarely at the end of the wide, long main street. It has a fine modern screen with forty carved panels and an old open-timbered roof. Modern glass. Big Royal Arms, too high to identify.

Herne 11 is repeatedly reminded that Ruskin said that the flint tower of its church was one of the few perfect things in the world. Its beauty lies in its colour and texture: the areas of black knapped flint contrasting with orange and whitestone and shore pebbles, set carefully in mortar. It *is* beautiful. The whole building has good texture. The interior is very much restored—there are large areas of tile and Victorian stained glass, not very worthy. But the wide screen is effective, and old in parts—stalls also. Otherwise Herne suffers inevitably from the development of

HADLOW Tower

Herne Bay just to its north. But the back of Herne Bay is less repellent than that of most resorts, and the village remains a clean and cheerful outskirt.

Herne Bay 11 is a classic Victorian seaside watering-place, now swollen by the homes of thousands of commuters. It has its passionate advocates, but it needs a connoisseur of resort amenities to distinguish its virtues (apart from its greater proximity to London) from those of the other resorts in Thanet.

The town is symmetrically laid out with broad promenades, boating and beaches, bandstand, pavilion and kiosks. Behind these connecting streets join roads with shops parallel to the sea. There is a splendidly ornate clock-tower put up to celebrate Queen Victoria's coronation in 1837. Indeed everything dates from about then: the parish church, also of 1837 (used as a Congregational chapel till 1841), and the better houses along the front, white and bow-windowed. For the railway had arrived in 1833, and this seven mile strip of coast began to be developed, independent of the old village of Herne inland, to cater for the new holiday public. It was done without any Regency crescents so striking as those of Ramsgate, or Victorian show-off as ornate as Folkestone. But the general effect is solid and friendly.

This can be appreciated from the end of the pier, nearly a mile long, and the pride of Herne Bay, although it had to be breached in two places during the war, for defence purposes. But to sea, at night, are the lightships on the Thames Estuary, and inland, always, valleys and rich woodlands.

Hernhill 14 is a small village high up to the east of Faversham, looking down to the Graveney marshes. The fifteenth-century church stands with lime trees high on a small green, which has white weatherboarded houses beside it. It is basically a very elegant building, with slender columns to arcades, but it has been much restored, and the interior effect is largely Victorian. The whole district is one of woods, winding lanes and unexpected clusters of cottages.

Hever ("He-ver") 5 is in pleasant country south-east of Edenbridge. It has a reconstructed Tudor inn with front and back views of Henry VIII on the sign, and a church with a fourteenth-century tower, shingle spire, barrel roof, and the large table-tomb of 1538 of Sir Thomas Bullen or Boleyn, the father of Anne. There are also two wonderful brasses, a Jacobean pulpit and a modern lectern of convoluted ingenuity.

Hever Castle. This lies below the village on the River Eden and was, when built in the thirteenth century, just a fortified farmhouse and yard, surrounded by a moat and reached over a wooden drawbridge. It became the property of the wealthy Boleyns in 1458, who made it into a complete small Tudor manor house, still with some of the fortifications of the late Middle Ages. Here Henry VIII probably first met Anne Boleyn, daughter of Sir Thomas, after having already had an affair with her elder sister Mary. He became a frequent visitor and the rest is history and in the excellent guidebook. After Anne's execution her old father was allowed to live on at Hever until his death, when the property reverted to the crown, and Henry settled here his fourth queen, by this time discarded, Anne of Cleves. The property went downhill, became a resort for smugglers, and by Victorian times was used as a farm, with its kitchen in the Hall, geese in the moat, farm tools in the guard-house and potatoes in the gardens.

William Waldorf Astor, the American millionaire whose personal story is highly dramatic, and who became a naturalized British subject and first Lord Astor in 1916, rescued the building and created the lavish reconstruction that exists today. His grandson, the Hon. Gavin Astor, is the present owner of the castle. Lord Astor employed 1,500 men for five years diverting the course of the Eden to form a new lake of 40 acres, laid out splendid gardens, and built a mock Tudor block for his guests which has recently been converted into individual houses. The manor itself was rebuilt with elaborate care: observing such details as authentic rather than modern pointing. A new drawbridge was made and the keep, where not authentic, put into the best possible reproduction of an exquisite early Tudor fortified manor. Inside were lodged a collection of Renaissance pictures and other treasures. Most of this, and the Italian garden, topiary and grounds are frequently open to a delighted public, but also constitute a home. Hever Castle is not of course a typical small Tudor Manor in perfect preservation, full of works of art, and surrounded by a moat. It is more magnificent and much more comfortable than anything known to the Boleyns. But it is not a film set either—rather an enhanced historic fantasy, re-created with dedication, the best possible advice, and unlimited resources: splendid fun, and visually delightful.

Higham 3 is a scattered industrialized and dormitory development stretching up north of the western end of the Strood-Rochester-Chatham-Gillingham conurbation, and south-east of Gravesend. It merges, almost indistinguishably, three former hamlets. The old part is at the north, where there are indeed a medieval church and some early cottages. The newer part has a Victorian church with a spire, built when development began because this was the terminus of the Thames and Medway canal. Marshes and saltings to the north, but to the south, on the main road from Gravesend to Rochester, *Gad's Hill.* The old church is in flat orchards near the Thames. It is built of bands of flint and stone, is two-aisled and has medieval woodwork—door, pulpit, screen. Here is the Sir John Falstaff Inn, and Gad's Hill was the setting for the Falstaff robbery episode in *Henry IV, Part I.* It preserved its reputation for violence, and Defoe quotes it as a place where seamen were waylaid after being paid off at Chatham. (A "gad" was cant for a vagabond.) Almost opposite is a Georgian red brick house called Gad's Hill Place, now a school. It was here that Charles Dickens lived and worked from 1857 until his death in 1870.

High Halden 16 is a pleasant Weald village with a green in its old centre, surrounded by weatherboard façades and decent unsensational shops and houses. The church has a great timber tower of about 1300, with a curious wooden entrance lobby,

HEVER Castle

rather than porch, built on about 200 years later. The timber work inside is remarkable. Church very much Victorianized otherwise.

High Halstow 3. Perched up in the very middle of the Hoo peninsula. Overgrown, and touched with the industrial overspill of the area. But from outside the church (the inside of which is rather plain and Victorianized) are fine views of the whole peninsula, with the curving fields of orchards set off by the gigantic stick of pylons stretching across towards the oil refinery of Grain. A nature reserve centred here has one of the few remaining heronries in Kent, and the whole of Hoo is a great breeding ground for water birds.

Hildenborough 5 is an arterial conglomerate of a place on the main road to London north of Tonbridge, with one or two Georgian cottages showing that there was a hamlet here before development. This came early, for there is a Gothic Revival church of 1844, by Ewan Christian, with shingled spire, in sandstone; apsidal.

Hinxhill 13 takes its name from Hengist. It is a tiny village quiet amongst lanes and beautifully wooded country about three miles from Ashford. A small plain manor house in white stucco, a few cottages, and a church famous for the snowdrops in its churchyard in spring, with inside in the sanctuary a big Elizabethan monument to members of the Edolph family, with kneeling figures under a canopy (1631).

Hoath 14 is an unremarkable hamlet now in the coal area but not obliterated by Chislet Colliery to the south. A dull little church has however the typical shingled tower with a spire, and a good modern oak reredos.

Hollingbourne 6. A beautifully placed village on the Pilgrims' Way along the lower slopes of the North Downs, with steep woods behind and the Maidstone to Ashford road below. Standing by the hillside is a high chimney-stacked brick Tudor manor house. Farther down are more timbered houses, an old inn and a pond. The church is fifteenth century, and notable for monuments to the great Kent family of Culpeper. There is a life-size marble effigy by Edward Marshall of Lady Elizabeth Colepepper, who died in 1638, and an earlier one in the chancel with kneeling figures. This branch of the family lived at Greenway Court, now a farm south-east of the village. But the church, so beautifully placed in relation to the North Downs behind, and of such good presence and texture externally, is disappointingly Victorian and dark within.

Beyond the church modern buildings, many of them clean, tile-hung and appropriate, and then suddenly beyond the railway another street of old houses, which represent the once separate hamlet of *Eythorne Street*.

Hoo St. Werburgh 3 is the "capital of the hundred of Hoo", but was, for the centuries it proudly claimed this title, only a village. Nominally it is one today, but it is overshadowed by a gigantic chimney and is a stretch of contemporary industrial development—houses, schools, garages and concrete. Evidences of the old village remain to the south of the main road round the thirteenth- and fourteenth-century church of St Werburgh, a Kentish princess thought to have founded a nunnery here. The shingled spire used to serve as a landmark for sailors on the Medway. The building is more attractive outside than inside.

97

Horsmonden 6 is a large, busy, trim place in hop and orchard country in the Weald. It is very much developed, but has an agreeable green called "the Heath" in the middle, surrounded by decent if individually uninteresting houses. The centre of the parish has moved since the church was finished in the fifteenth century and this is now marooned beside a farm two miles away, on rising ground to the south. There is a fine brass under a canopy to Henry Groshurst, priest, of 1330, and a bust to the discoverer of the stomach pump. The church is much rebuilt, but has a handsome yellow sandstone Perpendicular tower. There are two windows full of dashingly-coloured twentieth-century stained glass. Northwards is a chapel of ease of 1869, by R. Wheeler: brick, apsidal.

Horton. See Chartham.

Horton Kirby 2. A large village on the Darent too near to Dartford to have escaped extensive development. It has a church of about 1220, probably built by the masons working on Rochester Cathedral. There are Roman tiles in the walls, and a Roman settlement was found on the river to the south towards Farningham. Today, it is a cruciform flint building showing much rebuilding. The central brick tower is late nineteenth century. There is a good brass (a lady with a horned head-dress), some delicate cartouche tablets, eighteenth and nineteenth century—one signed Gaffin, Regent Street, and a most unusual Royal Arms, a half-circle, Hanoverian, with flags for backgrounds. *Franks Hall* is dignified red brick and of Elizabethan origin. Neo-Elizabethan predominates in the village generally.

Hothfield 13 is a village three miles north-west of Ashford, in beautiful parkland country. There are still attractive old red brick houses, and a few good ones, although the village is spreading, mainly to its disadvantage. Hothfield Common is a piece of heathland designated as a nature reserve, with notable wild flowers and insects.
The late medieval stone church has a short shingled spire. It has been whitened and tidied inside. There is a

fine monument to Sir John Tufton, his wife and family with alabaster effigies on a marble table tomb. "He re-edified the aisles of this church after its was burnt." Other nearby houses of significance are *Swinford Old Manor*, the home of the least honoured Poet Laureate, Alfred Austin, and the Jacobean *Godinton Park*. This is much visited for its good panelling and carving, and for the pleasant gardens, laid out in the eighteenth century and altered in the nineteenth by Sir Reginald Blomfield.

Hougham 15. A scatter of houses with a broach-spired church in the high land behind Dover. The church has a Trans-Norman arcade, nice thirteenth-century work, a good timber roof and wall tombs. Royal Arms: Queen Anne.

Hucking. See Bicknor.

Hunton 6 is a scattered hamlet in the magnificently rich hop country south-east of Maidstone: orchards, chestnuts, and the ash trees that provided the hop poles. Essentially the cottages are those related to the big house, *Hunton Court*. This is a plain classical building in a 100-acre park with fine Wellingtonias beside a lake. It was the home of that neglected Prime Minister, Sir Henry Campbell-Bannerman. He has a characteristically undemonstrative plaque in the church, which stands at the park gates, behind yews and fir trees. There is a vast sixteenth-century alabaster tomb of Sir Thomas Fane and his wife, with recumbent effigies and a splendid canopy. Also another Fane tomb of 1692, with a great build-up of scrolls and mouldings and a bust. There is old glass, of Canterbury type, mixed up with later armorial glass, all mounted with bold and rich glass of *c*. 1840–50.

Hurst. A lost Romney Marsh parish.

Hythe 17. An ancient market town and one of the five original Cinque Ports, now mainly a resort. It has all the regulation amenities of fishing, bathing, boating, golf, cricket and general seaside activity. But it is much more. By freak of the changing coastline it is a strip of shingly beach and promenade, behind them a belt of fairly modern buildings along the

Military Canal; and back again, the long High Street and the old houses, once lapped by the waves. Then there is development up into the skyline. Summer traffic pours relentlessly one way along the basically eighteenth-century High Street, and past the Town Hall of 1794 with a white portico and a projecting clock: but the town remains attractive.

Originally Hythe ("the landing place") was New Hythe, and water covered what is now the whole sea front of the town. It was silting up by 1230, and by 1450 the Harbour was lost. But it won a charter in 1575 and continued as a prosperous market town. The church, St Leonards, superbly perched back on the hill and floodlit at night, is that of a medieval centre of importance. It is one of the finest in Kent, with an astonishing high nave of the peak period of the town, about 1225. An ambulatory, miscalled a crypt, contains a popular but macabre peep-show at thousands of medieval skulls and bones stacked here some time before 1500. In the churchyard lies Lionel Larkin, the inventor, in 1785, of the first lifeboat.

Below the church and down to the High Street are lanes and old houses. Beyond this is the development to meet the demands of the Victorian seaside holidays—gardens and shaded walks beside the *Military Canal*. This starts here and stretches 23 miles down the coast, petering out at Cliff End, a few miles from Hastings. It was an important part of the crash defence programme against Napoleon, when he was massing troops at Boulogne. It was both a canal and a defence line, tying in with the Martello towers some of which still remain. Pitt himself superintended much of the work, staying at Walmer Castle down the road. Now it is an amenity (a water carnival is held in the Hythe stretch every two years) and a setting in H. G. Wells' *Kipps*. But it was an enormous undertaking, and the atmosphere is retained by various street names like Barrack Hill and Battery Road. The occasional rattle of musketry off, however, has nothing to do with Boney. It is the School of Musketry, with a camp on the London Road and ranges in the marshy sea-girt land behind the road to Dymchurch.

17th-century monument in IGHTHAM Church

The Romney, Hythe and Dymchurch Railway, "the smallest public railway in the world", starts in Hythe, and steams across the Romney Marsh out to the lighthouse at Dungeness. It was built by Captain Harvey, a railway enthusiast, in 1927, and remains a magnet for other enthusiasts and countless children. Hythe was originally attached to *Saltwood*, which is now an agreeable residential extension of it steeply inland to the north. Here, on the edge of a valley, is *Saltwood Castle*, founded by the Normans and rebuilt about 1160. Later building included the gatehouse, which is fourteenth-century work, and now the main residential part of the castle. The murderers of Thomas à Becket are said to have completed their plans here on the eve of the crime, December 20th, 1170. The ruins were restored in Victorian times and the castle is now the home of Sir Kenneth Clark. It is gravely impressive, much is authentic, and it is at times open to the public.

Ickham 14. An undisturbed straggling village on the Lesser Stour, east of Canterbury, with a red Georgian mansion, and an over-restored parish church with a shingled spire. Also *Lee Priory*, praised by Horace Walpole as a rival to Strawberry Hill. This had been a simple seventeenth-century building, but was rebuilt in full Gothic by James Wyatt in 1782. It was subsequently re-Gothicized by Gilbert Scott. It has an octagonal library intentionally imitating Ely Cathedral.

Ide Hill 5. A hamlet gloriously placed on the Greensand Hills, among a crop of beech trees which crown the Darent valley, and are visible for miles. It consists of a few respectable little cottages and an inn round a green, with a small Victorian church perched on the edge of the wood. From just below it a path leads past the old Rectory, with gardens, to a National Trust viewpoint. From this, and from the whole escarpment along to Bayley Hill, there are two miles of woodland, with huge vistas over the tops of the trees to the Weald below.

Ifield 2. Pylons, cabbages and fruit trees. A little 1838 church, partly weatherboarded. Nave and chancel. Box pews with low doors, and an 1860-ish coloured east window.

Ightham ("I-tam") 5 is a pretty village, which suffers from over-exposure to visitors. There are several fifteenth- and sixteenth-century half-timbered houses and others anxious to be: a notable timbered Town House, now an hotel, the "George & Dragon", all in a pleasant hollow, with a nice row of tile-hung cottages climbing up on one side. The church stands away from the main road, on a rise east of the village: not now alone, because there is development, but on the verge of orchards. It is twelfth to fifteenth century, with notable oak roofs and Jacobean pews. There are effigies and monuments, including in the brick north aisle of 1639 one of Benjamin Harrison, who died in 1921. He was the village grocer here, the discoverer of "eoliths", and first to explain these

99

IGHTHAM MOTE

as early stone implements. His archaeological interest was developed by the Iron Age earthworks in *Oldbury Hill*, towering 600 feet high above the village. These, constructed in or about the first century BC, represent the oldest hill-fort in Kent, originally covering 120 acres. Ightham Court, north of the church, is a Tudor house with a good garden.

Ightham Mote 5 is well south of Ightham village and the main road, near to a small hamlet of a few cottages agreeably round an inn, called *Ivy Hatch*. The mote (probably named from being at some Saxon period a meeting point or "moot", not because

it is moated) is reached down a heavily wooded lane. It sits in a little valley below the road, one of the most attractive, and admired, of all Kent's pieces of early domestic architecture. It is in form a square courtyard surrounded by a moat, with the walls mounting sheer from the water. Some of the house, including the Hall, is of the mid-fourteenth century, and so is the crypt. The entrance tower and some of the timber work is rather later, and the domestic chapel was finished about 1530. There are half-timbered stables facing the lane, with the original entrance. It is a beautiful moated grange, in a grey Tennysonian way,

but must have been, in its hollow, dank and dark when it was built. It is now beautifully cared for, looks comfortable, has delightful gardens, and is on occasions open to the public.

Ivychurch 16. A typical isolated village of Romney Marsh, surrounded by sheep, rhines, and winding lanes flanked with trees bent by the wind. The magnificent long low church, mainly late Decorated, is grey outside, and light inside. Inside it is big, bare and striking, with mostly empty stone-floored nave, aisles and chancel. There is some original woodwork, fine open timber roofs, well-textured walls, splendid Royal Arms of 1775 and oval text-boards on the walls, characteristic of the district. It was damaged by flying bombs and is now one of the group of Marsh churches jointly administered and all owing much to the generosity of a London firm who own local property and are providing funds for restoration. There are wide views from the tower.

Iwade ("Eye-wade") 10 is on the Sheppey Way, perched amongst the last of the orchards, and descending to the north into the marshes that lead to Kingsferry bridge across the oozy Swale. It has farms and a few old buildings without distinction round its pretty little thirteenth- and fifteenth-century church with foreign sixteenth-century glass of the Crucifixion. Mainly new estates, with garages and amenities on the main road, geared to the needs of the traffic streaming through from Sittingbourne to the Isle of Sheppey.

Kemsing 5. Much of the village is now an overspill of Sevenoaks. The older part is to the east, and has some agreeable houses, with beautiful lanes. Off the outlying hamlet of *Heaverham* is the large park of *St Clere*, a seventeenth-century red brick manor house with a battery of chimney stacks and attractive gardens. Kemsing's own pretty church, with a fourteenth-century timber porch, stands back from the road. There is a half-figure brass of a priest, fragments of fourteenth-century glass, and a good deal of modern glass. The interior is dominated by the High Church twentieth-century screen and chancel decorations. There is a modern ribbon wall on the south side of the churchyard—like older ones in Suffolk.

Kenardington 16. A small village just below the ridge bordering the Romney Marshes. There are earthworks, optimistically attributed to Alfred the Great, and for centuries there were fishermen. The church itself stands high above, up a long lane away from the village, and overlooking the Military Canal, with lovely rolling country away to the north, as well as the Marsh to the south. It is small and bare, the south aisle of a larger building struck by

IGHTHAM MOTE

lightning in 1559. It is usually dismissed as "mean", but has a stark sort of charm, and is wonderfully placed.

Kennington, near Ashford 13. Limestone church among orchards in the outer fringes of Ashford. Slight medieval features, decently restored and incorporated in to a Victorian interior. Fifteenth-century tower and glass fragments. Kingpost roof.

Keston. *See* Hayes.

Kilndown 9. A tiny place down lanes south of Goudhurst, and with fine views looking back towards it. It has

a Gothic revival church of 1841, originally Salvin, advised upon by Carpenter, Butterfield and Willement, under the supervision of Beresford Hope. Dark, dramatic "Munich" glass; that on the south destroyed by a stick of bombs in 1940, which narrowly missed the church.

Kingsdown (near Deal) 15 has a seafront of variegated villas and bungalows which stretches down the road south from Walmer. It ends in Old Kingsdown, which is nautical and attractive, with a beach of boats and tackle. A hill climbs up through older cottages, and the top of the

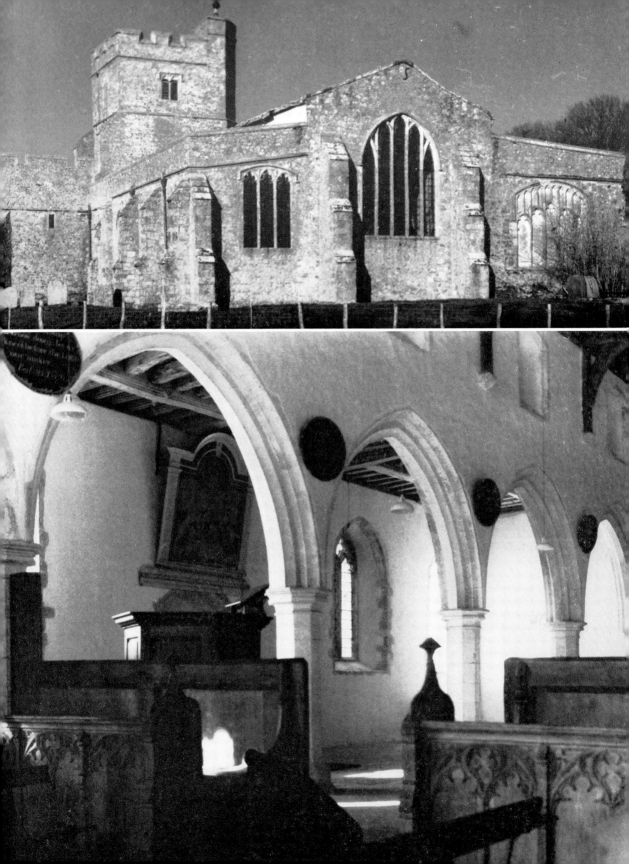

cliff has a strip of residential maritime villas with wooden balconies. On the cliffs to the south are the links of the Walmer and Kingsdown Golf Club.

Kingsdown (near Sittingbourne) 13 consists almost entirely of a farm, a rambling old rectory and little Victorian church hidden in flat farmland four miles south of Sittingbourne. The church was built here, on an older site, in 1865. It is effective if incongruous, and turns out to be from the designs of E. W. Pugin (son of A. W.). The inside is miserable.

West Kingsdown 5 is a strip of appalling main road development, semi-detached cafés and filling stations, on the A20 north of Wrotham corner, but with newer buildings rather better than those of the '30s. A gaunt windmill stands beside the road, preserved as an attraction or a sop to conscience. Unexpectedly, up a turning north, past an old-fashioned village post office, the lane becomes peaceful and re-absorbed into the countryside all about. A pathway through the woods leads to the little Norman church of St Edmund, with medieval glass (two figures complete, and fragments), early paintings, and a tower curiously half way along the south side. It is unspoilt and quiet—except when a meeting is taking place at *Brands Hatch* motor-racing circuit which lies just to the north, when the growl of engines is incessant.

Kingsgate 12 is a resort on the tip of Thanet at the extreme north-east coast of the county. From the map and the air it appears simply as another spread of clean little bungalows and villas, their avenues leading down to the sea and the sands. It is indeed a new place, but does not lack its own character. It developed at what was once called Bartholomew's Gate—the gate or gap in the cliffs here. It became the King's-gate after Charles II landed here in 1683, with his brother the Duke of York, afterwards James II, on their way by water from London to Dover. An actual gate to commemorate the event was blown down in the last

IVYCHURCH
on Romney Marsh

century, but re-created in the grounds of a nearby convent.
The coast road from the North Foreland goes beside the grounds of Kingsgate Castle, one of several ingenious conceits of the first Lord Holland, who built this one in 1760, "to represent Tully's Formian Villa". Of several distinguished owners, one was the Lord Avebury who was responsible for the institution of Bank Holidays, and who died here in 1913. Battlemented on the north side of the bay, again a sham castle, is the Captain Digby Inn. There are golf courses, walks beneath the cliffs in both directions, rocks, smugglers' caves and all that Lord Avebury's beneficiaries can desire. Kingsgate is largely residential, as well as a popular resort.

Kingsnorth 13. A typical and so pleasant Wealden village 2½ miles from Ashford, without particular historical interest. The plain little church has a good stained glass picture of St Michael and the Dragon, made about 1400.

Kingston 14 is a quiet village just off and below the traffic of the Canterbury-Dover road, which runs, broken by a windmill, along the skyline. New houses blend uncomfortably with old cottages, presided over by a long narrow church, with Perpendicular features, amongst trees. Nave, chancel and west tower. The exterior is well-textured and the interior quite attractive, whitewashed, with a Jacobean pulpit and good wall-tablets of various dates.

Kits Coty House. *See* Aylesford.

Knockholt 4 with its larger extension Knockholt Pound is a notably spick and span place (Best Kept Village in Kent, 1966) with a green, a few old houses, villas, lamp-posts, and road edgings and patently is not in the heart of the country. But it has great trees everywhere, hiding, at least from the main road, the fact that it is the highest placed village in Kent (725 feet). The originally thirteenth-century church is badly restored, but the village retains character and obvious pride. Knockholt Beeches, a tall clump to the south, are a landmark for miles, said to be visible from Harrow-on-the-Hill.

Knole. *See* Sevenoaks.

Lamberhurst 9 is a pleasant Weald village on the Sussex border and the small Teise, flowing here through a rich valley. It is also on the Hastings road, and suffers accordingly. But there are old houses with boarded and tiled fronts along the village street, and a half-timbered Tudor house, *Coggins Hall*, opposite the "George & Dragon". Off the main road at the bottom of the hill are other attractive village houses, climbing to *Lamberhurst Down*, scattered round a green.
To the north-east is the fourteenth-century church, much restored in the nineteenth century and re-ordered in 1964. There is a very large, painterly Royal Arms of Queen Anne. Also there is a well-standing Georgian house called *Court Lodge*, now the club house of the golf course, and views of the valley. Lamberhurst was once a centre of the Wealden iron industry, and provided the railings for St Paul's Cathedral. With iron, the stage coach, and now the through traffic of the motor-car, it must always have been prosperous.
Just off the road past the village is a drive to *Scotney Castle*. This, of which the gardens are often open to the public, is a place of great beauty and historic interest. The "modern" castle is a remarkably successful Gothic building of 1837 by Anthony Salvin. It stands on high ground, and from the terrace of the house paths wander downwards through an alpine garden ingeniously formed in a quarry, to reach a lake and the ruins of the earlier castle. This was a fortified fourteenth-century manor house, added to in Tudor and Stuart times. Only the shell of the seventeenth-century house is now readily distinguishable, but the whole composes finely round the remaining fourteenth-century tower, reaching up out of the water against the superb backcloth of trees and shrubs. The whole scene, with its fine planting and carefully planned walks and view points is a splendid monument of the English picturesque genius. Its site was suggested by Sawrey Gilpin, nephew of William Gilpin, the "Picturesque" author and theorist, and has been greatly enhanced and carefully preserved by Christopher Hussey, the author of the standard

work *The Picturesque* in our own day. It has been in the possession of the Husseys, ironmasters, for generations.

Langley 6 is four miles from Maidstone, surrounded by orchards and hopfields, with a Victorian church with a stone spire, 1855, by William Butterfield. It also possesses a splendid gabled Tudor timber-framed house, *Rumwood*. *Langley Green* is scattered, and has numberless little bungalows screened by furze and heavily wooded lanes. Where undisturbed, the country is glorious.

Langton Green 5. Church by G. G. Scott, after 1860's. Nave and chancel, bellcote over chancel arch, south

aisle and two transepts. Sandstone. Beside the main road into Tunbridge Wells.

Leaveland 13. An attractive farmhouse in whitewash and black half-timber neighbours a small church of flint and stone with a tile-hung bellcote. The inside is Victorianized, but has an old kingpost roof and a tiny Jacobean monument.

Leeds 6. An irregular village in lovely orchard country east of Maidstone, rising above the little River Len and the wide grounds of Leeds Castle. *Battle Hall* is a restored and enlarged fifteenth-century house, and the church, on a corner, has an extremely sturdy eleventh-century

tower, no doubt once used as a refuge. Only the lower part was ever built. The entrance to the church from it is under an immense Norman arch. Inside there are tall slender arches, late fourteenth century, a restored fifteenth-century rood screen which goes right across the church, and seventeenth- and eighteenth-century marbles, one with cherubs, another with pedimented head. *Leeds Castle* is visible from a public footpath through the Park, and is revealed as an almost idealized spectacle of the medieval castle of tradition. It is striking and magnificent, and if only part of it is "real", the romantic effect is a credit to the skill of its successive owners. The castle rises from a lake created by damming the River Len, leaving two islands. The first, which is natural, is reached by an Edwardian bridge and gatehouse leading into a walled bailey. At the far end is the main building, largely rebuilt, most effectively, in 1822. Beyond this, reached by a bridge with a chapel above it is, on another island, a medieval building, the Gloriette. The work of the different periods harmonizes delightfully, and the surrounding park, laid out by Capability Brown, is glorious with trees, more lakes, wildfowl, and in springtime, daffodils.
The original castle was built by Robert de Crevecoeur in the twelfth century. Later it belonged to the crown, when it was often used as a prison, as it was for Richard II. Later it belonged to the Culpeper family. It has much history.
Technically the castle is in the parish of *Broomfield*, a hamlet which lies, with a little restored church, away to the south-east of the Park. Attractive outside, of good texture.

Leigh ("Lie") 5 is a pretty, rather contrived village with a fine green, trees round it, and some trim houses and cottages. The church stands back high above the road : restored (almost rebuilt) thirteenth-century, mostly 1862 (G. Devey, architect). Also works of 1892. It has some good woodwork and a "quaint" brass of *c.* 1580. By it are the self-important Victorian gates of *Hall Place*, an Elizabethan red brick house damaged by fire but restored in the mid-nineteenth century by the wealthy and philanthropic industrialist, Samuel

KILNDOWN Church, 1841

KINGSGATE Castle

Morley. He largely re-shaped the village as well, often in undeceptive half-timbering, and died here in 1866. There is a large park. The general effect is of a place open, pleasant, and well-endowed.

Lenham 13 was a small market town and staging post on the coach road. Now it is fortunate to be by-passed. It has a pleasant market square, with the Old Market House, converted for shops on the ground floor, still in the middle. Three sides have good eighteenth-century or half-timbered houses, one of them, on the corner of the Maidstone road, outstanding. On the fourth side of the square is the fifteenth-century church, with some interesting details, including good stalls, a carved oak pulpit of 1622, with a canopy, a wall painting of St Michael weighing souls, and monuments.

Leybourne 6 is just west of Maidstone on the London road. From this it appears simply as a continuation of built-up map points of which the next is *Larkfield*—bungalows, filling stations and traffic signs. In fact Leybourne proper lies to the north. Here are large new estates, but some older cottages, and a modern house which incorporates part of the fourteenth-century castle. The church was badly restored in 1874, but well in 1967, after lightning had struck the

tower. This now has a new and bright little steeple. Inside is an unusual "heart shrine", said to contain the heart of Roger de Leybourne, who died in Palestine on a crusade in 1271.

Leysdown-on-Sea 10 gives pleasure to thousands. It is a twentieth-century agglomeration of holiday camps, caravan sites, garages, hotels, little red-box houses and their appropriate amenities, enjoying the seashore on the eastern edge of the Isle of Sheppey.

For the less gregarious, it is surrounded by marshes and sea-birds, with away down lanes to the south the desolate *Isle of Harty*. Here in rich pastureland is Sayes Court, originally built by the first Lord Saye and Sele. Nearby is a humble but delightful twelfth-century (and later) church with a wooden belfry and old woodwork in an oil-lit interior: charming and so far isolated. It has a fifteenth-century Flemish chest of intricate workmanship, dredged up from the Swale. This shows two knights tilting.

To the north of Leysdown lie Warden Point, and the Thames Estuary.

Linton 6 descends the steep hill where the road south from Maidstone to Hastings first dips down into the Weald. Pleasant, unimportant, often old houses cluster up the street. Back from it, up steps, is the largely

Victorian church. This is plain, restored, and with a modern tower, but has some interesting monuments, 1615 (Mayne) and 1627 and white marble nineteenth-century ones, including one designed by Horace Walpole for his friend Geoffrey Mann, who died in 1758. "Simplicity and decency, with a degree of ornament that destroys neither", he thought. Others are to the Earls of Cornwallis, who owned Linton Place. This and its park lie behind the church, and are visible as a landmark for miles below. Although not architecturally exceptional, Walpole was right in saying that the house "stands like the citadel of Kent. The whole county is its garden." The trees are superb, and there is a public path through the park, with a pretty sunken lane at the end.

Littlebourne 14. The first village out of Canterbury on the route to Sandwich, and built up accordingly. But it still has a green, a mill, a long thatched barn, the little bourne itself, the Lesser Stour, and some pleasant coloured cottages, with a church behind a big lych gate made by local craftsmen, off the main road. This is thirteenth- and fourteenth-century, much restored, and is flanked by a thatched barn as long as itself.

Little Chart 13 is an attractive village,

Two views at Dungeness (see LYDD)

not cowed by its small factory, with some late medieval timbered houses. The old church, some way from the village, having been bombed during the war, a new and more accessible one has been built (H. Anderson, 1956). The outside is plain brick, with a tower, simple Gothic, but the inside is light with some good use of arches, and incorporates various furnishings from the original, including monuments to the Darell family, and a Crusaders Saracen's Head from one of their tombs.

Longfield 2. A developed place between Dartford and Rochester. The church is nearly all modern, and not very interesting. Fragments of fifteenth-century glass, with a good head.

Loose 6 is carefully pronounced LUSE, but none the less is probably from the Old English leose, a pigsty. The little River Loose still flows attractively through the village, once operating numerous mills. Although only just out of Maidstone, Loose preserves character and has pretty timbered and tile-hung houses, with half a mile to the west a fine fifteenth-century Wool House, now belonging to the National Trust. The church is a restoration of 1888, and development is of standardized inevitability, but the great charm of the village lies in its clustered roofs, and climbing steep hills, surrounded by oast-houses and orchards.

Lower Halstow 10 is in a creek on the Medway estuary: rich orchards above and then suddenly the mud banks and marshes where once the Romans had potteries and everything looks old and melancholy. Ships stand in the little wharf almost beside the church, then there is the slimy water, and across to the north Slaughterhouse Point and the chimneys of the Isle of Grain. Looking out at all this the church itself is gay and pretty, flint flecked with Roman tiles. It is rather like a church on Romney Marsh. Inside, there are a twelfth-century leaden font, discovered in 1921 when the plaster covering it disintegrated as the result of gunfire during the first world war, frescoes, a seventeenth-century pulpit with sounding board, and a good timbered roof. Remains of box pews. Splendid brass chandelier. The main village, farther inland, escapes the desolate charm of the marshes, has new buildings, and is cheerfully undistinctive.

Lower Hardres 14 has a church by Richman, 1832.

Luddenham 13 is a grouped church and manor house, lying between scattered farms on a long looping road north of Faversham: orchards, agricultural activity, low marshes and grazing sheep stretching north to the Swale. The church has a long, nearly rebuilt Early English nave and chancel, and a little red brick Victorian tower.

Luddesdowne 3 is in glorious forested country, rather hard to find. There is a very early manor house, in private hands, containing Saxon, Norman and Tudor work. The church, classically adjacent, is usually locked. It was virtually rebuilt in 1868, but still has traces of Roman tiles in the walls. There are magnificent trees, especially chestnuts, in the churchyard.

The whole area to the south, down to the line of the Pilgrims' Way, is wooded and hilly country, reticulated with narrow lanes with remarkably good surfaces. It is quiet, beautiful and unintruded country, with cottages, mainly nineteenth-century, but occasionally earlier, grouped as at *Priestwood* or *Harvel*, and a sprinkling of farm houses.

Near the group of cottages called *Great Buckland*, and the superb viewpoint of *Holly Hill* is the site of a village abandoned after the devastation of the Black Death. It is *Dode*, now one or two houses and the shell of the little Norman church, restored in 1910 and now the property of the Roman Catholic Church.

Lullingstone 2. *The Castle* is reached by a drive up from the main road, or, most agreeably, by a public path

across the park from the Roman villa. Like many "castles" this was never more than a fortified Tudor manor house, and much of the present building consists of additions of the beginning of the eighteenth century, when the west front was added. It remains a handsome house of brick. Henry VIII and Queen Anne were both visitors. It is the property of Sir Oliver Hart-Dyke, whose family have lived here since about 1500.

Naturally their tombs and memorials are in the fourteenth-century church of *St Botolph*, on a lawn in front of the house. There are also memorials of the Peche family, who lived here previously. One tomb has painted effigies and standing allegorical figures at the corners—Work, Peace, Death and Resurrection. Another, a wall-tomb, is Gothic. A third is a handsome table-tomb against the south wall of the chancel. The screen that dominates the interior seems to be sixteenth century, though it looks new. There is fourteenth-century glass, and many weathered remains of 1754. Cut down box pews and pulpit. Plaster ceilings of note. There is also a classical porch, and the house and church together make a memorable group.

The *Roman Villa* is half a mile away, and outstandingly well displayed. The site was known in the seventeenth century, but was rediscovered, and its importance revealed in one of the major archaeological discoveries in

Britain since the last war, in 1949. The villa, standing on the banks of the Darent, seems to have been started about AD 90, probably as the home of a farmer. Later is was expanded, often as the county residence of officials. It was burned down about AD 400, by which time it must have been a sophisticated pocket of civilization in the disintegrating province. The central room has a fine mosaic floor, there is a "Deep Room" with a natural spring used for worship, and above it, and later, a Christian chapel. There is much more, admirably described in a Ministry of Public Building and Works pamphlet by Colonel Meates, who has been in charge of the investigation. The most important area is covered over by a well designed functional building of wood and glass.

Lydd 16 stands out, a landmark, remote in the middle of Romney Marsh: a little town of historic importance which consorts without grave detriment with an Army camp, a nuclear power station, and its nearby airport. It has a good High Street with an eighteenth-century rectory, a Town Hall, some houses of preserved authority, and a green called the Rype. The Manor House of Westbrook is a seat of the Devening family.

Its glory is the church—the longest parish one in the county. This, like

the whole neighbourhood, suffered badly from bombing in the last war, but is beautifully restored, with colourful lancets to the new choir by Leonard Walker. It is light and airy, thirteenth to fifteenth century, with suggestions of earlier work. There is an effigy of a fourteenth-century knight in armour, and many brasses, some hatchments and a Royal Arms of 1732. New parquet floors, and much restoration. The tower, 132 feet high, was commissioned by Cardinal Wolsey.

Lydd is a subsidiary Cinque Port. Its maritime importance evaporated with the medieval fluctuations of the River Rother, and it turned to the wool trade for new prosperity. It is now 2½ miles from the sea. In spite of this, and the impact of war and modern industry, it still retains integrity. Windswept, it can be bitterly cold.

Dungeness (pronounced "Dunjeness") 17 is the geographical name for the unique triangle of land which points out into the English Channel, a ledge of loose shingle covering some 6,000 acres. It forms more than half of the parish of Lydd, and grows at the rate of about 18 inches a year. The whole formation has come from the curious action of two opposing currents, and it appears likely to go on growing, as it has for centuries. Dungeness has its own mysterious life, with special fauna and flora and a bird sanctuary. It has an old lighthouse, and a new one built in 1963 and visible for 17 miles. In 1944 Dungeness was a starting place for "Pluto", the petrol line to the invading forces on the Continent: the Central Electricity Generating Board's fifth Nuclear Power Station was completed here in 1965. Another one was added, 1968. Amongst the gorse and the shingle surrounding these activities, and laced by the pylons which lend perspective, are abandoned workings, fishermen's huts, tarmac strips and a sort of shanty town spread which reaches up to Lydd-on-Sea, where the bungalow belt begins to Greatstone. To the west it is wet, bare and windy, and still solitary.

Lydden 15. To the motorist, a strip of development on a bend a mile or so from Dover, on the London road. The cottages of the original hamlet lie to the north, in a fold of the downs fringed with trees, with an over-restored twelfth-century flint church—attractive outside—still agricultural and comparatively peaceful. Houses are creeping up.

Lyminge 14. A large built-up village of mainly undistinguished modern houses, and a lesser business centre. A few Georgian houses and a pleasant old rectory survive. The church is on a rise to the south-east. It is a fine flint one with a somewhat fortified look, a sixteenth-century tower, and an odd external arch. The Normans built on the site of a Saxon abbey church dedicated to St Ethelburga, widow of the king of Northumbria, who came here in 633. When the Danes sacked the abbey the Archbishops of Canterbury progressively built the building that now survives. It has several points of interest, including a massive chancel arch, which is late thirteenth century, and an odd recess of Roman bricks in the south wall of the nave, not fully explained. The wide-arched, very late medieval north arcade is attractive. So is the gay Victorian east window by Gibbs. Alas, the walls are scraped of their plaster. The pews are worked by local craftsmen. Traces of the original abbey, excavated in 1859, show disconsolately in the churchyard.

Lympne 17 is pronounced "Lim", and was once, although now high inland, the Roman Portus Lemanis, one of the first of the Saxon Shore. It still rises majestically on a skyline overlooking Romney Marsh, that once was a cliff with the sea breaking below. Now there runs here the Military Canal. The remains of the Roman Castrum, tumbled by landslides, lie beneath the escarpment down a path. They are called *Stutfall Castle*, and Roman cement work is still visible. Lympne Castle is magnificently placed on the crest. It incorporates parts of a fortified manor house of the early fourteenth century belonging to the archdeacons of Canterbury. Now, much and ably restored, it is a private house, but is frequently open to the public.
The church, on the castle doorsteps, is Norman, and has a severe tower, a font of Bethersden marble, and the same wonderful views across the marshlands. Overhead are often aeroplanes, and Lympne Airport is busy just down the road. Northwards the Roman Stone Street runs straight and unbroken to Canterbury, 16 miles away.
At a road junction out of Lympne on the way to Hythe is a modern cross. This is the Shipway Cross, put up in 1923 by Lord Beauchamp, then Lord Warden of the Cinque Ports, to mark the traditional meeting-place of the Barons of the Cinque Ports. From this symbolic site most of the Marsh villages can, given favourable weather, be identified.

Lynsted 13 is still a pretty village on the North Downs, particularly in the spring, with orchards in blossom, and still has a number of red brick and timbered buildings, old cottages, and an Elizabethan manor house. But the church was damaged by a bomb in 1940, and although repaired is now faced by white council houses. It is three-aisled, of attractive texture outside, and stands in a delightful and unspoiled churchyard. The tombs inside are remarkable: these have recumbent figures, two have kneeling figures. The best, signed by Epiphanius Evesham, is to Christopher Rooper, 1622. It has him lying and his wife kneeling behind: big, life-like and well carved, in a fine decorated setting. There is a candelabrum of 1688.

Maidstone 6 is the county and assize town of Kent, on the Medway and at the foot of the North Downs, halfway between London and the coast. It has 60,000 inhabitants. It is a go-ahead provincial centre visited for its shops and its market. It has civic pride, great industrial and commercial activity, incessant traffic and a pervading and balmy smell of malt. It is ugly but has character, and modernization does not yet disguise the fact that the centre of the city is an architectural palimpsest, with sturdy Victorian work overlaying and developing a medieval town. There are a surprising number of interesting survivals of the past, and a vigorous sense of belief in the future.
This past is amply documented and cherished by the authorities and the "Friends of Maidstone". The first notable inhabitant was an iguanadon, a twenty-foot reptile which many millions of years ago lived on the shores of the Wealden Lake. It was discovered as a fossil in 1834 in the ragstone quarry of Messrs Benstead and Higgens, and subsequently destroyed by gunpowder. It remains in the coat of arms of the City. There are evidences of Bronze Man, of the Iron Age, of the Romans and of the Anglo-Saxons, from whom perhaps (learned controversy) derives the name Meddestane, "Maiden's Stane", in Domesday. By Norman times the city belonged to the Archbishops of Canterbury, who made a country residence here during the reign of King John. Shire moots and great assemblies were held on *Penenden Heath*, to the north-west, now a recreation ground, and Maidstone was deeply involved in the insurrections of Wat Tyler in 1381, Jack Cade in 1450, and the unhappy Sir Thomas Wyatt, against Queen Mary, in 1554. After the last, Wyatt lost his head and Maidstone, temporarily, its charter. In the Civil Wars the Kentish Sir Byng's forces rose against Parliament in 1648, and were brought to a halt at Maidstone when Fairfax took the town after a five-hour siege and fighting in the market place. Disraeli dropped his apostrophe here and secured his first entry to Parliament in 1837 as member for Maidstone. The town bitterly opposed the coming of the railways, but got a line (to what is now Paddock Wood) in

1844, and profited accordingly.

Indeed the cherished historical highlights are against a background of increasing prosperity as a market centre for the rich produce of the farms and orchards of the Medway Valley, easily conveyed by river to the growing metropolis of London. All this redoubled in the sixteenth century, when refugees from Flanders brought in improved methods of hop cultivation and new fruits and vegetables. They also brought the trades of weaving, fulling, dyeing, and the making of linen thread. Fullers earth was available locally, and the cloth trade flourished. Meanwhile the Quarry Hills provided and do provide, ragstone, the hard bluey-grey limestone used in most of the early buildings of the county. Oak also grew round Maidstone, which sent much timber to the dockyards at Chatham.

Thread-making declined and flax-fields were turned to hops, but the mills were converted for paper-making. Brewing developed, flour-mills, and more recently have come toffee-making and automobile engineering. Victorian and modern Maidstone produced a varied economy, as well as creating a vast residential centre. But the sense of a market town still remains.

From the Medway bridge the High Street rises to a cross-roads that is the middle of the town, presided over by a monument to Queen Victoria. The façades are those of shops and banks, many of them eighteenth or nineteenth century with modern frontages or Tudor disguised as mock Tudor: others modern: one, Blake's shop, an early example of a building erected on an iron frame. At the top of an island of buildings with a remarkably ugly bank at the bottom is the Town Hall, a very plain building of 1763 with mid-Victorian cinquecento decorations in the Council chamber by the Italians Galli and Gotti. The most justly famous group of buildings in the town is down the river to the right—the church of All Souls, the College of Secular Canons, and the Archbishop's Manor House. Seen (and incessantly photographed) from the far side of the river they make a pretty and impressive group. The great Gothic *All Saints* was begun by Bishop Courtenay in 1395, and

ended as a very fine example of early Perpendicular work, with wide nave and aisles, high and airy. There are excellent carved stalls with misericords, four canopied sedilia, and other interesting details. A 78-foot tower over the south porch, perhaps gains from having lost its spire in the eighteenth century. To the south, still in the group, are the remains of the *College of Secular Canons*, completed in 1397, and now used administratively. Best of all is the *Archbishop's Manor House*, or Old Palace, built in the fourteenth century but altered by the Elizabethans, and with a remade east front of the early seventeenth century. The gatehouse, which may have been a mill, is the office of the Inspector of Weights and Measures. Away from the river, part of the group but the other side of a sweeping new main road, Bishop's Way, and cheek by jowl with the bus terminus are the *Archbishop's Stables*. They look like, and were long thought to have been, a huge tithe barn. But the rooms at the top of the unusual external staircase suggest grooms and stable boys. The building is used to house a notable collection of eighteenth- and nineteenth-century carriages.

Other medieval evidences are dotted about: a crypt in Gabriel Hill, a fourteenth-century bridge over the little River Len under Mill Street and early timbered houses at 16 and 62 St Faiths Street and elsewhere. In St Peters Street, dwarfed by breweries, is the thirteenth-century chapel of St Peters, belonging to an early hospital, set up beside the Medway for travellers. This was suppressed in favour of Bishop Courtenay's College in 1395, and only the chapel, restored and re-dedicated in 1836, remains. The Early English work is not spoilt, and there is some unusual modern glass. At the bottom of Earl Street, parallel with the High Street, is a fifteenth-century building which was originally the hall of the Brotherhood of Corpus Christi, and at the Dissolution became a grammar school. In Faith Street, parallel again, is the museum, housed partly in Chillington Manor, an Elizabethan building restored, enlarged, and added to by a wing from the Court Lodge at East Farleigh in the nineteenth century. The Museum has

a valuable collection of county objects and pictures, displayed in an old-fashioned convention. It also has special collections of the works of the water colourist William Alexander, who was born in Maidstone, and of relics of William Hazlitt. The Unitarian Chapel where Hazlitt's father was minister, stands in an alley off the High Street. The building is charming, which compensates for the fact, stressed in the guide books, that Hazlitt left Maidstone in 1780, at the age of two. There is a pargeted house of 1611 at 78 Bank Street, and no less than three eighteenth-century almshouses—the Edward Hunter one of 1757 in Mote Road, the John Brenchley one of 1789 in Kay Street, and the Sir John Banks Almshouses of 1700 in St. Faiths Street, with numerous other Georgian and Regency houses. The Prison is a severe building by Daniell Alexander of 1818, and in no time industrial archaeologists will be claiming for history the massive eyesore of the Medway Brewery. One or two late Victorian gin-palaces are in almost mint condition.

There are good modern libraries, schools and other buildings, and vast housing estates which have swallowed whole villages like Barming and Tovil, and continue their now more regulated spread.

Mote Park is 558 acres of breathing space bought from Lord Bearsted in 1929. The house and the Pavilion were both designed by Daniel Alexander at the turn of the eighteenth century; the lake is used for yachting; and the county cricket ground, in the Mote, is part of the history of the game.

The best of very urban Maidstone is observed from the towpath of the Medway, with the great laden barges coming up the river from Rochester.

East Malling ("Mawling") 6 has vast development off the London and Maidstone road, and conspicuous but not unharmonious modern buildings even beside the green, which is a cradle of Kent and English cricket, famed in esoteric history. The village remains however a fine one, with tall trees, open spaces and some good Kentish cottages by the church. This has a pleasant interior, with whitewashed walls and much restoration. Brasses (including a lady in butterfly head-dress), wall tablets—a seventeenth century one has a nice forward-facing bust—and fourteenth-century tracery light stained glass in two windows. To the east is the Horticultural Research Station. This possesses at *Bradbourne* a large and nearly perfect Queen Anne manor house, which long belonged to the Twysdens, one of the oldest of the Kent families. It makes effective use of bricks of different colours to give contrasting surfaces.

West Malling 6 is also called Town Malling, and indeed it is large for a village: fine eighteenth-century façades and individual houses of merit and authority both in the High Street and Swan Street. The High Street is particularly wide. Some of the houses have creepers on them, the shops are bright but not garish, but it remains a local centre of character without self-consciousness. There is an appropriate church, with a massive Norman tower and a spire added in 1838. Oast houses.

St Mary's Abbey (with a typical small Georgian house, Abbey View, opposite) incorporates bits of a Benedictine nunnery founded in 1090 by Bishop Gundulph of Rochester, including a square Norman tower and a fifteenth-century gatehouse. Made habitable by the Akers family, the rest of the building is again a nunnery. A stream, passing through the gardens, cascades ornamentally through the wall out and under the main road. Farther south, off St Leonards Street, stands the ruin of a Norman keep and gatehouse, said to be more of Bishop Gundulph's work, and probably the remains of a fortified manor house.

Marden 6 is very much built up round its railway station, but possesses an attractive open High Street with some Kentish tile-hung houses, and some timbered ones. The church is fourteenth-fifteenth century, and has a porch of old beams with a priest's room over it. Three chancel windows by Patrick Reyntiens, 1964.

Margate 12. Population 46,000, and the largest resort in Kent, with a deserved reputation for cheerful vulgarity. It has spread out all along the north coast of Thanet, from the indescribably ornate Clock Tower at its centre, its fun-fair image of

picture-post cards, Margate rock, bingo, funny hats, conferring politicians, and mass amusement. This garishly and unashamedly overlays remaining evidences of the architectural grace of the early watering-place of the eighteenth century.

The old town, now diminished by a huge modern biscuit box of flats, rises from the harbour, once busy with a fishing fleet and boats going to the Continent, but now mainly used by yachts. This is circled by the pier, built of Whitby stone by Rennie in 1815, with its lighthouse. Much more visited is the jetty, with a pavilion at the end: 240 feet long, jam-packed in summer, with steamers coming and going, and the lifeboat. Behind is Cecil Square, business, and the shops. North-east is an early nineteenth-century Grotto, adorned with sea shells and stories of smugglers, and to the west the Royal Sea Bathing Hospital, sponsored by George III. South is a forbidding building of 1875, the Royal School for the Deaf and Dumb. In the middle of all this there is a sixteenth-century timbered house in King Street, restored in 1952, and the tower of Holy Trinity Church, all that remains of an 1825 Gothic building bombed during the last war. The old church is St John's, a Norman village edifice extensively and expensively spoilt in 1879. All about are hotels, boarding houses and shops, mainly Victorian, but sometimes Regency or eighteenth century, with bright curtains, coffee-coloured muslin ones, anachronistic aspidistras or contemporary neon invitations. The Marine Parade, and the front generally, have of course every expected enticement and the self-renewing sands. Behind them lies, fun-dedicated and frightening, the Dreamland Amusement Park.

Margate was never smart, but it was always jolly. The joys of the old Margate "hoy" and the trip by daily packet from London are a literary footnote to Lamb, Dickens, and *Mrs Caudle's Candle Lectures*. Its rise began about the middle of the eighteenth century, at the beginning of the vogue for seaside resorts as opposed to inland spas. 1753 is given as the date of the introduction here of the first bathing machine by a local Quaker, Benjamin Beale. This is disputed by Scarborough. But the

innovation proved popular, although Beale ruined himself. Soon there was the full complement of Lending Libraries and Card Rooms, and the lovely theatre still in Addington Street. Cecil Square was built in 1769 and Harley Square "in a contiguous field". They remain respectable evidences of the early glory. Most of the later building, enormously increased after the coming of the railways in 1863, is progressively undistinguished. It merges into *Cliftonville*. This is the residential and more ambitious end of Margate, intended originally as a Hove to its Brighton, or St Leonards to its Hastings. Unlike the old town it is laid out in parallel streets, and has its own sands, bathing pavilion and lawns along the front. Also miles of hotels and boarding houses, many of them hideous. A wide sweep of the whole Thanet coast can be seen from the Flagstaff Promenade, popularly known as "Hodges". Whole blocks of Cliftonville are operated, clearly to widespread satisfaction, by Butlins. *Westgate-on-Sea* is the western extension of Margate, as Cliftonville is the eastern. It too has its own bay, boats, sands and amenities, with grass above the cliffs and lines of cheerful little seaside suburban houses, many with the regulation half-timbering of the 1920s. There are two bays, called St Mildred's and West Bay, a pavilion, gardens, a church of 1883, views, and many schools for various educational ends. A hundred years ago there was one farm house only. Off the Canterbury road, to the left is the early fifteenth-century gateway of the Dandylion— the one-time castle of Dent-de-Lion or Daundelyon.

The whole area is strenuously and successfully dedicated to recreation: not to retrospection.

Mark Beech 5. A high hamlet which hived off Cowden and Hever and became a parish with its own little Victorian church of 1852, by D. Brandon, with a chancel designed by Bodley forty years later. An inn, a few cottages and outlying farms, with tremendous views north to the Greensand Hills and south across the Weald into Sussex.

Matfield 5 was long an outlying hamlet of Brenchley (to the south), and only became a parish in its own right, with a new church, in 1875. This is well-detailed, small, by Basil Champneys. There is Kempe glass. None the less, it has all the character of an old village: a green, with a pond, a wide main street with weatherboarding and a Queen Anne manor house with a fine turreted stable block. There are new buildings round about, some very well designed, but also orchards, and the general effect is of colour and content.

Meopham 2. An admirable village of cottages and inns with some typical if not outstanding Kentish façades, straggling 500 feet up on the road from Gravesend to Wrotham. The church tower, flint with brick and white stone buttresses, stands out for miles. The building is spacious but rather dull and over-restored. John Tradescent was born here in 1608—the naturalist whose collections formed the basis of the Ashmolean Museum at Oxford. Amongst other things he first introduced into England the lilac, the plane tree, and the acacia.
Farther south, at *Meopham Green*, is one of the famous Kent cricket grounds, and a remaining windmill.

Mereworth ("Merryworth") 5 village has no very old houses, for good reason. In the 1740's John Fane, later the Earl of Westmorland, destroyed the existing hamlet and church, to use the site for his Palladian "castle". He built a model village beside a new and exotic church down the road half a mile towards Tonbridge. This is the basis of the village today, with the incongruous but attractive spire of the church a landmark for many miles amongst the hopfields. The whole operation is frequently quoted as a major example of aristocratic arrogance and despoliation. There is small evidence that the people of Mereworth greatly resented their new amenities, much as modern villagers usually prefer contemporary bungalows to the homes in which they were born. Now, at all events, we can be grateful for the high-handed whim which gave us the castle.
The church, possibly by Colen Campbell, and of 1746, is loosely classical: a Tuscan nave with an elegant

western portico. The inside has fine proportions: Doric, with a painted barrel vault in the nave, and plaster ceilings to the aisles. There are some monuments, from the older church, tucked away under the tower. They include late brasses and a splendid seventeenth-century composition with reclining marble figures under a canopy, with flying gilded cherubs holding a crown and palm branches, suspended from its soffit (Despenser). There is much armorial glass of the eighteenth century—handsome and golden in effect.
C. Henry Warren, author of *A Boy in Kent*, was born in the village, and describes it, as Fladmere, in his book. *Mereworth Castle* has its entrance half a mile down the road towards Maidstone. The gardens have great charm, and the castle is one of the most interesting buildings, architecturally, in the county. Having cleared the site by transferring the village, Lord Westmorland commissioned Colen Campbell to build him a place based on Palladio's own Villa del Capra at Vicenza, but much larger. It was started in 1720, and completed by 1748. It has a central hall and rooms with decorations of stucco and painted ceilings under a dome 60 feet high and 38 feet in diameter. It may have meant dignified discomfort, but it impressed even Horace Walpole so much that he wrote in 1752 that Mereworth was "so perfect in the Palladian taste that I must own it has recovered me a little from Gothic". Its formality we still enjoy and in Kent it is unique in its period.
There are fine trees all about, and an avenue which disappears amongst lodges on the other side of the road.

Mersham 13. About four miles southeast of Ashford, off the Folkestone road. It has much modern housing development, and some pretty farms and houses. The church, of various styles, is set prettily beside a huge barn, and a large house near it has early mullioned and tracery windows. Inside is a most unusual fifteenth-century west window, with old glass, and fine monuments to the Knatchbull family, including the Carolean Sir Norton Knatchbull who built Ashford Grammar School.
Below to the south lies the valley of the East Stour, and a rich view. To

the north, on the other side of the main road, is *Mersham-le-Hatch*, where the Knatchbulls lived from the time of Henry VIII until recently. The big house here was built by Robert Adam in 1762–72, and lies behind a fine line of trees, which protect it from the road. It is a simple and beautifully proportioned building, now the home, since 1946, of the Caldecott Community, who bring up homeless children.

Milsted 13 is an attractive village. There are bungalows, but with Sittingbourne only three miles away it retains remarkable freedom from ugly exploitation: there are pleasant cottages, farms, brick and timbered Tudor buildings and a fine manor house of half-timber and brick opposite the church. The church was enlarged and restored in 1872. It is well textured outside, of flint and stone, with a west tower. Inside, Transitional to Decorated, pleasant in atmosphere, and not overdone.

Milton (Chartham). *See* Chartham.

Milton (Gravesend). *See* Gravesend.

Milton Regis 10 on the Swale, just north of Sittingbourne, used to be a small market town flourishing on its oyster fisheries. The High Street still retains a self-conscious little fifteenth-century half-timbered Court House, there are a few old houses, and a Port Reeve is still elected to a purely nominal position. But the Swale here silted up, Sittingbourne became an industrial area, and Milton is now a northern suburb, lacking in charm. The big church, looking its size from the Kingsferry road above, on its way to the Isle of Sheppey, is almost entirely fourteenth century. From the front it surveys housing estates, and little brick homes for the factories and paper mills which surround it. It is impressive, and built of dark flints and light stone. Grand interior. Fine candelabra. Brass.

Minster (in Sheppey) 10 is named from a Saxon nunnery here which was sacked by the Danes in 835. This was re-established about 1130, when the present church was built, incorporating and still showing parts of its Saxon predecessor and even Roman tiles. It is splendidly placed on the highest point in the Isle of Sheppey, its heavily buttressed tower looking out over the Thames and the Medway. There are good early brasses, and on the south of the chancel a fourteenth-century tomb recess with the effigy of Sir Robert de Shurland, Lord of Sheppey, who served with Edward I. At his feet are his squire and the head of a horse, emerging from the waves. This is the origin of the story of Grey Dolphin in the *Ingoldsby Legends*. The churchyard has been made bare and municipal-looking by the placing of the stones round the side walls.

A large block of masonry in the churchyard is what remains, restored in 1933, of the original nunnery.

The buildings in Minster itself are generally dull and utilitarian, with bright modern residential develop-ment looking out to sea on the low cliffs to the north.

Minster (in Thanet) 15. Superficially an unattractive sprawl of mainly new houses four miles from Ramsgate, its skyline taking second place to the nearby power station at Richborough. In fact it is the heart of Thanet, which was a real island until the Middle Ages. Minster is named from the abbey founded here in 670 by King Egbert of Kent. This was sacked by the Danes, but passed into the hands of St Augustine's Abbey at Canterbury, who started building the existing church in 1027. The interior is impressive: nave fine Norman, chancel and transepts vaulted, thirteenth century. But the effect of the interior is much spoiled by clumsy electrical equipment, and the churchyard by a wholesale tomb-stone clearance. Fifteenth-century choir stalls with exotic misericords. A Manor House down the road is known incorrectly as *Minster Abbey*. It was built in the twelfth century as a grange by the monks of St Augustine, and now, much restored, houses a community of nuns. The village is surrounded by marshes and, in spite of few visual evidences, a sense of history.

Molash 13 is a hamlet of a few scattered farms and cottages amongst fields and orchards, condensing on to the main road from Canterbury to Maidstone. The small unremarkable medieval church stands back. It is pretty enough, with a little brick-topped tower and buttresses, and a long red-tiled roof. Its walls are mainly of flint, and flints glisten thick in the fields round it when they are

MEREWORTH Castle

ploughed. The interior is plain, cream-washed and attractive, with some old stained glass, including a figure of a late fourteenth-century bearded man, and old clear glass in other windows. The Royal Arms (1790) is in the proper place over the (renewed) screen.

Monks Horton. *See* Stanford.

Monkton 12 is a hamlet in inland Thanet, dwarfed historically by nearby Minster, and aesthetically by road development: a few oast houses and early farms and cottages jostled by light industry. North lies the road to Canterbury, and south the marshes. It was given to the monks of Christ Church, Canterbury, by Queen Edgiva in 961, which accounts for its name. The church, long and rather bare, is mainly thirteenth and fourteenth century. Dull inside.

Murston. *See* Sittingbourne.

Nackington 14 is a collection of farms and orchards, two miles from Canterbury. The small church, almost in a farmyard, is a building originally Norman, with later medieval alterations and much Victorian attention, but of note for its thirteenth-century glass related to that in the Cathedral. The Marriage at Cana forms a complete panel, and there are figures from a tree of Jesse, like those at Westwell.

Nettlestead 6. A noble house and church beside the bank of the Medway, and not many other buildings. They lie, with a cricket ground, south of the road from Wateringbury to Tonbridge, and make, in spite of a modern barn, a most charming group. Nettlestead Place is of ragstone, much but agreeably restored at various periods from a fourteenth-century original. It has a vaulted undercroft dating from the first building. The garden, which is often open to the public, is entered through a medieval gatehouse, and has a rose garden above a water garden, dropping delightfully to the river. The church is a graceful mature Perpendicular building, with a thirteenth-century tower, and a great deal of stained glass windows in the wide aisleless nave

MEREWORTH Church

with arms of Kentish families and figures of saints. The windows have all their original glass. Others have some. Two monuments with kneelers: Elizabeth Stafford, 1598, and Katherine Smith, 1616.

Newchurch 16 is a typical inland village on Romney Marsh, the centre of a large parish of scattered farms. It has a group of cottages round the church, SS Peter and Paul, spacious and largely unspoilt. The tower is fifteenth century: the inside earlier, with some good glass fragments. Spacious, though largely unremarkable. To the south *Blakmanstone* bridge preserves the name of a vanished medieval village, and tall fragments of a tower to the east are remains of the church once at *Eastbridge*.

Newenden 9. A hamlet on the Sussex border, with an eighteenth-century bridge over the Rother, a garage, a white weatherboarded inn and a miniature late medieval church on a mound, with grotesques on the large square Norman font. The Norman style chancel was built in 1930.

Newington 10 straggles along the Roman and business road from Gillingham to Sittingbourne, but has a few older houses round the crossing with the lanes going north and south. The thirteenth- and fourteenth-century church, picturesque in cherry blossom time, lies north. It has a splendid Kentish tower of the fifteenth century carefully banded in flint and stone, and the pedestal of a shrine to St Robert le Bouser, killed in the parish in 1170. It was brought here from a roadside chantry. Also a good screen and some wall paintings, a brass and a wall monument with a kneeling figure, seventeenth-century. A light attractive interior, with old floors.

Newington-by-Hythe 17. Although the Folkestone road goes through it, and has absorbed the next parish, *Cheriton*, in its outer spread, Newington remains a pretty village, poised behind the Hythe-Folkestone conurbation. It climbs up north from the road towards the Downs and has an attractive church dedicated to St Nicholas. It is long and squat with a wooden belfry and a lead cupola.

Newnham 13 lies between orchards and private parkland five miles from Faversham. It is essentially a long street of decent little cottages of all periods, but there is an outstanding Tudor building called *Calico House*, because the material was made there. This has pargeting, which is unusual in Kent. Above the road is a *Court House* and an avenue of larches. The church was tragically over-restored in 1868. It has pews with doors of that date, but is all cream and cement colour inside. *Eastling*, just down the road, was practically re-built in 1856 but has giant churchyard yews. Edward Hasted (1732–1812), the early historian of Kent, was born in this hamlet.

New Romney 17 has only a small population and is now over a mile from the sea. The town remains, however, the chief of the Cinque Ports, and retains a mayor, although it lost its maritime importance when a terrific storm destroyed the harbour in 1287 and permanently diverted the course of the Rother.
The long High Street has a pleasant general effect, and there are individually attractive Georgian houses, with an important little Town Hall. The glory of the town, and one of those of Kent, is the church of St Nicholas. For centuries the ships used to anchor just below it, and sometimes the water broke in. Even now its splendid amber tower, in five stages, and 100 feet high, stands as a landmark for this part of the Marsh. It is fine Norman work, and inside the church is light and spacious. The flowing tracery of the three east windows makes a splendid contrast with the Norman architecture. The church as a whole has pride and atmosphere. The floor of old stones with brasses, and varied textures, is one of the great attractions. Arrays of pews with doors.
An avenue of trees flanked by modern houses leads ambitiously to the shore, where some Victorian marine villas have become *Little Mongeham* (*see* Great Mongeham).
Littlestone-on-Sea. Here indeed is the uninhibited seaside, a parade, and the concrete edifices of organized enjoyment, with a long road, built up with beach dwellings and bungalows,

to be named further down *Greatstone-on-Sea*, in a continuous string of hotels, boarding houses, and residential villas. Celebrated golf course.

Nonington 14 has a much tiled and pitchpined church in a developing village in the coal area.

Northbourne 15 is a Kent country village by the sea, with windmills, capacious barns, and a large country house, *Northbourne Court*. The grounds of this include seventeenth-century terraces and the house has traces of a grange of St Augustine's monks of Canterbury. All beautifully kept up. There are views out to sea and widely inland, over the obtruding foreground of Betteshanger Colliery. The large park of *Betteshanger* previously belonged to Lord Northbourne. The house, a freakish Jacobean imitation built in 1824, is now, enlarged, a school. A tiny church is another unfortunate whimsy: imitation Norman, built in 1854, but with some rescued Norman masonry and a monument by Scheemakers.
Another ornate monument, this time by Thomas Green of Camberwell, is in the rebuilt church of *Waldershare*, another estate to the south. It is to Sir Henry Furnese, the first owner, who died in 1712, and has life-sized supporting figures.

Northfleet 2 is part of the industrial belt that stretches along the south coast of the Thames west from Gravesend, and on the main road you cannot tell where it begins or ends. In fact it is a town with history and some character. The centre is less forbidding than the approaches: a little square, ugly but unpretentious, and behind it the old and somewhat depressed church, its overgrown churchyard backing on to chalk pits. It has a fourteenth-century rood screen which is the earliest in Kent: and a seventeenth-century flint tower built inside the ruined walls of an earlier Norman one. From the distance what catches the eye is, however, the nearby Roman Catholic Church of Fletton brick built by Sir Giles Gilbert Scott in 1915. Across from the square the road overlooks the ships, wharves and movement of

NEWCHURCH, Romney Marsh

114

NEW ROMNEY Church

the river. Also works and chimneys. Northfleet was a shipbuilding town in the eighteenth century, and also exported chalk in quantity for dressing the land. Its industries today include cement, paper, and cables. Portland cement (so-called because it was supposed to resemble Portland Stone) was first developed here by William Aspdin in 1834. Chalk and clay were available locally, and the river was the obvious means of transport to London. The results of the development of cement are self-evident. Locally its effect on the atmosphere contributes unkindly to the industrial patina of the countryside. The church is a handsome cruciform building of stone and flint, of character outside and in, though the inside is much re-furbished. Norman and thirteenth century. Aisleless, but of good proportions. There is a splendid white marble monument of 1628 (Sandys family) with two lying effigies in a grand architectural setting.

Norton 13. A hamlet down a country lane off Watling Street. The modest medieval church is reached by a long field path, and backs on to Norton Court, which was built by Inigo Jones in 1625, modified, and was altered again recently.

Nurstead 2. Undulating green fields; country near suburbia. Pleasing nave and tower; early church with attractive stone floor with old ledger slabs. First War memorial east window. Small Kempe window. Royal Arms of George III, 1801–16, with electoral cap of Hanover.

Oare 13 stands above Faversham Creek, and has a nautical air, with views of the shipping below, and low-lying marshes to the Swale on the north. A dilapidated windmill and a few old houses, but the general effect is rather messy, and the bellcoted church is nearly rebuilt, with some Early English fragments.

Offham 5 is much visited because of the quintain standing on its cheerful little green. This tilting-post consists of an upright and a cross-bar. The cross-bar is on a swivel, and lack of dexterity in hitting one end meant being hit by the other. This is the only example still extant on a village green in England of what was a common village sport up to the eighteenth century. Here it has been restored through time by the lords of the manor. The village is wide and pleasant, with at least two good Georgian houses and a number of eighteenth- and nineteenth-century cottages. There is a pretty if plain church some way north from the village, down delightful lanes. Orchards all round, and fine views.

Old Romney 16. A tiny village, small even in 1377, when it had 133 inhabitants to 1,400 at New Romney.

NEW ROMNEY Church: the south aisle

116

The proportion is much the same today, with a few farms and sheep grazing. The remote little church, secluded off the road, is mainly thirteenth century. Inside are box-pews west gallery, and furnishings, recently well restored. There are west gallery, original reredos and commandments, Chinese-taste chancel gates, Royal Arms of 1780 over chancel arch. Altogether a proper Georgian interior. It is a diminished village, but not a depressing one.

Orlestone. *See* Ham Street.

Orpington 1. The railway came in 1865, not at once destroying a village wistfully remembered as straggling along a High Street often flooded in winter by the springs of the little River Cray, famous for its trout, and its church the mother one of several nearby parishes. It was only 14 miles from London, on the edge of lovely country. By the turn of the century the population was 5,000. Now Orpington is a town that is the administrative capital of a population of over 80,000. There are still poultry farms, where the Buff Orpingtons come from, but the place is best known as a political barometer, a shopping centre, and an outer suburb proud to be at once select and progressive.

It is not Kent at all, except to the assiduous antiquarian. There are one or two old houses, notably the so-called Orpington Priory, below the church, and now municipal offices. This, once a Manor House of the priors of Canterbury, has a great hall of 1471, with a panelled ceiling. There are streets of well-built unexceptional Victorian houses of the first railway development, and rows of villas of the continuing ones, on the whole bright, brick and indistinguishable. There are in many of the side roads trees and grass verges, the little gardens are gay with flowers in summer, and there is a peppering of decent but strictly utilitarian places of worship for various denominations. The parish church of All Saints stands high and well, with an aisleless nave and a chancel with a north chapel, and a tomb under the north side of the porch with a beautiful crocheted canopy. It has a good modern screen, and outside a large churchyard with fine yews.

The High Street is modern, busy, multiple-stored, and the shops favour mock Tudor.

Ospringe 13 is now almost absorbed as a western suburb of Faversham, but retains some good houses, on and off the main street, and a fifteenth-century half-timbered house

called Maison Dieu, well restored and displayed by the Ministry of Works. This stands on the site of a hospital founded by Henry III in 1234, and contains pottery from a nearby Romano-British cemetery. There is the spring which gave the place its name, and made it an attractive stopping place for pilgrims to Canterbury. There are Norman remains in the church, which was rather ostentatiously rebuilt in 1866. The interior is dark and over-furnished. It has a fine, well-carved recumbent marble effigy under a canopy (James Masters) of 1631.

Otford 5. On the main road from Sevenoaks to Dartford, and with a number of well designed modern estates. Fortunately, they hardly impinge on the middle of the old village, which has a pretty green with a pond in it, trees, a Georgian house and generally acceptable shops, inns and cottages. The church stands back from the green, with a squat Norman tower. It suffered fire in the seventeenth century and restoration in the nineteenth. Splendid marble group (Polhill family) on north side of chancel, 1687, with life-sized figure of a man and two allegorical female figures, seated. Also a wall monument, with bust. The seventeenth-century timber work in the porch is attractive. Fine Royal Arms, 1697.

But the most interesting thing is the ruin just south of the church. This, made of red tiles with stone facings, gains, at least temporarily, from being left somewhat wild. This octagonal tower, the wing of a gate-house, and some other work incorporated in nearby cottages, is all that is left of the so-called Castle of Otford. This was for centuries one of the favourite palaces or manors of the Archbishops of Canterbury. Thomas à Becket lived here, Archbishop Winchelsea in 1313 died here. It was enlarged and at its peak is mentioned with awe by Erasmus and other visitors. Henry VIII stayed at Otford with a vast retinue on his way to the Field of the Cloth of Gold, coveted it, and wangled it out of Archbishop Cranmer. Then he coveted Knole as well, said that he found Otford "rheumatic like unto Croydon", and so took over Knole for himself and left Otford for part of his court. The Princess Mary was

allowed it as a residence. The building began to deteriorate soon after Henry VIII's death, and was early stripped of its lead roofing. The ruined tower is now all that remains of Knole's great rival and neighbour, although bits of panelling are said to exist in some of the older houses in the village.

There are no physical evidences that Edmund Ironside defeated Canute and the Danes here in 1016 (it is a strategic point where the road leaves the Downs and comes down to meet the Darent), but traces of a Roman villa have been found off the road to Kemsing.

Otham 6 is a charming village, surrounded by hop gardens and orchards, south-east of Maidstone, on the other side of Mote Park. The church, half a mile from the village, in an isolated position, has little of interest, but the cream-washed interior has eighteenth-century wall tablets. There are any number of beautiful half-timbered houses—one of the best groups in the county. *Synyards* is a well-restored building of 1663, and *Wardes*, also in the long High Street, includes fourteenth- to sixteenth-century work. To the east is *Gore Court*, rather later, standing in a park. The prize building is, however, *Stoneacre*, up a steep lane to the east. This is an outstanding example of a yeoman's house of about 1480, with sixteenth-century adjustments and careful modern restoration in the 1920s by Mr Aymer Vallance, the Kentish antiquary, who presented it to the National Trust. Its internal timbering is easy to see and appreciate.

There are glorious views of the North Downs.

Otterden 13. A tiny place in a lovely setting with nothing much besides the big house and the church. The big house is *Otterden Place*, a fine Tudor brick mansion, with Georgian alterations. Here, as early as 1729, Dr Stephen Gray and the Rev. Granville Wheler experimented successfully with electricity, throwing it from rubbed glass along a string supported by silk threads for no less than 886 feet. The church is also Georgian, built in 1753, with some tombs inside from an earlier building. Victorianized, alas; with the

addition of an absurd Gothic chancel in the 1870s or 80s.

Paddlesworth 14 is a tiny village lying on high ground inland north of Folkestone. There are tremendous views. The Saxon church, of orange stone and flint, only 48 feet long, set back in a field, is unusually dedicated to St Oswald. There is Norman work, too. A scatter of military outbuildings, farther down the hill, condenses into the headquarters of "The Royal Air Force, *Hawkinge*".

Paddock Wood 6 is best known for its station, from which wealthy commuters spray into converted Tudor houses all over the area. The place itself is large now and industrialized, the headquarters of hops, with busy mechanized development down a main road, bungalows off, and a modern red-brick church of St Andrew. At *Five Oak Green*, to the west, also built up and a nineteenth-century creation, is a piece of kindly red-tiled ugliness called the *Little Hoppers Hospital*. The romantic hop season is largely superseded, now that 90 per cent of the picking is done by machinery, but a hop festival is still held at Paddock Wood every September.

Patrixbourne 14 is three miles from Canterbury on Watling Street, and much visited for its church, which is not perhaps as fine as Barfreston, having more late accretions, but is nevertheless extremely good late Norman work, with an outstanding south doorway and small priest's door. It was built about 1160, and stands amongst trees in the village, with a shingled spire rising unexpectedly from the middle of the south aisle. The interior is very much Victorianized (G. G. Scott, 1851). There is a lot of colourful and quite good nineteenth-century glass in the church, and many pieces of foreign glass, sixteenth and seventeenth century, well placed in two windows. Also many nineteenth-century wall tablets.

There are several "Tudor" houses in the village, well and cleverly built about 1860, and not unpleasing.

East Peckham 5 is in beautiful country, but largely industrial, particularly towards the hamlet of *Hale*

Street to the north. The old church stands two miles away from the village (which has a church in it of 1841 by Whichcord and Saunders), on top of a hill among beeches, and from it are views to the south and west over all the wealth of the Medway valley. The building has been much restored, and contains nothing remarkable. It has a shingled spirelet on a stuccoed tower. Eastwards is a very large red Elizabethan house, *Roydon Hall*. This was much altered in Victorian times, but the garden is remarkable, and the setting delightful. This was long the home of the Twysden family.

West Peckham 5 has near the church, on the way to Mereworth, a group of ancient tile and timber cottages, called Dukes Place, restored as a private house. This may represent the site of a manor of the Knights Hospitallers, who certainly existed here. There were wild boars in the district until the time of Queen Elizabeth I. Now there is a village green, with cricket pitch, decent cottages, a manor farm, an inn, and

an over-restored church with a Norman tower. There is a remarkable raised pew and mausoleum called the "Geary Pew", over a vault. It has a screen, hatchments and monuments, including a large white marble composition with husband and wife (Culpeper) reclining, in conversation. Round about are hops, Kentish cobs, and numerous big houses. One of the finest, to the north-east, is *Yotes Court*, built of red brick in 1658 with white stucco quoins, with a lovely garden, and framed by trees. To the west is *Gover Hill*, a National Trust viewpoint 450 feet up, looking over the Weald, and below this, to the south, is *Oxen Heath*, with an alphabet avenue, open to the public, of trees stretching from Acacia to Zelcova.

Pegwell Bay 15 is renowned for Hengist and Horsa, St Augustine, and shrimps. Here, at the southernmost point of Thanet, the Stour, after infinite convolutions, at last reaches the sea, through a wide expanse of saltings. Now the cross-Channel hovercraft terminal. To the north is

Pegwell, absorbed into Ramsgate, and a few characterless buildings at Cliffsend. To the south is marsh and sea-birds. Here, invited to defend the land in which they eventually settled, Hengist and Horsa traditionally landed in AD 449, under what must still have been the towers of Richborough Castle. Their individual existence is now discountenanced, but there is no reason why the first Saxons should not have landed at this spot. And here at *Ebbsfleet* St Augustine and his forty monks also traditionally landed in 597 to bring Christianity to the court of King Ethelbert. Here, indeed, as J. R. Green put it, "English history began".

On St Augustine's golf course, inland from the road, is St Augustine's Well. Down a lane, by some lavender gardens and on the supposed site of his landing, is a stone cross to St Augustine, put up by Lord Granville in 1884.

Pembury 5, the first village out of Tunbridge Wells on the Hastings road, is sprawling, busy and residential. It has a triangular green,

OLD ROMNEY Church inside and outside

with one or two buildings beside it of an older prosperity, and two modern churches. The true centre of the village lies to the north, with an old if not exceptional church and a manor house that is now a girls' public school. All round here are Pembury Woods, with walks under the leaves: quiet and very beautiful.

Penge 1 means "woodland", and was for centuries where the people of Battersea, of which it was a subsidiary hamlet, grazed their cattle on the common land. In 1821 it still had only 228 people. Then the railway came in 1851, and city merchants began to build their homes among the fields. In 1861 the great Crystal Palace was re-erected to dominate the new main street, and the population increased again. By 1936, when the Palace went up in flames, Penge was a vast suburban sprawl. It had only become part of Kent in 1900, by Order in Council, and now it is administratively re-submerged into Outer London.
Victorian houses still survive, usually rather shabby, but still with dingy trees, briefly bright in the spring, in what were once the rich merchants' gardens, looking out on to the Weald. The main street still climbs towards the Park, where the metal Palace has gone, but a huge aerial mast still dominates the skyline. There are new shops and houses, and a busy life. At the bottom of the High Street are a Home for Thames Watermen, with battlemented towers, and alms-houses in memory of William IV for the widows of Naval officers. St Paul's church, built in 1865 to the design of G. Bassett Keeling, is high Victorian Gothic.

Penshurst 5 is a delightful small village sitting where the River Eden joins the Medway. It is dominated by its great house, Penshurst Place, and, if overcrowded in summer, is not unduly spoilt by the stream of visitors. The most conspicuous group of cottages is at the entrance to the churchyard: late fifteenth-century timber-framed buildings through one of which a gateway is made, with an infilling of oak boarding. There are other interesting buildings, some

The Robert Sidney monument,
PENSHURST

PENSHURST Place

early, some skilful mock-Tudor houses by George Devey, and there is delightful country all round to walk in. The church of St John the Baptist, almost within the Place itself, is attractive without being of great architectural distinction. It is Norman, with late medieval additions and a drastic re-treatment by Gilbert Scott. Monuments in the Sidney Chapel: the best is a seventeenth-century white marble monument to Robert Sidney. There is a splendid seventeenth-century rectory.

Penshurst Place is a rewarding goggle for the tourist and also a joy to the discriminating: the most fascinating show place in Kent. Both approaches to it, through the churchyard or from the side-road, up steps and through the wall into the Italian garden on the south side, are impressive, and a good view of the whole of the west front can be had from the road. From here it is easy to distinguish the roof of the Great Hall in the middle which dates from the fourteenth century, surrounded by the sixteenth-century and later extensions. The same local stone was used at most periods, and has mellowed with its red brick into a delightful warmth: Tudor materialism softened by time.

Penshurst was originally called Penchester, and the Penchester family held the manor at the Norman Conquest. During the reign of Edward II it passed to Sir John de Pulteney, a merchant prince who was four times Lord Mayor of London. It was he who started the present building in 1340, and set up the Great Hall, per-

haps the best remaining example of the period in the country. After much history the property came into the hands of the Sidney family in the reign of Edward VI. After its great Tudor days the structure fell into decay, and by the end of the eighteenth century was very nearly a romantic ruin. But several generations of Sidneys (created Lords de L'Isle and Dudley in 1835) carried out sympathetic reconstruction and rebuilding. The present owner, the Rt. Hon. Viscount de L'Isle, v.c., is a collateral descendant of the Sir Philip Sidney of *Arcadia*.

The whole place is, of course, permeated with the legend of that Sir Philip Sidney, who was born at Penshurst in 1559, who wrote about it in *Arcadia*, and whose relics remain in the house, although his tomb is in Westminster Abbey. The Black Prince, Henry VIII feasting, Queen Elizabeth dancing, are all in the excellent guide book. But Sir Philip, the "perfection of men", the "observed of all observers", is the principal ghost and host. The gardens are superb.

Petham 14 is a small valley village with a few half-timbered houses and more modern ones, in beautiful country south of Canterbury. Chartham Down provides the skyline above it. The well-placed church has a tower with a good brick-top stage of 1769, and is pleasantly light and unencumbered inside. Early glass was removed to the Cathedral.

Petts Wood 1 proper is forest land,

a lung stretching up into Chislehurst Common, purchased for the National Trust in 1927. As an address and home for thousands, however, it means an extension of the suburban conurbation south-east of Bromley. It is contiguous with Orpington, with if anything wider grass verges, larger villas, deeper garages, bigger rose-bushes, and a "Tudor Way". It has one of the more ambitious of the several new Congregational churches in the area, and a general aura of middle-class affluence. Its cherry-blossom is not for fruit, nor its eyes for past history.

Platt 5 is generally unsung, perhaps because it has no old church, and for centuries existed as an outlier of Wrotham. It has, however, a good modern church (Whichcord and Walker, 1841), and is a most attractive hamlet with tolerable buildings, old and contemporary, with a heavily wooded lane leading to it from Offham. To the west it merges into *Borough Green*: a large new semi-industrialized semi-commuter development round a railway station.

Plaxtol 5. A large attractive hilltop village. There is a particularly pleasant group of cottages round the church, a curious pseudo-Gothic conception of Archbishop Laud, finished in 1649, the year of King Charles's execution. It was devastatingly restored in 1894, but still has the proportions of the original. There is a long village street, from the Papermakers' Arms to a timbered house on the crossroads, and also a forge, making the wrought iron gates and weather-vanes now democratically popular.

South-west of the village is *Fairlawne*, lived in and traditionally haunted by the Parliamentarian Sir Harry Vane the younger, beheaded by Charles II in 1662. The poet Christopher Smart was born here in 1722, the son of a steward of the house. This is impressive, and has fine gardens and outbuildings in a thickly wooded park. There are also racing stables.

Away to the east of Plaxtol, up a long twisting uphill lane, is *Old Soar Manor*. This is a well-preserved

Old Soar, PLAXTOL

example of a thirteenth-century home, once owned by the Culpeper family, and now by the National Trust. There is a solar, an undercroft and a chapel, all of which can be visited. More of the building is absorbed into an adjoining eighteenth-century farm, itself attractive but in private hands.

Pluckley 13 has many new houses on its outskirts, but its centre, on a side of the Greensand Hills, is delightful. There is a tiny square in front of the church, with some charming cottages, and tremendous views across the Weald. The spired church is very

much restored. It has some German glass and a chapel of the Kentish family, the Derings of Surrenden; is lined with plain tablets. There are brasses.

Postling 17. A quiet village, well placed in a fold of hills two miles north of Hythe. It has a small church, with high nave and chancel; simple whitewashed interior, with kingpost roof. One deep-splayed window. A distinctive pointed cap on the tower. It sits beside a manor house and farm buildings. At *Pent Farm*, a little to the north and on the so-called Pilgrims' Way, is a house once lived in by Joseph Conrad, and visited by Shaw, Wells, Henry James and other friends. Below the Downs here the East Stour rises, some five miles from the sea, finally to reach it far away up on the east coast at Ebbsfleet.

Preston (by Wingham) 15 is a pretty village high above the marshes between Canterbury and the east coast. West of the church a Roman burial ground was discovered. The church has some Saxon masonry, and is Early English and Decorated, restored. Old glass in window heads; Royal Arms of Queen Anne; bright O'Connor glass in east window. Attractive Soanesque farmhouse beyond a pond opposite. To the east, rising above the marshes, the hamlet of *Elmstone* has a pretty little church of its own; small, Early English, restored, with a bright and attractive east window of the 1860's by Gibbs; also a lively bust of 1684. *Elmstone Court* is moated.

Preston. *See* Faversham.

Queenborough 10 is now an industrial area, sitting greyly on the western edge of the Isle of Sheppey. There are some bright-looking new commercial laboratories, but the general effect is depressing, and the wide High Street, ending at the water's edge, has a somewhat run-down appearance, scarcely relieved by the old Guildhall and one or two other buildings of lost authority. The name is derived from Queen Philippa, wife of Edward III, who built an elaborate fortress here in 1366, and a church. There are good tombstones, dominated by a great obelisk, packed into

the small churchyard. Little remains of the castle, and the locked church was restored in 1885. The town had for a time considerable importance, being the only wool-staple in Kent other than Canterbury, and the Wardens of the Cinque Ports had this as their official residence from 1582. It returned two members to the unreformed Parliament, and was the starting point for the boat service to Flushing.

Iron pyrites were found here, and a Mathias Falconer of Brabant set up a factory in 1579 for the making of brimstone and copperas. Today Queenborough has glass and chemical works, iron foundries and potteries, and boats on the Long Reach winding in from the Medway. Some find its eighteenth-century memories and waterside activity endearing. But the brimstone seems to cling.

Rainham 3 has a long High Street of mainly nineteenth-century cottages, with a few earlier ones, to show that it was once a large village. Now it is along the main road, where cars cannot stop even to allow their passengers to visit the fine fifteenth-century church. This has in fact amongst other things a good rood canopy with the badge of Edward IV on it, and an effigy to a cavalier member of the Tufton family. There are remains of wall paintings, and an admirable fifteenth-century parclose screen. North and south stretch

housing estates that serve Gillingham, into which Rainham is being inevitably absorbed.

A vast estate is at *Wigmore*, where there is also a new church, St Matthew, consecrated in 1964, one of several built recently in the Rochester Diocese. This has a 66-foot tower supported by a lower belfry, and angular lines. It is of red brick, with a waterfall from the font into a baptismal pool, other remarkable innovations, and merges into a community centre.

Ramsgate 15 means their first boarding school to numbers of small boys of the middle classes, a shrine to admirers of A. W. Pugin, something to students of early Victorian marine architecture, home to 37,000 people, and a holiday by the sea to many more. For the last it rivals Margate as the most popular Kent resort and its illuminations, the "Festival of Light" from July to September, are vivid and renowned. It has hotels, boarding houses, terraces, gardens, entertainments, a pavilion, two piers (the east pier of 2,000 feet, the west of 1,500 feet) and sands. Unlike Margate it has a southern aspect, and there are chalk cliffs on either side of the "gate" or gap which gives part of its name. (The "Ram" is probably "Ruim", the British name for Thanet.)

Above all there is the harbour, 46 acres, still of some commercial im-

portance, with a non-tidal inner basin, and a Yacht Club. It was a front-line naval base in the second world war, and played a large part in the evacuation of allied troops from Dunkirk. In earlier times Ramsgate was used by the Romans, and was populous and a member of the Cinque Ports by the time of Edward I. By the time of Elizabeth I it had declined again, only to pick up from a prosperous trade with Russia and the East in the eighteenth century. In 1749 it was selected as a port of refuge for ships coming through the Downs, and in 1750 John Smeaton (who built Eddystone Lighthouse) designed a new pier. But it still subsisted largely on fishing and smuggling.

Renown came with the discovery of sea bathing at the end of the century, when Ramsgate vied with Margate in attraction and popularity being, however, regarded as slightly more select. The extension of the railway in 1846 brought new visitors, less refined but equally avid. The best buildings date from the first period: the Esplanade and West Cliff, with the Paragon and the Royal Crescent (near the Regency Hotel). These, and some individual hotels and boarding houses, are good Regency work. The town climbs up from the sea, but the general rhythm of the skyline is spoilt by a vast modern block of flats. Past the Crescent on the West Cliff is the Roman Catholic church of St

125

Augustine, built by A. W. Pugin in 1847–51. It is what he considered his best work, and he paid for it himself: his ideal Gothic revival building. Next door, flint-built and prickly, is his house, the "Grange". He is buried here, near what he thought "the only things worth living for"—the sea and Christian architecture. Pugin also designed the older buildings (1860) of the nearby St Augustine's Abbey, founded shortly before by Benedictines from Italy.

The back of Ramsgate from the sea is congested and undistinguished, and new building has made a complete suburb of *St Lawrence*, which has a Norman church, and *Dumpton*, which leads, brick-red, north to Broadstairs. Inland is *Manston* aerodrome. South lies *Pegwell Bay* (q.v.) where, as T. R. Green put it, "English history began".

Ramsgate's contemporary vulgarity is vigorous and popular: its visual memories of an early Victorian watering-place are sometimes delightful. Its new extensions are wide and standardized contemporary.

Reculver 11 is the site of the Roman fortress of Regulbium, which guarded the northern entrance, as Richborough did the southern one, of the Wantsum—the channel which made Thanet into an island. The castrum occupied some eight acres. Signs of occupation have frequently been dug up, and parts of the south and east wall still remain, often unvisited because down a path, beyond the church. The other walls, and some third of the area, have been eroded by the sea.

The famous church of St Mary was built, in the middle of the decaying Roman site, about AD 670, when King Egbert of Kent retired here and built a monastery and a palace. The early church was of the same design as the other earliest Christian buildings in Kent, notably the church of SS Peter and Paul built by St Augustine at Canterbury. After resisting the sea down the centuries "as a monument of the downfall of paganism and the triumph of Christianity" it was demolished in 1809, in an act of well-intentioned vandalism (they were afraid it was becoming a peepshow) by the vicar and his parishioners. The Board of Trinity House stepped in and rescued the two towers, recognizing their value to mariners, restored them, and they stand, prominent on the headland, now carefully preserved by the Ministry of Works.

They do not stand in beauty and isolation. Round them are a few ugly houses, and the gay vulgarity of a vast caravan park and its attendant needs.

Some parts of the old church were incorporated in an otherwise plain little bellcoted church when it was built in 1879 (J. Clarke, architect), up the lane behind at *Hillborough*.

Richborough Castle 15 stands on a bluff of high land north-west of Sandwich, on the western bank of the Stour. It was once an island in the Wantsum, the mile-wide channel which cut off Thanet from the mainland. It guarded the southern end, as Reculver guarded the north. To the Romans they were Rutupiae and Regulbium. It is now approached by a narrow lane, and its size and height are not apparent till you get there. But it is the finest Roman monument in Britain south of Hadrian's Wall. Rutupiae was the principal landing place and military depot for the Roman occupation of Britain by the Emperor Claudius in AD 43. It grew to be a city and commercial and administrative centre. Here the legions continued to land for 400 years, and from here Watling Street took them to London and the rest of the province. In the third century, when Rome was under attack, and Saxons began to raid the coasts, the 2nd Legion was moved back here from Caerleon, and a huge fortress was built as headquarters of the several strongpoints on the south-east coast: the base for the "Count of the Saxon Shore", who also operated a naval force from here as part of a combined defence operation. It was the last station to be evacuated in the 5th century, and although human occupation lingered on, the Wantsum silted up and the Saxons, when installed, preferred Sandwich.

What is now visible are the walls of this fortress, surrounded by two lines of defensive ditching. Originally 25 feet high and 11 feet wide, they have lost their facing through the depredations of time and medieval builders, and much of the stone is gone. But the double rows of flat red tiles, bonding courses of Portland stone and squared grits, are still powerful. In the middle of the fort a cruciform mass of concrete in the grass is thought to be part of the main foundation of a building of AD 85, perhaps for supporting a gigantic triumphal statue. It is enormous and not entirely explicable.

The whole site and a small museum are excellently kept by the Ministry of Works, and the full story is available in a guide book.

There are also ruins of a Saxon chapel dedicated to St Augustine, who landed not far away below. Mental reconstruction, kindled by all this, is restrained by the vast edifice of the Richborough Power Station of the Central Electricity Generating Board, starkly dominating the foreground.

Near it, in 1916, to relieve war traffic through Dover, an army of men were set to work to deepen the Stour, build a canal, reclaim land and fit up a great wharf for sending material to France and the front. That is the significance of Richborough port, near Ebbsfleet where Augustine landed, and lying derelict below the Roman ruin of Richborough Castle.

Ridley. *See* Ash (near Wrotham).

Ringwould 15 is on the Deal to Dover road, but rises above it in both senses: it is largely unspoilt, with some pretty cottages and a church perched up to command the view to the sea. It has a red-tiled roof and a Kentish "onion" on the tower, which can be seen from far out in the channel. The old tower of flint was handsomely buttressed and ornamented with brick in the eighteenth century. The interior is much rebuilt.

Ripple 15 is a hamlet lying 2½ miles west of Walmer: now becoming a dormitory, but still with ragged hedgerows and woods. The little church is modern, of 1861 (A. Ashpitel). Norman Revival. In its churchyard is buried Sir John French, Lord Ypres, Commander of the British Expeditionary Force in 1914, who was born here.

Roman defences at
RICHBOROUGH CASTLE and
RECULVER

ROCHESTER

Riverhead. *See* Sevenoaks.

Rochester 3. An ancient and historic cathedral city, a shopping and commercial centre for a population of over 50,000, and heart of the Strood-Rochester-Chatham-Gillingham industrial complex along the south bank of the Thames. It needs a guide or a most discriminating eye to pinpoint the old amongst the teeming and contemporary. Even though the M2 takes away much of the through traffic the High Street is always busy and crowded. There is, of course, every kind of available documentation, from full histories to Dickensian monographs, but although the castle is a landmark, Rochester does not display itself as so evidently of interest as Salisbury, Canterbury, or many cathedral cities.

The historic importance of the site is due to its being on an elbow of the Medway at the lowest point at which this could be bridged (although until Tudor times the bridges were notoriously dangerous) and so a key point on the road from Canterbury to London—Watling Street. There was an extensive Roman castrum called Durobrivae (signs of the wall are near the Esplanade) and a Saxon settlement which gives the name: Hrofe-caestre. It was one of the first places visited by St Augustine's mission, and a Christian church was built in 604. There was fire and

sword, Mercian and Dane, and inevitably the Normans saw this as a necessary place for a considerable strongpoint. William I built the great castle, and Gundulph established the important monastery of which only traces survive. The story of the town in the Middle Ages is that of the castle (*infra*). When this fell to a new faction the wooden houses of the town usually went up in flames. But the place grew during this period in both commercial and ecclesiastical importance, keeping roughly to the rectangular plan of the Romans, which the medieval walls of 1225, some of them extant, closely followed. The first charter had been obtained from Richard I in 1190.

The importance of the city, ecclesiastical, municipal and naval, remained even after the Tudor dissolution of the monastery. But it was still not large, being almost confined to the original 24 acres within the walls. Even by Dickens' time Mr Jingle's eulogy was not unduly selective: "Ah, fine place, glorious pile—frowning walls—tottering arches—dark nooks—crumbling staircases—old cathedral, too—earthy smell—pilgrims' feet worn away the old steps—little Saxon doors— . . . fine place—old legends, too—strange stories—capital!"

And capital, rightly, they still make of it. But the whole area had suffered an economic revolution by the middle

of the nineteenth century, and huge factories sprang up particularly on the banks of the river, with wharfs and cranes dwarfing the old pattern of roofs. Heavy goods went by water, but railways came in the sixties, and in addition to the general heavy and maritime industries of the area Rochester became, and remains, a centre for boat building and repairing, sail-making, iron-founding, welding, cement, chemicals and now such things as plastics, portable buildings, electrical and radio equipment. There is a prodigious fruit and vegetable trade with the Continent, and by motor barge with the industrial Midlands: heavy coastal traffic by water, and thundering coastal traffic by road. The population increased and the town spread, relentlessly, over the hills to the south, a creeping tide of suburbanization, or, as the Official Guide Book prefers to put it, "the attractive estates stretch into the delightful Kent countryside". The old bits remain, all fairly close together, in the bustling shopping and commercial area round the bridge, the castle and the cathedral.

On arrival from London and Strood over Cubitt's iron bridge, a sharp turn to the right follows the river along the Esplanade. Here is the *"Bridge Chapel"*. There was a chapel, here for pilgrims and other travellers, built by Sir John Cobham in 1397, but it was rebuilt in the eighteenth century to house the records of the Bridge Wardens and restored in 1879 and again in the 1930s. Nearby is a length of the *Town Wall* and through a mock-Norman *Water Gate* are the gardens of *Rochester Castle*.

What now dominates the city is not strictly a castle, but a Norman keep, 104 feet high, 90 feet square, and one of the best castellated ruins in the kingdom. Its very thick walls are made of Kentish ragstone. Part of the fourteenth-century curtain walls exist, and so does the Barbecue, the northern entrance. But only the keep remains comparatively intact. It is largely unaltered, and the real entrance, as was common when it was built, is not on the ground floor, but through a square fore-building at first floor level. Inside there is a central hall, with a rich arcade, and a small chapel. There are passages through the walls, which are in some places 13 feet thick. The building rises to five stories, with a buttress tower at each corner, and there is a winding staircase to the battlements, from which are views of the whole Medway scene. Underneath are the gardens, on the site of the bailey of the original castle, now a public park.

This first castle was built on the Saxon and Roman site by the great builder Bishop Gundulph about 1080, and formed with Dover and Canterbury a key protection for the road from London to the coast, as also a dominating military centre over the surrounding countryside. (There had been a Kentish rising against the Normans the year after the Conquest.) The keep itself is later, built by William de Corbeuil, Archbishop of Canterbury, about 1130, and repaired in 1461. It was captured in 1215 by King John, in his war with the barons, resisted Simon de Montfort and his supporters in 1264, when it was held for Henry III, but was taken by Wat Tyler the rebel, to the enthusiasm of the citizens, in 1381. It never afterwards fell to direct attack, but began to be broken up in the seventeenth century, and by the nineteenth century was a ruin, with the ground let out as allotments. It is now vigilantly cared for by the Ministry of Public Building and Works.

The *High Street* is so congested that a general view is difficult. There are many houses of all periods and disguises. Early on the left is the *Guildhall*, red brick of 1687, supported on coupled Doric columns. It has the city arms embellished on the front and on the roof a cupola with a copper weather-vane of 1780, a full-rigged ship, five feet high. The hall inside is well-panelled, with portraits and city treasures. Opposite is the *Bull Hotel*, an old coaching inn with a colonnaded yard and fine staircase. It is a pull-in for Dickensians, for it is a setting in *Pickwick Papers* and *Great Expectations*. There is the "elevated den" where Mr Tupman found the musicians, and in-fighting exists amongst the higher critics as to whether Mr Pickwick slept in room 11 or room 17. Anyhow, Queen Victoria as a Princess stayed here in 1836, and the hotel is really the Bull and Royal Victoria. *The George*, opposite, is also old, and has a fourteenth-century undercroft.

A little beyond is the Old Corn Exchange, or *Princess Hall* (the new Corn Exchange is in Northgate Street). Sir Cloudesley Shovel had it built in 1701. His arms are on a clock wheel projecting on an ornamental bracket from the red-brick façade, and are several times referred to by Dickens.

The *King's Head* hotel is another old inn, standing in the High Street at the bottom of Boley Hill. Opposite to it is the fifteenth-century *College Gate*, one of the three surviving entrances to the cathedral precincts. It is the "Jaspers Gate" of *Edwin Drood*. A Gate House Tea-Room has good sixteenth-century linenfold panelling, and farther on at No. 97 is *Watts Charity*, a three-gabled hospital building founded in 1579 by Richard Watts "for poor travellers": also the *Mathematical School*, most of it of 1737. The High Street becomes Eastgate Street at the Chatham end, and here is *Eastgate House*, a good three-storied domestic town building of 1590, with oak and ornamental ceilings inside. It is used as a museum and since 1961 has had re-erected in the grounds the chalet in which Dickens used to write his last works in the garden at Gadhill. It is itself "Westgate House" in *Pickwick Papers*, and the "Nun's

House" of *Edwin Drood*. *Restoration House*, on the Maidstone road, was or was not the "Satis House" of *Great Expectations*, and did or did not house Charles II in 1660: but is a handsome enough brick town house of 1587. The real "Satis House", with its own anecdote of Queen Elizabeth and a visit in 1573, is a large white building, the home of the wealthy Richard Watts, at the top of Boley Hill. Near by is the delightful eighteenth-century *Minor Canons Row*, a terrace of seven brick houses. *The Vines* is a public park on the site of the old monks' vineyard, and although its Victorian buildings are unattractive, the King's School is of proud and ancient foundation. Near by to it, through the fifteenth-century Priors Gate, are the precincts.

Rochester Cathedral
The Cathedral Church of Christ and the Blessed Virgin Mary is one of the most interesting buildings in the country: it is not one of the most beautiful. It has no great close to insulate it from the traffic, it is small for a cathedral (305 feet long, about 24,000 square feet in area and the spire 156 feet high), there is no external harmony of styles and, perhaps due to the prevailing cement in the atmosphere, it seems dingy. Inside is another jumble of styles, the less fortunate Victorian ones readily catching the eye. Yet it is this confusion of period which makes it fascinating to the student of church architecture, for whom it is claimed that from one point in the Lady Chapel it is possible to see work of every period from the eleventh century to the twentieth. He will wish to enjoy the building in detail and there is ample available documentation.

For the less dedicated visitor, too, there is more than is immediately apparent. King Ethelbert and St Augustine in 604, only six years after the foundation of the See of Canterbury, appointed a bishop and built a modest stone cathedral dedicated to St Andrew at Rochester. The only traces of this are in and under the floor of the present nave. The building was sacked by Danish raiders and was soon afterwards "utterly forsaken, miserable and waste". A new cathedral was started by the Normans, at the time of Bishop

Gundulph, the architect of the White Tower in London and of the nearby Castle. This was in 1077. His work remains in the crypt, the south aisle of the nave, elsewhere, and particularly in what is called Gundulph's tower. This, only part of its original height when it was a place of refuge and then a belfry, is on the north side of the choir, just inside Deanery Gate.

The cathedral suffered numerous disasters. Gundulph's conception was extensively altered by his successors, Bishop Ernulph (1115–1124), and John of Canterbury, and the new building was consecrated, still unfinished, in 1130. There were disastrous fires in 1137 and 1179. It was looted by King John, Simon de Montfort, and indeed the citizens of the town, during disputes with the monks. After the abbey was dissolved in 1540 the monastic buildings were pulled down, the glass in the cathedral itself smashed, and the altars destroyed. Cromwellian soldiers did further damage. Various Victorian restorations included a highly unsuitable Decorated central tower by Lewis Cottingham in 1823. This was itself removed, and the nineteenth-century tower brought back to something more like its original shape, to the designs of C. H. Fowler, in 1904. Meanwhile Sir Gilbert Scott had been at work during the 1870s on the interior. Recent attention has been sympathetic and less drastic.

What remains of general interest is of two main periods: middle Norman and thirteenth-century. The rich thirteenth-century work is due to the brief prosperity won by the cult of William of Perth. Rochester was not unnaturally jealous of the wealth flowing to Canterbury with pilgrims visiting the shrine of St Thomas à Becket. It was therefore highly fortunate when a conspicuously pious baker from Perth, having spent a night with the Benedictine monks of Rochester, was next morning murdered a few miles outside the city, and miracles were observed when he was brought back to the Cathedral for burial. In 1256 this good man was canonized as St William of Perth. But even earlier pilgrims were attracted to his shrine in the north-east transept, and their offerings helped

in subsidizing the new building work. The Romanesque west front is striking and elaborate, although only the central part is original: three of the four turrets date from 1892. The Tympanum, with a headless Christ in Majesty, supported by figures and symbols, is particularly beautiful. Inside the nave the stout Norman arcade has pillars in a number of forms and a rich triforium opening into both the nave and aisles. In the choir the choir screen is fourteenth century, and the figures on it nineteenth century. The thirteenth-century stalls were spoilt in restoration. There is, however, a fascinating fragment of wall painting illustrating the Wheel of Fortune. The carved doorway to the present Chapter House is a particularly elaborate piece of fourteenth-century carving. There is much monumental sculpture, with a Grinling Gibbons panel, and the medieval tombs include that of Bishop Walter de Merton, the founder of Merton College at Oxford.

The crypt is one of the largest and finest in England, and has some early thirteenth-century graffiti.

St Nicholas Church is beside the Cathedral and the main road, and looks bleak and redundant. It was built in 1423 as the parish church, when incessant disputes between the monks and the citizens made use of the Cathedral nave for this purpose impracticable, and the Pope ordered a site in the monastery cemetery to be made available. The tower and west end are of this period, but there was a rebuilding in 1624 and a disastrous one, after a fire, in 1892.

From Boley Hill St Margaret's Street goes up to a pleasant part of the city, with some Georgian and Regency houses and views across the roofs, the cement works, and the river. Here is *St Margaret's Church*, with a freakish body of 1840 joined to a fifteenth-century tower.

Ryarsh church is Perpendicular, and beautifully placed looking across an orchard westwards. Much renewed inside. There is an excellent head in yellow-stain, fifteenth-century stained glass, framed on a window sill.

Strood, on the London side of the bridge, is huge and urban. Its importance, when it was an old town, was local not national, and it was

incorporated into Rochester in 1836. The High Street is crowded, narrow, useful and ugly. In it is the parish church, which has a fourteenth-century tower, the rest being a rebuilding of 1814 by Robert Smirke. To the south, amongst housing estates and factories, is *Temple Manor*. This Manor House of the Knights Templar was largely ruined, but has recently been carefully restored: it is a thirteenth-century hall on a vaulted undercroft of three bays, with seventeenth-century brick extensions at either end, and an external staircase. To the north, uphill, is *Frinsbury*, another industrial wilderness, based on cement. Its church stands away high on a bluff, grandly surveying Rochester, Chatham and the whole Medway scene. It was founded in 1075, has suffered successive restorations but retains a Norman chancel arch and windows, an early thirteenth-century tower of flint blocks, and some early paintings on the window splays, including one of St William of Perth.

To the south of Rochester is *Borstal*, high above the motorway. What catches the eye is Fort Borstal, one of a chain of fortresses built as part of the Medway defences against Napoleon. The penal settlement which has become part of the English vocabulary lies away behind it.

The M2 motorway itself crosses the Medway along the fine sweep of the new bridge—not suspension, but cantilevered prestressed concrete. The casting was done *in situ*, the main span is 145 feet, and it is a notable contribution by the twentieth century to the general somewhat scarred, if still maritime, prospect of the area.

Rodmersham 13. A little village with a green and one or two old houses, two miles from Sittingbourne. The chimneys of the brick factories are in the distance, but the foreground is cherry orchards. They are round the church, which has a dark flint tower of the fifteenth century, and inside a medieval chancel screen, reassembled in 1880, of Spanish walnut. The interior is rather gloomy, and tiled.

Rolvenden 9. A large prosperous-looking village in orchard and hop

ROCHESTER Cathedral

130

country. It is much developed, but has enjoyable old houses, and a central group with hung tiles and weatherboarding. *Great Maytham Hall*, south of the church, was the home of Frances Hodgson Burnett, who wrote *Little Lord Fauntleroy*. It was said to be the setting of her *The Secret Garden*, but the present house is a large neo-Georgian mansion by Lutyens. The church is mainly fifteenth-century work, with an elevated pew like a box in a theatre, for the Lord of the Manor, and a new and admirable oak revolving door at the west end for the warmth of parishioners today. Good eighteenth-century monuments are obscured by side altars or tables at east end of both aisles. Fine Royal Arms, 1713.

Ruckinge 16. A small nondescript village, with startling red brick development, beautifully placed just below the ridge overlooking Romney Marsh. The church has a Transitional Norman tower and south door and a somewhat spartan interior, with attractive fragments of early glass and fourteenth-century choir stalls on one side of the chancel.

Ryarsh. *See* Birling.

St Margaret's at Cliffe 15 is itself a village without special distinction, although with a few weatherboard houses and a particularly fine late Norman church, lofty, powerful, and light inside. It is the mother parish, however, of
St Margaret's Bay, a still delightful seaside resort, perhaps undesecrated because the approach to the little cove is so steep for motor-cars. The beach is unspoilt, with a fine headland to the north, and the South Foreland away to the south. The balconied houses above are cheerful and prosperous looking. It is one of the most charming places in Kent for a conventional and unexploited holiday of bathing and enjoying the sea.
On the cliff a mile to the north is the granite obelisk which is the Dover Patrol Monument.
The South Foreland Lighthouse, which can be visited, flashes three times every 20 seconds, and is one of the most powerful on the English coast. The Paris and Brussels tele-phones enter the sea here, and channel swimmers sometimes come out of it.
A mile farther west, and not on the cliff at all, is *West Cliffe*, a few small houses with an Early English Church.

St Mary Cray 2. The most southern of the four Cray villages: St Mary's, St Paul's, Foots Cray and North Cray: all old places on the stream eight miles long which rises near Orpington and flows north to join the Darent in the marshes north of Dartford. It was scheduled as in the Green Belt, and a delightful valley. The Brick Belt won. For a time the little waterways marked the outer edge of suburbia. Now the spread has engulfed it, and description of the Crays is a sad essay in comparative desecration.
St Mary's has paper mills and other industry, high blocks of modern flats, and a few converted eighteenth-century and nineteenth-century houses, usually grim and municipal. The High Street is a welter of offices, car parks and conveniences, dominated by a viaduct. The old church adjoins all this, not even keeping its head above the tide, for it is next to a factory with a dominating chimney. Inside are some late eighteenth-century brass engravings, rare in period but feeble in design.
St Paul's Cray, downstream, is more open, but largely a place of modern factories and houses, although still attractive by the river-side, and having indeed a common of 100 acres, with trees and gorse bushes. Away from the main housing development is the little church dedicated to St Paulinus, one of St Augustine's missionaries: basically thirteenth century, with some Roman brickwork.
Foots Cray has a pleasant fourteenth-century church standing back in a remaining patch of green land from the main road traffic and the stretching fingers of Sidcup.
North Cray survives precariously, with parkland about it, on a comparatively undamaged stretch of the river. The church, much restored, has some medieval choir-stalls with Flemish carving.

St Mary's Hoo 3. A hamlet standing on high ground in the middle of the Hoo peninsula. The country round is flat, dropping to marshes in the north, and the whole area, although still agricultural, has industrial manifestations. The few houses themselves escape this, and they and the little church, rebuilt save for the fifteenth-century tower, lie amongst trees, grouped out of the wind.

St Mary-in-the-Marsh 17. A remote and enchanting village in Romney Marsh, quite self-contained amongst the flats round it, with sheep pasture and a pylon skyline. St Mary's Church, standing beautifully over a little rhine bridge, is good Early English, double-aisled for its full length. It is small, harmonious, and has little incident, but is mellowed, yellowed, and well kept. Late box-pews and Royal Arms of 1775, a pair to the one at Ivychurch. A little over-tidied up, perhaps. Tablet to E. Nesbitt, author of children's books, who spent her last years here.

St Michaels 16. An agreeable northern suburb of Tenterden, with a few old houses, tidy new ones, and a Victorian church with a tall stone spire, widely visible. It is dull, lofty and full of dark stained glass. By G. M. Hills, 1864. There are glorious views of the Weald all round it.

St Nicholas-at-Wade 12 is a delightful village in Thanet, only three miles from Birchington but off the main traffic routes. It has many houses of old brick, and a long Norman church with a tower visible for miles across the marshes. Inside it has much thirteenth- and fourteenth-century work, and a Jacobean pulpit. Fine candelabra (1757), Royal Arms of George III and elegant wall tablets. A "wade" is a ferry, and there used to be one here across the Wantsum.

Saltwood. *See* Hythe.

Sandgate 17 is for practical (i.e. motorists') purposes a built up resort strip between Hythe and Folkestone, continuous with the sea-fronts of both towns. But its long main shopping street retains some character and for its devotees it is a resort in its own right, although administratively absorbed by Folkestone. Remains of Sandgate Castle lurk darkly on the seafront just off

SANDHURST

the High Street: a bastion of Henry VIII's coastal defence scheme of 1539, adapted in 1806 to meet the Napoleonic menace, and still in grave danger from the encroaching tides.

H. G. Wells came to live in Sandgate in 1899, and settled at Spade House. Nearby is Radnor Cliff House, with a fine terraced garden, sometimes open to the public. It is off the Lower Sandgate Road, by far the most

attractive approach to Folkestone.

Sandhurst 9 has a green, some old white wooden houses and many new red-brick ones, and is about three miles from Hawkhurst. The church

SANDWICH: the Barbican

stands remote from the main road, improbably large, and harshly restored. But the massive fifteenth-century tower is of golden sandstone, and from it are magnificent views of the Weald on one side and Kent Ditch, Romney Marsh and the French coast beyond, on the other.

Sandwich 15. Although now two miles inland is a Cinque Port. It is also a resort with some of the finest golf courses in England, a market town, and a piece of history. Its winding streets are usually inevitably and oppressively crowded. To see it, it is essential to walk, and particularly to walk round the charming promenades which mark the line of the medieval walls.

Sandwich, then an anchorage in a wide and sheltered bay, was developed as a port by the Saxons, when the sea was already receding from the Roman Richborough to the north. King Edgar gave it to the monastery of Christ Church Canterbury, and it flourished in spite of Danish depredations. Sweyn and his son Canute indeed landed here with a large army in 1013, before taking over the English throne and for a

time attaching England to the Scandinavian Empire. As one of the more important ports in the country it had a turbulent history in the Middle Ages, being burned by the French in 1216 and again in 1456, and sacked in 1458 by the Earl of Warwick, in the course of the Wars of the Roses. Becket had fled from here to France, Richard I arrived here from exile, and the huge expeditionary force of Edward IV here set sail for the Continent in 1475. It was prosperous, the first of the Cinque Ports, and the most important naval base in England.

The sea receded from 1500 onwards, and the harbour became choked with sand, made worse by the sinking of a large papal ship in its mouth. Prosperity was rescued by the provident settlement here by Elizabeth I of Protestant refugees from France and the Netherlands. These introduced the manufacture of serge, baize, and flannel, and the cultivation of vegetables. Also their surnames, some of which still survive, as do Flemish words like "polder" for the marshlands to the north of the city, and the distinctive Flemish architecture which can be seen in many of the buildings.

Sandwich is not self-consciously

"quaint", or a film set. There are good and bad modern buildings. But there are many medieval and Tudor ones not always of individual distinction, but collectively effective: noticeably in Quay Street. Some that have particular interest include: *The Bridgehouse*, or *Barbican*, with a toll over the swing bridge of 1893 is a restored Tudor building with a chessboard pattern at the bottom and red tiles at the top; the nearby *Fishers Gate*, through which Becket passed on his last journey to Canterbury: built in 1384, restored in the sixteenth century, and the only one remaining of the five original gates to the town; the sixteenth-century *Dutch House*, in King Street; the *Guildhall*, built in 1579, much restored, but with some interesting things inside; the half-timbered *Weaver's House*; the *Old House*, also Tudor but partly refaced in brick about 1750, Henry VIII and Queen Elizabeth both used it; *St Bartholomew's Hospital*, now a group of little houses, founded at the end of the twelfth century by Sir Henry de Sandwich; *Manwood Court*, dated as 1564 (but restored), first endowed as a free Grammar School by Sir Roger Manwood, son of a local draper who made good as Queen

Two views of Knole House, SEVENOAKS

Elizabeth's chief Baron of the Exchequer; the seventeenth-century *White Friars* in New Street, on the site of an early Carmelite priory. *The Salutation* is a famous house by Lutyens, with a Jekyll garden.

There are three notable churches: *St Clements*, amongst elms and limes just round Hog Corner, had an arcaded Norman Tower, and various treasures inside, including fourteen very old stalls, a seat for the mayor, a rich roof and remarkable font: *St Peter's*, built in the thirteenth century by Carmelite monks from Normandy was added to, and then partially ruined when the tower collapsed in 1661. It was rebuilt with a bulbous cupola, again showing the Flemish influence. It is now used as a chapel by the Grammar School, and the curfew is rung from it every evening at 8 o'clock: *St Mary's*, on a site where a church is said to have stood since the seventh century. Again the tower collapsed, this time in 1667, and for long the church was derelict. Now restored.

There is much interest within the

Knole House, SEVENOAKS: the Cartoon Gallery

small and somewhat overcharged perimeter. Industry and development have been largely isolated north of the town, at Great Stonar, on the Ramsgate road, but nothing stills the traffic.

Sarre 12. On the main road half-way between Canterbury and Margate. It had some importance when Thanet was still an island, but declined and became an attachment of St Nicholas-at-Wade. The church disappeared. The stage coach put the village back on the map, and the inn derives fame from Charles Dickens and cherry brandy. The stretch of road from here to Upstreet is called the Sarre Wall, and is the line of a fifteenth-century drainage scheme by Archbishop Martin.

Scotney Castle. *See* Lamberhurst.

Seal 5 is now a sophisticated locality in country that is still wooded, on high ground near Sevenoaks. Some of the planned development is good —and there is an attractive wide High Street with agreeable evidences of the original village. The church stands high, with a fine fifteenth-

century tower, but it is much restored. Fine brass of a knight, 1395. There are beautiful views of the Downs. The *Wildernesse*, perched to the south, is an early Georgian house, built for Lord Chief Justice Pratt. The golf club is here. Fine woods to the south-east, across to Ightham Common.

Seasalter. *See* Whitstable.

Selling 13 is an extremely pretty village, well away from main roads, in delightfully wooded country laced by small lanes. The church, which has notable fourteenth-century stained glass in its east window, is perched amongst red-tiled roofs, yews and cedar trees. *Perry Wood*, to the south, has a mound called the Pulpit, famous for views.

Sellinge 17. A village on a bend of the main road from Hythe to Maidstone, along which its bungalows spread avidly in both directions, but particularly to the south, where it becomes *Sellinge Lees*. The church has a low Norman tower with a tiled pyramid on top. Inside white and agreeable. Glass fragments. A colourful window of 1851, by Gibbs. Seventeenth-century alabaster monument (Heyman) and a good wall tablet of 1664.

Sevenoaks 5. A prosperous country town and shopping centre of some 17,000 inhabitants, with a high proportion of commuters but too much character and sense of history to be called an outer suburb of London. The south coast traffic streams through it uncomfortably and incessantly, but it is to this road, and its great house, Knole, that the town owes its importance. It is beautifully placed on the northern slopes of the Greensand Hills, and there was a road junction here in the early Middle Ages which made it develop early into a market centre amongst a ring of farms, on the northern edge of the largely impenetrable clay and forest of the Weald. It only emerges into text-books as the scene of the defeat here, in 1450, of the royal troops under Sir Humphrey Stafford, who was pursuing the rebel forces of Jack Cade. The site of this engagement, Sole Fields, is now under bricks and mortar on the way to Sevenoaks Weald. More specialized text-books dwell on the victories and defeats at The Vine cricket ground, one of the oldest in England, presented by the third Earl of Dorset in 1773. It is at the top of the hill from the Bat & Ball station.

In general the story of the town is that of the Sackvilles of Knole, and of one or two other families of large landowners, including the Lambardes. William Lambarde (1536–1601), the author of the *Perambulation of Kent* (1570), the first real county topography, has his monument in the church. The town remained cheerful and prosperous, unaffected by the Dissolution of the Monasteries, because there were none, but stimulated by the development of the turnpikes and the post-roads to Tunbridge Wells, when the spa became popular. It was a comfortable Cranford of gentlemen, retired people, and tradesmen: "a very genteel little town" as the Guide of 1839 puts it, happy in its position and under the shelter of its great house: proud of its school and church, busy with the through traffic.

The railway came in 1868, and life changed. Now a man could go to London and back in a day, and many men did. Their large Victorian villas still exist (with some excellent modern ones) on the way to the station. It was, till the end of the century, the apogee of the first-class ticket holder. The gas had come in 1840, and the original gas works still stand, now a laundry, at the corner of Hartland Road and Holly Bush Lane. Population increased, the town spread, the Regency market house became a public convenience, cars grew thicker on the roads. The Southern Electric train service started in 1935. Now the main streets are crowded, there are dormitory villas everywhere, and on the outskirts it is a suburban sprawl. But much of the old remains, and the prevailing cheerfulness. And there is still the Park, Knole itself, and the gorgeous surrounding countryside.

The old part of the town consists mainly of two streets, the High Street, entered from Dartford, and the London Road. In the High Street the Chequers Inn is sixteenth century, and there are other old buildings behind the modern façades: a White House, with a Regency façade, and a fine Red House of 1686. The best bit is at the top of the hill, where the two roads converge. Here there is a group of eighteenth-century houses, with conspicuously on the left the Sevenoaks Grammar School and Almshouses. The school was founded by William Sennocke, a friend and contemporary of Dick Whittington, and also a Lord Mayor of London, in 1418. It is one of the oldest in the country, but the somewhat severe buildings, credited to Lord Burleigh, are Georgian. They are of grey ragstone. Old houses nearby include the Royal Oak Hotel, the old Post Office, the Georgian House, and on either side of the church the seventeenth-century Chantry House and Old Rectory. The entrance to Knole Park, opposite these, is pleasantly unostentatious. The parish church of St Nicholas is mainly fifteenth century, with a fine fourteenth-century tower. It has been much restored, and lost the roof through fire in 1947, but retains a Carolean pulpit and good monuments, mainly to local worthies like Field Marshal Lord Amherst, who died in 1797, and including a tablet in the chancel to John Donne, who was rector of Sevenoaks from 1616 till his death in 1631.

Riverhead, to the north, is suburban, but has some Georgian houses on the Sundridge road, and a Gothic revival church of 1831 by Decimus Burton. *Chipstead* shows how pleasant it was before development and *Bessels Green* has old houses and a long terrace of early nineteenth century ones: *Dunton Green* is works, garages, and railway.

Knole House (named from the knoll on which it stands) has 1,000 acres of parkland, nearly six miles in circumference. It is one of the most famous sights in the county—if sometimes one of the more austere, when the huge block of ragstone masonry is not caught by the sunlight. It is so vast—"a town rather than a house", as Victoria Sackville-West called it—that it is difficult to gain a general impression of its lay-out, and an understanding is best achieved by an aerial photograph and a study of the delightful books by Victoria Sackville-West, who was born there: *Knole and the Sackvilles*, and more subjectively, *Orlando*. It is a vast Tudor and Jacobean Manor House incorporating Gothic and Renaissance features—gables, chimneys, battlements and cupolas. It is quadrangular, and covers about three acres. It provides the quoted if unverified extravagance of a courtyard for every day in the week, a staircase for every week of the year, and a room for every day in the year.

A medieval building on the site was sold in 1456 by William Fiennes, Lord Saye & Sele, to Thomas Bouchier, Archbishop of Canterbury. It was he who built here a vast archiepiscopal palace. Henry VIII made Thomas Cranmer resign it to him, but in the event did not like it, and hardly stayed here. Eventually, Queen Elizabeth I gave it to her wealthy and important cousin Thomas Sackville, Lord High Treasurer of England, in 1566. For legal reasons he could not take it over until 1603. Then, created Earl of Dorset, he started to spend enormous sums to make Knole as splendid as his rank and fortune. Much of the present building is therefore late fifteenth-century work by Archbishop Bouchier, with the entrance tower added by Archbishop Wareham between 1504 and 1532,

Lees Court (see SHELDWICH)

and most of the rest the Jacobean display of the first Earl of Dorset. It remains the home of the Sackvilles: the fourth Lord Sackville gave the house to the National Trust in 1946, but leases part of it and the private gardens for his own use, and remains owner of the park.

Knole is frequently open and constantly visited. Its furniture, pictures and other treasures are on show, and there are full guide books. A visit, to do them justice, not unnaturally takes a considerable time. The park, which is always open to the public, is a delight: red and fallow deer, partly undulating grassland in the middle, and on the edges avenues and

groves of beech, chestnut and oak. For pedestrians there are entrances at River Hill, Fawke Common and Godden Green.

Sevenoaksweald 5 is naturally affected by its position just south of Sevenoaks, from which, already with a plain little church of 1820, by J. Carter (chancel by T. G. Jackson) it separated to become a separate parish in 1861. Material circumstances draw it back again. Meanwhile it is still a village in lovely wooded country below the Greensand ridge, with its magnificent views. Here, in *Else's Farm*, beside the railway, lived the poet Edward Thomas.

He befriended the then destitute W. H. Davies, installed him in a cottage in Egg Pie Lane, and here Davies wrote *The Autobiography of a Super-Tramp*.

Sevington. *See* Willesborough.

Shadoxhurst 16 must have been a tiny hamlet. Now the whole district, and *Bromley Green* to the south, is peppered with individually inoffensive overspill houses for people working in Ashford. The core of Shadoxhurst remains unspoilt, with a small green and the church lying back behind an odd Gothic church-school of about 1800. The small nave and chancel church of stone with a wooden turret and a brick porch incorporates some slight medieval features, has a parquet floor, and contains a grand 1760 tablet in variegated marble (Molloy) with bust and symbols of naval command and of Trinity House brotherhood.

Sheerness 10. A garrison town, naval base and aspiring resort of 14,000 people. It is on the extreme northwestern tip of the Isle of Sheppey, with a long canal behind it making it almost an island itself. Its character is indeterminate, for it is a place of some interest, but with little history and that without much visible evidence.

The town is divided into Mile Town, which is the shopping and business part round the High Street: Marine Town, east of this and stretching to the sea-front and esplanade, a mile and a half long: and Blue Town, the old Naval Quarter. The Dockyard was founded in 1665 by Charles II, who also built a fort here. It covers 60 acres and is severely out of bounds to visitors, fronted by defensive cement fortifications. Blue Town all leads to the pier, which faces across the Medway to the Isle of Grain. The beach is of sand and shingle. Apart from the late Georgian Royal Fountain Hotel the hotels and boarding houses are utilitarian, and as marine architecture do not compare with the older resorts of Thanet. Sheerness is said to be very healthy, and is brisk and busy.

Sheldwich 13. A quiet hamlet south of Faversham, with a much-restored church. There is a shroud brass.

Window by Burne-Jones in SHOREHAM Church

Nothing else of interest. It is north-west of *Lees Court*, built in Inigo Jones style between 1640 and 1652. This was gutted by fire in 1912 but restored to a replica of the Italianate original. It has flat pilasters on its severe and handsome front, and wide eaves on slender braces.

Shepherdswell 15 is a folk corruption of Sibert's-wold, which is Sibert's-down. It is now mainly suburban houses, built when the Dover to Canterbury railway made it the centre for a wide area, and has a little church built in 1867 (by Benjamin Ferrey), when the old church was demolished. A very ancient one

remains, however, at its sister parish, *Coldred*, standing on a rectangular earthwork that is perhaps Roman. This has a thirteenth-century bell gable, and a couple of small Norman windows high up. Restored and re-roofed by Victorians.

Shipbourne 5. (Pronounced "Ship-burn" and meaning the stream where sheep were washed.) A scattered village standing high on the road north from Tonbridge to Ightham. There is a large green, a few houses looking across open country, and a Victorian church (by Mann & Saunders, 1881), standing beside the road. Inside is some of the old church, and

in the crypt the coffin of Sir Harry Vane of *Fairlawne*, the big house down the road at Plaxtol (q.v.). It is a place of pilgrimage for visitors from Massachusetts: Sir Harry was Governor there for two years at the early age of twenty-four.

Sholden 15, by Deal, has a little church, over-restored in 1872–6.

Shoreham 5. It is often visited, because it is charming, and it is increasingly lived in. But current building development is still decently off-stage, and despite week-end crowds it remains delightfully quiet, unassertive and attractive. It is a chalk village, on the clear narrow Darent, in a valley to the west of the main road from Sevenoaks to Dartford. All along the stream are willows, up above are the heavily wooded downs, and the mainly red-roofed cottages are various and attractive. There are several eighteenth-century façades, representing a prosperous community in Georgian times, and presiding over them a warm red-brick church tower of 1775. The rest of the church is mainly fifteenth century, with a splendid wide, black, rood screen of this period. There is good vaulting, a noble timber porch, a Burne-Jones window, and portrait busts by Cheere on a well-composed monument. Below the church and the old inn opposite, over the bridge, is Water House, a handsome eighteenth-century building. Here lived and painted the artist Samuel Palmer, affected by and reflecting in his work the beauties of the valley of trees and landscapes. William Blake, aged and ailing, came here to stay with him. At Dunstall Priory, conspicuous amongst the trees on the downs above, lived the poet and creator of fantasy, Lord Dunsany. Farther on a cross carved in the chalk, and widely visible above the village hidden below it, is Shoreham war memorial to its fallen in the 1914–18 war.

Shorne 3 retains a green peace in vulnerable country between Graves-end and Rochester. There is a picture-postcard church with roses round the door. A fine cross-legged

Samuel Palmer country in winter, SHOREHAM

effigy to Henry de Cobham who fought for Edward II, inside. Also a Jacobean monument with four kneeling figures. When Dickens lived at Gadshill he had a tunnel under the main road to his garden on the other side, where he sat in a chalet writing. This brought him into Shorne parish. There are some old cottages. Shorne is now a first and second wave dormitory—the first wave of rather rich houses, with rhododendrons, the more recent with contemporary emphasis on the garage rather than the garden. But it is beautiful wooded country, fortunately by-passed by the main road.

Sidcup 1 is a modern creation, developing from *Ruxley*, which it has swallowed and is now a major road junction on the other side of the Cray river. The population in 1860 was 300. This grew rapidly in late Victorian times round a station built on what was then the Dartford Loop Line. Sidcup understandably prospered as an outer suburb of the better sort: with tennis clubs and tea on the lawn, a discreet and manageable distance from the capital. It is now part of the Bexley conurbation of Greater London, with a population of some 81,000. A certain sense of style and gaiety remain. It is open,

has a green, and many houses both Victorian and contemporary are well built. The Romanesque church of St John, built for a wealthy but limited congregation in 1844, must at the time have seemed advanced and architecturally ambitious. It has incorporated an admired but heavy Flemish pulpit of the seventeenth century.

Sissinghurst 9 is really part of Cranbrook, although it became a separate parish in 1839, when its church was built. It has a fine open street of mixed Kentish façades of all periods, and individual large houses, including Sissinghurst Place, with gardens open to the public and a 500-year-old oak tree, and Sissinghurst Court. *Sissinghurst Castle*, also on show as one of the great sights of the county, is off the main road to the east. It was built by Sir John Baker ("Bloody Baker", the adherent of Mary Tudor and persecutor of Protestants, who died in 1558)—a large house round three courtyards. French prisoners were kept here during the Seven Years War, in what they appropriately called the château, with the young Edward Gibbon for a time in disgruntled charge of them. The castle was subsequently destroyed, and all that now remains is

the moat, the mellowed red-brick gatehouse, with octagonal towers, and parts of two wings used as cottages. But behind it lie the enchanting gardens built when the ruins were bought and restored in 1930 by Sir Harold and Lady Nicolson. Lady Nicolson, the poetess Victoria Sackville-West, was descended from the original owners. The highly individual gardens are particularly lovely in springtime, and their roses in June, but at any time there is much to enjoy.

Sittingbourne 13 has become a considerable industrial centre, and is visually unprepossessing. It was a staging post for the pilgrims to Canterbury in the Middle Ages, then a market town of declining importance, but had a brisk re-emergence with the coming of the stage coach. All this can be guessed from the façades, some of them eighteenth century, of the busy two-mile High Street. Most, however, are covered with unsympathetic shop signs and the general effect is depressing. At the foot of the hill the fifteenth-century church has a massive tower, but the inside, which suffered from fire in 1762, is unimportant.

Industry started with the paper mills, established about 1840, leapt ahead

Milton Creek, SITTINGBOURNE and (below) *Naval boathouse at SHEERNESS*

with the coming of the railway in the 1860s, and has expanded ever since. Now the industrial area lies almost entirely to the north of the town: the paper mills, cement and brick works, with chimneys, and fruit-preserving factories. The fruit is locally available, and the bulky brick cargoes can go by water to London. Oil interests have also come and the district continues to develop.

All round about the country is delightful with orchards, and the dormitory villages, like *Bapchild*, which has a church with a shingled spire of Norman origin, much restored, back on to this. But the urban area, and the works and mills round the creek, are uncompromisingly utilitarian.

At *Murston*, in the dock area to the north, All Saints is a development church of 1874 by W. Burges.

Smallhythe 16. A modest and attractive village down the hill south out of Tenterden. On the slope itself is the church, a curious red brick Flemish building, bare inside, and much Victorianized, but with old roof and screen, which was built in 1515 to replace an earlier chapel destroyed by fire. Victorian glass by Clayton and Bell and others. Next to it is a black-and-white timbered Priest's House, and lower down the village the timber and brick Yeoman's house of 1480, which Ellen Terry made her home from 1919 until her death. It had been the harbourmaster's house when the sea ran in as far as this, and afterwards a farmhouse. Now it is a National Trust memorial to the actress, and with its barn a place of summer pilgrimage for people interested in theatrical relics.

Smarden 13 is a particularly lovely village, with numerous wooden gables and black-and-white timbered and white weatherboarded houses, many of them unselfconscious and not over-garnished, and with no uncongenial buildings in its centre round the church and delightful churchyard. The church stands finely and has been called, in admiration of the wide span of its roof, "The Barn

above: *SMARDEN*

below: *Ellen Terry's House at SMALLHYTHE*

of Kent". Inside it is indeed rather bare: late medieval and lacking in interest. The chancel has been scraped of its plaster.

Smeeth 14. The name means the "smooth clearing" and is one of the origins of the surname Smith. Not many from here though, for it must always have been a tiny place, detached on rising ground just off the road from Ashford to Folkestone. A squat church with late Norman doorways and chancel arch, and Jacobean and other relics from the home of the Scott family, of whom Sir William Scott was Knight Marshal of England in 1350. A scattered parish of rich farmland.

The Priest's House and chapel, SMALLHYTHE

Snargate 16. A church, a few houses, and scattered farms on a crossing of the road leading into Romney Marsh, between Appledore and Old Romney. The fifteenth-century church is fairly large, but not outstanding. Its rector was once Richard Barham, Man of Kent, later Canon of St Paul's Cathedral, and author of *The Ingoldsby Legends*. His facetious verses are out of fashion, but his scholarly antiquarianism was genuine, as was his love of the county. He lived three miles north, in the parsonage at Warehorne.

Snave, away to the north-west, is as lonely, and even smaller. It has the charm of possessing the marsh all about it. The church is attractive in

K

its setting, tree-surrounded. it has good proportions inside, old king-post roof and Royal Arms of 1735, though it was refurnished by Victorians and is marred by the greenish light from ripple-glazed windows. How splendid it would be to see the marsh through clear glass here!

Snodland 6 is an extensive parish, and has a long main street of ugly industrial buildings on the west bank of the Medway, usefully dedicated to cement works and paper mills. Here, as at *Halling*, to the north, a few older buildings are dotted reproachfully amongst the rows of Victorian cottages and more modern bungalows. But the cement in the air does not weather buildings attractively. The church is cement-coloured too, but not unattractive. It has Norman fragments, a Perpendicular tower and brasses in its renewed interior. There is the incidence, however, of quarries and lorries, the river itself, and steep lovely wooded country climbing up behind.

Southborough 5 is little more than a northward extension of Tunbridge Wells (q.v.), the "south" in its name however referring to Tonbridge. A suburb, but not without character, with a high wide green, some old houses, and St Peter's, of 1830, is by Decimus Burton in yellow brick with a spire. There are two other modern churches, amongst the busy commercial sprawl (St Thomas, by F. H. Pownall, 1860, and St Matthew, by R. H. Hill, 1902).

Southfleet 2 appears from any distance to be like its neighbour *Betsham*, absorbed into the magnetic field of Gravesend. Its church tower stands dark under the pylons that impinge on industry and the coastal industries. In fact, at the crossroads in its centre are one or two pretty timbered houses, and the fourteenth-century church has some interest, including an octagonal font with the signs of the Zodiac. There are orchards and hop gardens all about, but building development inevitably continues, even to the south, in great suburban estates like *Longfield* and *Hartley*.

Speldhurst 5. An attractive village, just north-west of Tunbridge Wells,

residential, but by no means a suburb. It has an old inn, the George & Dragon, and a Gothic revival church, by J. Oldrid Scott, careful and Kent-conscious, of 1891, with ten windows by Burne-Jones. The colour of these is fine—in the east window blue and sharp pink contrast with the predominant grey-green. The village is high up, has views, is approached through several heavily wooded lanes. One of them is from *Langton Green*, in the south, also much built up, but still having a green, and surrounded by woods and parkland.

Stalisfield 13. Lovely country of bluebells and narrow winding lanes. Victorianized church, tiled. Louvred belfry. Flint and stone.

Stanford 17. Once, as the name implies, a stone ford, it is now a macadamized strip, not disagreeable but lined by mainly suburbanized housing on the main road from Hythe to Canterbury. The church is Victorian: by E. and W. H. Nash, 1879. It is just north of *Westenhanger* station and Folkestone Race Course.
Just beside Westenhanger station and the River Stour are the ruins of what was an extensive fortified house of the fourteenth century. One of the towers has legendary associations with Fair Rosamund, the mistress of Henry II, and is unreservedly called Fair Rosamund's Bower.
More factually a stone house away to the left, three miles north, is a Tudor mansion incorporating a Cluniac priory. This is *Horton Priory*, or *Monks Horton*. There is also a small medieval parish church, much rebuilt.

Stanstead 5 is hidden in rich undulating country north of Wrotham, and approached down narrow lanes. It is itself scattered on a hill, with a tiny green with an ambitious war memorial, old farm buildings, a few modern ones, a dull little church perched behind trees, and enviable seclusion.

Staple 15. An untidily scattered village, on the downland west of Sandwich, holding out against the evidences of the Kentish coal industry round about it. Amongst new bungalows are pleasant timbered cottages and somewhat decrepit

thatched ones. There is a dignified little grey church with a seventeenth-century lych-gate and a sculptured fifteenth-century font, and pleasant wall tablets. No chancel arch. One continuous roof over nave and chancel.

Staplehurst 6 has behind it a spread of new housing estates. But the shops for them fortunately stand back discreetly from the main road, and do not affect the fine main street. This has mellowed Kentish houses with a few outstanding ones of restored half-timbering, including *Fuller House*, at the Cranbrook end, opposite Iden Park, and *Maplehurst* ("hurst" is a clearing in the forest, and a common name in the Weald). Part of the pavements on each side of the street are raised.
It is a district of fine country houses, including *Spilsill Court*, a fourteenth-sixteenth-century building, to the north, and *Loddenden Manor* beyond it.
The spacious, much-restored church has a twelfth-century south door with Kentish ironwork of Viking emblems (now inside), a good late brass, and a handsome tower with dramatic views from the top across the Weald.

Stelling. *See* Upper Hardres.

Stockbury 6. A scattered parish with pleasant unremarkable houses lying quietly in orchard country in the angle of two trunk roads, and benefiting by being unobvious of access from either of them. It is on high ground, but the church itself is higher, proud on a crest above the road from Maidstone to Sitting-bourne, beside a large farm. It is a thirteenth-century building with a fine flint tower. It has an attractive interior, with careful mouldings, fifteenth-century parclose screens and some stained glass. But much restored. From here are wonderful views of the Medway valley and the Isle of Grain on the horizon. Beside the church are, although not easily distinguished, the banks and ditch of an earthwork, the base of a Norman castle.

Stodmarsh 14. A delightful undeveloped place between the Great

Stour and Little Stour, where the seaward marshes begin. The small nave and chancel church, restored medieval, has a whole window and part of another glazed with thirteenth-century grisaille glass, in good preservation.

Stoke 3. Overlooks the Isle of Grain and saltings of the Medway estuary. The church has the stump of an unfinished tower. It was over-restored in 1898.

Stone 2 must once have been a delightful village, just behind the river and the Thames-side prosperity of Greenhithe. Now it is completely industrialized: a main road with the coastal traffic, works, mills, and quarries. It has, however, a church revered by ecclesiologists as one of the most interesting in the county. Stone Manor was given to the See of Rochester in 993 by King Ethelred, and the church was built with money received at the shrine of St

William of Perth, which Rochester hoped would rival the rewards as well as sanctity of St Thomas's shrine at Canterbury. This was about 1250. It was therefore remarkably richly decorated, and its proportions are delightful. The work is believed to have been carried out by the masons, if not the architect, of Westminster Abbey. The inside was damaged by fire in 1638, but restored with devotion by G. E. Street in 1859. His careful work in no way detracted

The Kentish love of white paint. SOUTHBOROUGH

from the earlier rich tracery, arcades with shafts of Purbeck marble, and other detail. There are contemporary paintings of the Virgin and the Martyrdom of St Thomas à Becket, a good canopied tomb of the sixteenth century, and murals, and good, colourful Victorian glass in the big chancel windows. In the churchyard, a fine rank of white limestone tombstones carved with flying cherubs, and so on.

Stone 13. The slight (flint) remains of a church in a field to the north of the Sittingbourne road outside Faversham are being excavated (1968). The church was built on a Roman site.

Stone-in-Oxney 16 is perched dramatically on the cliff of this land-island, for Oxney was for centuries a real island, surrounded by the sea. The fifteenth-century church has a Kentish hall-house beside it. Inside the church are old screens and a florid Royal Arms of 1814, signed by a painter (probably a coach painter) of Tenterden. The steep hill has many daffodils in the spring, and the church is of yellow sandstone amongst red-tile roofs. Preserved in the Victorianized interior is a strange monolith which may have given the village its name. It was certainly Mithraic, and once had bulls defined on it, and evidence of sacrificial fire on top. Later it was used as a mounting stone, and has a ring, no doubt used for horses. *Ebony* is a signpost name to an outlying hillock where once was a chapel. This was removed, stone by stone, and now stands unharmed at *Reading Street*, a mile or so away, on the road to Tenterden. Stone was long and pleasantly known as Stone-juxta-Ebony.

Stourmouth 15, East and West, form a scattered marine parish, roughly in a circle, at the ancient mouth of the Stour, which here poured into the Channel. Now the river deflects to Pegwell Bay. It is an unsophisticated spot, with untidy new buildings and a few old ones, but a delightful small ragstone church, hidden behind limes and chestnuts, with a wooden belfry, made originally of ships' timbers, a tiny steeple, and box-pews. A little old glass, and a fine Royal Arms of George III.

STOURMOUTH Church

Stowting 14. An undisturbed village amongst folds of the downs, some of them with Roman and Saxon burial mounds, with traces of a medieval castle just to the west. The almost rebuilt church has gigantic yew-trees outside, an early timbered porch and a window full of fine fifteenth-century glass with saints and kneeling donors. Also a Virgin and Child, the head of Virgin and figure of Child renewed.

Strood. *See* Rochester.

Sturry 15 was bombed in the war, and is now rebuilt and somewhat characterless, except for the church, which stands a little back from the main road from Canterbury to the Thanet resorts, and is symmetrical, with aisles, restored and not interesting. By it is a tremendous barn, of old brick, weatherboarded above, and behind this Milner Court. This was a grange of St Augustine's Abbey, rebuilt in the sixteenth century, also in brick. Later it became the home of Lord Milner, the statesman, and is now the Junior King's School of Canterbury. There are big additions, built recently. It is on the river, and Sturry means "Stour-y".

Sundridge 5 straggles along the

main road from Sevenoaks to Westerham, the stream of lorries bisecting a village still possessing its early nineteenth-century character, with several distinctive older houses: a rectory, manor house, Red and White houses, and Sundridge Place. These are a little way uphill from the Square. On the main road itself are Bishops Cottage and the very fine fifteenth-century half-timbered Old Hall, with the central hall itself still open to the roof, and very close studding. It is National Trust property. The thirteenth-century church is on rising ground to the south. Anne Seymour Damer the sculptress is buried here, and busts by her are inside. She was a friend and relation of Horace Walpole, and inherited Strawberry Hill. Combe Bank, to the north, has a park with the Darent flowing through it. It long belonged to the Dukes of Argyll, and afterwards to the Mannings. Cardinal Manning was born here.

Sutton by Dover 15. So-called, though lying back from the coast and really nearer to Deal. It is in undisturbed country and a pretty village with some flint and thatched cottages and a small church of Norman origin, apsidal, almost rebuilt in 1862 (A. Ashpittle). It has a Jacobean pulpit. Standing on a steep hill.

Sutton-at-Hone 2. A jingle used to say "Sutton for Mutton", and there is still agricultural land to the west. But Sutton today is a busy uncountrified place on the industrial left bank of the Darent, along the main road to Dartford. One or two houses show that there was an older village. To the east in the valley is the chimney of a huge works, and up a lane to the west the church, amongst beech trees. It is fourteenth century, and has a memorial to Sir Thomas Smythe, the first governor of the East India Company, who died in 1625.
Down by the river is a moated house, St John's Jerusalem. This was originally a commandery of the Knights Hospitallers, whose thirteenth-century chapel survives at the east end. Most of the existing house was built from 1665 onwards. It was altered, to his financial ruin, by Edward Hasted, the historian of

Kent, still widely quoted, who owned it from 1755 to 1766. It now belongs to the National Trust.

Sutton Valence 6, south-east of Maidstone, is on the ridge of the Quarry Hills. The name comes from a William de Valenc who held it in 1275. The boys' public school here was founded in 1576, but the red buildings at the top of the hill on arrival are new. Below, along two ridges of the hillside, are many modern villas but also a variety of old Kentish exteriors, and the general effect is bright and attractive, like a hill-slope Tenterden. There are great views across the Weald. The churchyard commemorates John Welles, 1777–1852, a pioneer who was "the first to introduce round-arm bowling into cricket". The church is of 1828: by William Ashendon.
At *East Sutton* there are more villas, a little grey restored church, and in its park a brick manor house of the seventeenth century, built for the Filmer family. They played a great part in the history of the county, and Sir Robert Filmer, who died in 1653, has his place in political theory as a defender of patriarchal government. Their monuments are in the church (not very imposing, the best by Chantrey). There is also fifteenth-century armorial glass. The interior of the church is scraped.

Swanley 2 was a tiny village, famous for its orchards and Henry Cannell, largely responsible for the development of the scarlet geranium. It acquired a railway junction in 1861, however, expanded into an industrial overspill, like *Hextable* to the north, and now has 13,000 inhabitants. Tucked away in a hollow down a path lined with pines, north of the main road and the main development, is a curious little locked church, built in 1862 with an odd use of red brick in stone. St Mary the Virgin, on the main road, is grander, more conventional red brick of 1902.

Swanscombe 2, behind a peninsular of mess and marsh, lies on the industrial bank of the southern Thames between Dartford and Gravesend. Its sprawl has a thin coating of the cement that, with paper mills, contributes to its livelihood, and its standardized streets might be any-

where. But it is an old parish, and has two churches of interest. The first is a modern Gothic one on the main road, built in stone and flint by Norman Shaw to cater for the Victorian development (the population doubled between 1860 and 1900). The other is now amongst modern houses but was once remote, even from the small agricultural village that Swanscombe was for hundreds of years. Although twice restored, it has a tower that is partly Saxon, a southern window with Roman brick in it, and a chalk font. Also a magnificent Jacobean alabaster monument, well restored and coloured. This is the tomb of Sir Ralph Weldon, Chief Clerk of the Kitchen to Queen Elizabeth I. He died in 1609, and the legend says "He hath well don, and so made good his name". Carved white limestone tombs in the churchyard.
At *Galley Hill*, here, in 1935, was discovered the first fragment of skull which has made the name of Swanscombe famous to archaeologists. Two other pieces discovered over the following twenty years, together with flints and animal remains, have established it, at the present stage of knowledge, as belonging to an Acheulian ancestor of man living perhaps 100,000 years ago. The chalk pit, and anything more it may contain, is now scheduled as a nature reserve.

Swingfield 15. Upland scatter behind Dover. Flint and stone church: nave, chancel, tower. Plain whitewashed interior with a nice kingpost roof. The ruins of *St John's Chapel*, north, are ivy-grown and derelict.

Temple Ewell 15 is so called because it once belonged to the Knights Templar. There was an abbey, and is a Victorianized Norman and later church with several panels of seventeenth-century (foreign) glass. The place is now essentially a respectable suburban extension of Dover, and has the Rural District Council offices.

Tenterden 16, in spite of incessant traffic, development, and being the busy shopping centre for a wide area, retains both integrity and beauty. It looks wealthy, and it always has been: a borough, a market town, and once a centre for the rich weavers and

ironmasters of the Weald. In the Middle Ages it was a subsidiary Cinque Port, with its dock at Small-hythe.

Development has been discreet and contained, and the long wide high street remains a delightful palimpsest of Kentish façades: Tudor, eighteenth century, bow-fronted Regency and tile-hung Victorian. The few eyesores only serve to stop it being self-conscious, and the grass verges along it are planted with trees and framed by attractive individual buildings.

Legend claimed that the steeple on the church tower of St Michael was built by money wrongly diverted from the funds raised for keeping the Romney sea wall in repair. The steeple went up, the sea came in, and hence the Goodwin Sands. This slander is now discounted. But envy is understandable, for the church, handsomely placed and with a tower of great beauty, is magnificent. The interior is spacious, over-furnished and dark with stained glass. There is a good Jacobean monument with two figures at a *prie-dieu* under a round-headed arch. The church lies back from the High Street but dominates discreetly the justifiably much photographed boulevard. Behind the churchyard, as indeed all round the town, spreads delightful wooded country of parks and farmsteads. There is an agreeable Town Hall, a good Unitarian chapel of 1662, and a Baptist church of 1767. Also, at one end of the street, is a *Caxton Inn*. The town claims William Caxton as its son, although all he himself said was that he was born in the Weald, "where I doubt not is spoken as broad and rude English as in any part of England".

Teston (pronounced "Teeson") 6 is inevitably very much a dormitory of Maidstone. It has a few old houses, a rebuilt church, and a fine Tudor bridge of six arches, below the main road, going over the Medway to West Farleigh. It is the eighth of the twelve bridges over the river between Rochester and Tonbridge, and perhaps the most beautiful of them all. The centre of the old village is near the church and small green, with some decent "infill": still pleasant. The church, as to nave and tower, is of 1710, and like a charming model or toy outside. Gothic transepts and chancel were added in 1848. Eighteenth-century reredos re-used. Royal Arms, 1811. This and hatchments adorn an attractive interior. Above the village is *Barham Court*, where the rector, a Mr James Ramsey, formerly a naval chaplain with service in the West Indies, met William Wilberforce in 1783 and interested him in the abolition of slavery. Tradition made a former house on the site that of Reginald Fitzurse, one of the murderers of Becket. Wonderful views of the Medway valley.

Teynham ("Tann-am", and piqued at mispronunciation) 13. Once a small town of local importance between Faversham and Sittingbourne, it now has a long plain village street, with behind a jumble of houses up to and round the station, where the road winds on to Teynham Street. Here there was once a manor house, and now are a few scattered houses and the Victorianized church, which contains brasses, and is surrounded by orchards. Although part of the parish is marsh, it is in fact the historic centre of intensive fruit industry: Richard Nairns, accredited purveyor to Henry VIII, planted over a hundred acres here with cherries, pippins and golden russets which he had bought overseas. The Kentish plenty of Flemish cherries developed from his orchards at Teynham.

Conyer, to the north, has a depressing group of houses, an inn, a brick factory and a busy yacht-basin. It looks bleakly across the Swale to the Isle of Sheppey.

Throwley 13 is a peaceful spot hidden away on the heights of the North Downs, surrounded by cherry orchards. It consists mainly of scattered farms, but the surprisingly imposing, though much restored, church served the great house at Belmont, near by, the home of the Harris family. One Lord Harris won Seringapatam: another captained England at cricket. There is a Harris Chapel, and splendid Jacobean and Georgian memorials to the Sonds family, two table-tombs have two kneeling figures each. *Belmont* is an early nineteenth-century house, handsomely set in a park, with domed corner pavilions.

Thurnham 6. A quiet village on the Pilgrims' Way, where a narrow lane heavy with trees bisects and goes downhill from the downs. There are one or two early timbered houses and an inn at the junction of the ways: and the rest of the houses and the church are below. The church has an elegantly buttressed, sturdy tower, is mostly late (and Perpendicular), but has a Norman window high up on one side. Nave, chancel and north chapel. Splendid kingpost roof to nave. Much restoration; but a good deal of atmosphere still, and quite a presence here on the wooded slope of the Downs. Alfred Mynn, the giant of Kent cricket, is buried in the churchyard. Above, the lane rises to 650 feet, one of the highest points of the Downs. On a bend at the top, where enormous views suddenly appear of the Weald, industrious investigation reveals the remains of an early Norman fortress, *Thurnham Castle*, with fragments of the keep. It was already a ruin in the sixteenth century. There are also hereabouts traces of Roman occupation.

Tilmanstone 15 was long just a hamlet off the road from Dover to Sandwich. There are still many trees, twisting lanes, a High Street, low street, and Norman church. Outside there is also Tilmanstone colliery—extraneous and disturbing, but with clean functional lines and not altogether disfiguring. The pit was started just before the 1914–18 war.

Tonbridge (pronounced, and anciently spelt, "Tun-bridge") 5 has, all on the main road, an ancient castle, a great public school; and a bottleneck for traffic. It was throughout most of history a small but prosperous market town on the Medway, and is still surrounded by rich and beautiful country of orchards and hopfields. It developed after 1741, when the Medway became a navigable waterway, but extended still more with the coming of the railways in 1842. This increased trade and made it an agreeable residential area for London businessmen. In recent years the motor-car and light industry have meant new and sprawling estates, especially to the north, and the middle of the town, particularly south of the bridge, is often virtually impassable from through traffic. Here the High Street is busy, contemporary and hideous. Over the bridge, and beginning with the Castle, there are however numerous buildings of interest. The cricket ground remains famous, and the making of cricket paraphernalia is a sizeable industry.

The remains of the *Castle* stand on a mound on the west bank of the river, surrounded by gardens which in Horace Walpole's time were "used for Mr Hooker's vinery". Here it commanded the road to Hastings and the south coast. Nothing is left of the great Norman keep built by the Clare family and besieged by William Rufus in 1088: it was dismantled by the Parliamentarians during the Civil Wars. What is left is the thirteenth-century gatehouse, elaborate for its date, a massive rectangular block with round towers and a hall on the second floor, built in yellow stone. The building next to it on the east, and merging surprisingly well, was put up in 1793, and is now municipal offices. Part of the moat survives, some of the curtain wall to the south-east, and a great earthen mound which was the motte, and has traces of masonry on top. Round about are some good houses, including *The Chequers* and the half-timbered *Port Reeves house* in East Street. Much of the High Street north of here, on the way to Sevenoaks, is eighteenth and nineteenth century, often with the ground floor spoilt by shop fronts, but often too with good brick and weatherboarding. *The Rose & Crown Inn* is sixteenth century, given a chequered brick front two hundred years later, and another old inn is the *Elephant & Castle*. This is at the beginning of the Bordyke ("borough ditch") where there are several agreeable buildings, and approaching *Tonbridge School*. This was founded by Sir Andrew Judd, a Member of the Skinners Company, in 1553. The buildings are severely institutional. The entrance quadrangle incorporates the oldest part of the school, built in 1760 and enlarged in 1826, but the main block of Victorian Gothic, in inoffensive yellow ragstone, dates from 1863 and 1894. The incongruous chapel was put up in 1902, but is not evident from the road. Two excellent Georgian town houses taken over by the school as boarding houses are Judd House and Ferox Hall, the other side of the street.

The large parish church of SS Peter & Paul is plain and much restored: a Norman chancel (the original church) extended by a nave of the thirteenth century, a north aisle of the fourteenth, a south aisle of the early nineteenth and an unwise extension of this in 1879. There is a thirteenth-century tower.

Tonge 10. A "tongue" or peninsular of land was a popular Early English physical/topographical description. This one is of orchard country, descending to marshland and the Swale, north-east of Sittingbourne. There is a restored medieval church, and was once a castle, but is no village centre of importance today. A small discreet hamlet.

Toys Hill 5 has a scatter of houses, but is really notable as a National Trust viewpoint. It is over 800 feet up, with sandy hills and much foliage, beautiful at all times of year. The view through the clearings in the trees, notably from a small public garden by the village well, is indeed superb, as it is from the Tally Ho Inn and from numerous National Trust properties along the steep ridge here above the Weald. A place for walking.

Trottiscliffe (slurred locally to "Trosley") 5 has a pleasant High Street of houses, many of them with weatherboarding (and one the home of the painter, Graham Sutherland). Its best spot is half a mile down a lane at the church. Here there was a manor of the Bishops of Rochester, and parts of the palace are built into an otherwise inexplicable but engaging building with a red-brick gateway, by the church itself. The group is, in certain lights, magnificent. Inside the church is dominated by a vast wooden pulpit and sounding board with angels blowing horns. This is a cast-off from West-

Sonds tombs, THROWLEY

minster Abbey, brought here in 1874, and earns sneers from ecclesiologists. It is fun. The church also has unusual squared brick work in the west wall, and nineteenth-century communion rails.

Half a mile farther on again by lane, are the *Coldrum Stones*. These are more properly designated the Coldrum Long Barrow, and are the exposed parts of a Neolithic burial chamber. They were given to the National Trust in 1926 as a memorial to the great Kentish antiquary, Benjamin Harrison.

Tudeley 5 is a tiny place just east of Tonbridge, on the road to Maidstone. There is a small church, and a lane leads north, through flat low fields to the Medway. The church, beyond a farmyard east of the road, has an eighteenth-century brick nave and tower (the nave re-Gothicized later)

The Swale, TEYNHAM

and a medieval stone chancel. It was completely refurnished in 1967 (Robert Potter, architect) when a very distinguished window by Marc Chagall was placed as a memorial in a renewed east window. Seventeenth-century monument. Eighteenth-century altar rails. Between here and Tonbridge to the west, the ground rises in a beautiful sweep of parkland, surmounted by *Somerhill*.

This is a Jacobean house with a fine sandstone façade, dominating the landscape for some miles. It was a favourite resort of Restoration notabilities visiting Tunbridge Wells, but fell into decay until the ancestors of the present owners restored it in 1849. The lake and formal gardens are sometimes open to the public.

Tunbridge Wells 5 acquired the prefix "Royal" in 1909. It is a bustling, beautifully sited, inland town of about 40,000 people, historically a spa, now a shopping and residential centre, with a pleasant common, a famous cricket ground, the Pantiles, and a few charming buildings dating from its period of high fashion. It has little architectural heritage to compare with other inland spas like Bath, Buxton or Cheltenham. Nevertheless, because it was a late creation, with no medieval predecessor, it has wide streets and pavements, and, with its triangular common in the middle, is cheerful and open.

Its early rise was fortuitous. The Weald here had been largely impenetrable throughout the Middle Ages, and this hilly district, still of rich woodland and common, 400 feet up, was then heavily forested. In 1606 Lord North, lost on his way back to London from a visit to Erith, stumbled on a spring whose waters betrayed "a ruddy ochreous track". It was an age of excited physical enquiry, and he took a sample of the chalybeate waters home for analysis by his physician. They were found to have gratifying medicinal qualities. Lord North publicised his discovery, and his recovery from consumption, at Court, and it became fashionable to make a pilgrimage to Tunbridge, down the notoriously muddy roads, to take the waters. The spa benefited from the patronage of Queen Henrietta Maria, who came here

with her court and who, because there was not enough accommodation, pitched pavilions for her retinue round about the spring like a military camp. Building began on some scale in 1638, and the fashionable world continued to flock down. Queen Anne often stayed here. Charles II paid several visits, and the Pantiles became a promenade for the social élite of the Restoration. Off and on its status was maintained for some two hundred years. Beau Nash was brought from Bath to become Master of Ceremonies in 1735, and the popularity of "the Wells" continued, even after the vogue for sea-bathing, and so for the new coastal resorts, arrived in the 1760s. All the celebrities of the eighteenth century thronged here, with their attendant quacks and toadies. Their successors of the age of the assembly rooms and lending libraries are described by Thackeray in *Henry Esmond* and *The Virginians*. Indeed, whilst Rochester and Broadstairs are all Dickens, Tunbridge Wells is Thackeray. He lived in a small square Georgian house, one of many pleasantly dotted on the other side of the common from Mount Ephraim. Queen Victoria liked the town, and the coming of the railway in 1846 increased its prosperity although it changed its character. It more recently suffered bombing and development of its outskirts, but survives attractively into contemporary society.

Arriving from London, the road diverges at the top of the common, the fork to the right becoming Mount Ephraim. Here, looking out over the grass and the great outcrops of sandstone which have delighted generations of children (but were forbidden by his mother to John Ruskin), are the main hotels and some villas: Regency and early Victorian, with the Mount Ephraim Hotel itself, surmounted by a great lion and unicorn, delightful. The road goes on to Rusthall Common and the High Rocks, a popular excursion into woodland and chasms ever since a visit there of the Duke of York in 1670. St Paul's, Rusthall, is in yellow sandstone, Early English style, by H. I. Stevens, 1850. The other fork of the road from London goes down the shopping street of Mount Pleasant, which becomes the High Street, and arrives at the older

part of the town, with the Pantiles, at the bottom.

Here is the church of King Charles the Martyr, opened in 1678, and its dedication insisted upon by the High Tory party. It is rebuilt externally, but remains an attractive seventeenth-century brick building, with a wooden cupola and clock of 1759. Inside it has a flamboyant baroque plaster ceiling by Henry Doogood and John Wetherill, and is altogether charming.

Opposite to the church is the entrance to the *Pantiles*, a terraced walk with shops behind a colonnade, and a row of lime trees—what would now be called a shopping precinct, but dating from an age of privileged elegance rather than standardized affluence. (The shops remain, in fact, particularly good.) In spite of being incessantly photographed, sketched and over-written, the buildings on the raised pavement remain attractive, and gain rather than otherwise from some late Victorian and other unpretentious façades above the level of the colonnades. The effect is of continuity rather than too-conscious period restoration. Individually indeed the houses are unremarkable, but the general effect is one of character. The arcade has existed since the first row of shops and houses at the Wells were destroyed by fire in 1687, and Queen Anne graciously provided funds whereby the "Walks" were paved from end to end with square earthenware tiles known as pantiles. They were replaced by Purbeck flagstones in a smartening-up movement in the eighteenth century, and these remain today. But after being for a time "The Parade", and for a lapse in the 1880's "Ye Pantyles", the old name survived. A nondescript building at one end masks the chalybeate spring. The bandstand has gone, and the Pump Room has been demolished: new block of flats on the site of latter.

On the Lower Walk, parallel with the Pantiles and below their embankment, is an excellent row of early

nineteenth-century houses, harmonious if individually unimportant, including the Royal Sussex Assembly Rooms. As the Royal Victoria and Sussex Hotel it was the centre of fashionable life at the Wells in Regency times and up to the middle of the nineteenth century. In 1880 it became a furniture repository: the Pantechnicon. The sign remains. Also on the Lower Walk is what was opened in 1802 as the theatre, became the Corn Exchange in 1843, and is now a second-hand furniture show-room. All about, at the back, and particularly in Mount Zion, are small groups of Regency and early Victorian houses, often of charm and distinction. There is a pretty Early Victorian house in Cumberland Walk, attributed to the Brighton architect Aman Henry Wilds, with his characteristic "ammonite" capitals.

At the top of the hill again, east of the road from London, is an area of municipal buildings, car parks and shops that might be anywhere. But below this and entered from Mount Pleasant lie Calverley Park and Calverley Crescent, the only attempts at stately spa architecture. They are by James and Decimus Burton, but cannot now be said to be particularly impressive. Calverley Crescent is a system of terraced houses, originally designed for shops behind the exiguous colonnade and unsatisfactory without them. The stone of the houses in Claverley Park has not mellowed attractively. They remain, however, evidences of style and a conscious attempt at distinction. In the Calverley Hotel, once Calverley house, Princess Victoria stayed with the Duchess of Kent. The Walk was built in the 1830s. Decimus Burton also designed Holy Trinity Church, Gothic, in local sandstone, with a fine interior, when in 1827 the growth of the town made the Church of King Charles the Martyr too small. There are also several Victorian churches, and a Congregational Doric temple in Mount Pleasant.

On the outskirts of the town are some prosperous Victorian houses with big gardens behind their laurels and rhododendrons: notably in Pembury Road. Inside the town are one or two narrow Victorian streets which are virtually slummy. But

Tunbridge Wells is generally bright, open and welcoming, the old fashionable world a memory (but an advantage to the antique business, for which it is a headquarters), and the new fashion cheerfully worn.

A by-product of the town's history, now much cherished, is Tunbridge Ware—elaborate trinkets and boxes of parquetry, contrived mainly in undyed local woods.

Tunstall 13 has one or two old rose-brick houses, new or red-brick ones, and a restored church standing well beside the road. It is now a dormitory of Sittingbourne, screened from it by orchards all round, in season gorgeous.

Ulcombe 6. A scattered and somewhat modernized village at the bottom of a hill, in lovely country surrounded by hopfields and orchards. The church, however, stands typically higher up, and has tremendous panoramic views of the Weald. Its exterior is handsome, and of good texture, and it overshadows a champion yew tree with a girth of 40 feet. Inside, the church has been restored in a model way with great sensitivity: a new platform in the chancel, good roof beams, and effective setting off of such features as its excellent brasses. There are some carved misericords, wall tablets, small old wall paintings and plenty of light. Armorial glass and fragments.

Upchurch 3 is a quiet attractive village although only five miles from urban Gillingham. It is on the shoulder of a little peninsula jutting up into the estuary of the Medway. There are spick and span new houses, rising above orchards. Presiding over the older houses, and a landmark in the waterways, is the odd little shingle steeple of the church. This has, inside, thirteenth-century paintings on the south wall, and some other good detail. The parson here was, in Tudor times, also the Chaplain of the Hulks—the disused ships laid up off this point in the Medway. A ships' Scripture reader appointed to this office in 1560 was a refugee from religious troubles in Devon called Edmund Drake. His young son, Francis, learnt his seamanship here in the Medway estuary. (One

feels Millais may have overlooked this in painting *Westward Ho!*)

The church has a symmetrical fourteenth-century interior, pleasantly whitened, and with atmosphere. There is some fine fourteenth-century glass, with figure work and grisaille. Brass. Crypt. The Romans made pottery here which was widely disseminated throughout the Empire.

Upper Hardres 14 is pronounced "Hards" and is named after the Hardres family, which started at the Conquest and died out with Sir William Hardries, who died in 1674 at the court here. It has become a generic term for a scatter of amiable development which spreads to include the once separate villages of *Stellis Minnis* and *Bossingham*, all south of Canterbury. There are pretty old farms and Kentish houses and a sprinkling of new villas, all amongst lanes and wasteland. Upper Hardres church is thirteenth to fifteenth century, thirteenth- and fourteenth-century stained glass, and a gallery. This is a good church, which also has two early seventeenth-century monuments, one with intricate engraved decoration and eighteenth-century tablets and hatchments, too. There is a gallery also at the old church of *Stelling*, down a long lane. The church is largely fourteenth century and has attractive late eighteenth-century box-pews and a three-decker pulpit also. The "Slippery Sam" Inn is named after a greased and so elusive smuggler of local legend.

Lower Hardres, farther north towards Canterbury, and now united with Nackington, is in a dip and the new houses blend agreeably enough with the old. On slightly higher ground there is a neat and respectable church of 1832, by Rickman. The Rickman fabric is largely in its original state, though pantiled now, and the spire has lost its top; but the pews and liturgical arrangements have been altered inside. There is armorial glass of Rickman's date. There is also an old rectory, castellated Gothic, and contemporary with the church in these very rural surroundings.

Upstreet 14 has a few old houses, but is very much a built-up strip of the road from Margate to Canterbury.

It lies pleasantly, however, and just south, on the Stour, is *Grove Ferry*, with an inn, beer gardens, and a bridge which has superseded the ferry. This is much visited and enjoyed.

Waldershare. *See* Northbourne.

Walderslade 3 which once was nothing, is now a vast expanse of modern houses stretching down south of Chatham to the knot of main roads under- and over-passing each other at *Bluebell Hill*. There are steep woods and beautiful lanes to the south, and another brick and concrete mass of avenues and crescents, called *Wayfield*, to the north.

Walmer 15 is now administratively merged with Deal (q.v.), and they continue as an unbroken line of building along this remarkably straight piece of coast. Insofar as they differ in character at all, Deal is the resort, and Walmer more residential. There is an old church of 1120 (Norman) and a "new" one of 1888 ("Early English"), and a number of well-proportioned houses of the Victorian development, as well as later ones, and some greensward. Sandgate Castle, a few miles to the north, was destroyed by the encroachment of the sea, but *Walmer Castle* has been stranded, and now lies back from the promenade, although once its moat was daily filled by the sea-water at high tide. It was built at the same time and for the same purpose as Deal Castle (q.v.). Its construction is rather simpler, but less easy to recognize, as there have been successive alterations throughout history, as its military significance declined and its residential needs increased. It is the official residence of the Lord Warden of the Cinque Ports, and visitors can admire relics of early and recent holders of the title, and notably the sparse personal requirements of the Duke of Wellington. Round the castle are attractive trees and gardens.
The Cinque Ports consisted originally of Hastings, Romney, Hythe, Dover and Sandwich. Rye and Winchelsea were added, and it became the confederation of the Cinque Ports and the two Ancient Towns. Smaller ports later joined as "limbs" or members, sharing the privileges and

the responsibilities. The arrangement was essentially feudal—rights accorded for service. The service was the provision of ships when called upon, for not more than fifteen days, to fight enemies or ferry the king's troops to his French territories. The rights were to be allowed to land and control the herring fleet at Yarmouth, which caused bitter rows, and to hold the canopy over the monarch at coronations. The Confederation also developed its own government, and the Court of Shipway was in existence by 1150. A charter came 100 years later.
The heyday of the ports, in spite of the constant sea changes to the Kentish coast, lasted some 200 years, but ended by about 1350. The Kentish towns continued with fishing, piracy and smuggling, but could not compete with the great ports of trade like London, Boston and Southampton, which took bigger ships. The sea receded. In 1572 of 135 ships of 100 tons and upwards only one, from Dover, came from a Kentish port. Meanwhile central government became stronger, and many of the administrative powers of the Cinque Ports were whittled away.
But the Confederation still exists, although most of the remaining privileges were mopped up in 1855. The churches of the old towns still have pews for its officials, the portsmen "barons" are still given special places at the Coronation, and the office of Warden remains a high and colourful if only ornamental office.

Waltham 14 is a somewhat built-up village in lovely country west of the Roman road that is now the route from Canterbury to Hythe. It was once Temple Waltham, for the Knights Templar had a holding here. The hilltop church, its flints glimmering above winter hedgerows and coppices, with views over the valley and up to the Downs, is bare inside and out, but has a remarkable timbered roof. Much nineteenth-century rebuilding, including the tower. Norman origin.

Warehorne 16 is a small straggling parish just south of the Hythe-Tenterden road and overlooking the Military Canal. It has an Early English church with a brick tower

and north porch of 1777. The original tower was struck by lightning. There is some thirteenth-century glass, box-pews, old tiled floor and not much visibly disruptive restoration. Like many of the churches in and on the borders of Romney Marsh it has no routine modern stained glass, and benefits accordingly.

Wateringbury 6. A pleasant village of old and new houses just outside Maidstone: a favourite spot for fishing and a centre for hop and fruit growing. The medieval church, with a shingled spire, has had many restorations but the interior has character. Organ on projecting west gallery. Splendid seventeenth-century monument (Style family), under a semi-circular arched canopy, with two reclining effigies. Kneelers on the base and figures of Life and Death hiding behind the canopy supports, all painted. Hatchments. Opposite the church is a picturesque house with a large, thatched, gabled section projecting, and supported on pillars.
Wateringbury Place, north-west of the church, is a fine Queen Anne house for formal and water gardens. The gardens, beautifully landscaped, are sometimes open.

Welling 2. No doubt a happy home to thousands, but a vast characterless spread of urban development past Woolwich at the foot of Shooters Hill, merging indistinguishably into Bexley and Bexleyheath. It can claim, with them, the breathing spot of Danson Park, south of the road, now a public park, with woods by Capability Brown and a sheet of water. Otherwise there are a few residuary village houses, a vestigial green, the Shoulder of Mutton, a red-brick modern church and miles and miles of red-brick villas. The main road, that was the Roman road, cuts a swathe through it.
It has swallowed most of *East Wickham*. But this still overlooks an unbuilt valley and has two churches: a thirteenth-century one with a wooden belfry, and a brick one of 1933. The old church has a fourteenth-century brass cross, involved with two half-effigies. To the north are Bostall Woods: elsewhere, hospitals, vast cemeteries, and brick-work.

Westbere 14. Much, fairly discreet, development east of Canterbury. The nave and chancel church has medieval bits only, and small fragments of old glass.

Westerham 4. An extremely pleasant country town on a hill in Holmesdale, near the Surrey border and the source of the Darent. Westerham Hill, above the town to the north, is the highest spot in Kent. The main east-west road flows through it, but the place retains character and a number of old buildings in spite of constant vibration. There is a tapering green, on a slope, dominated by a 1911 whitewashed brick statue of General Wolfe, who was born here in 1726. This event was in the Vicarage. The Wolfe's own house, at the foot of the hill, is now called *Quebec House*: a square brick gabled building of distinction belonging to the National Trust and used as a Wolfe museum. The seventeenth-century market place has two old hotels facing each other: one Tudor and one Georgian. Here and round the green itself are numerous old houses, which achieve a general harmony, dissipated the farther you go from the centre. The church stands back at the northern corner of the green, with a low thirteenth-century tower with a spiral staircase, and a short shingled spire. Inside it was badly over-restored in 1882, but is airy, with wide aisles running the length of the building. There are some good brasses, and fine views from the churchyard.

Another celebrated inhabitant was John Frith, the reformer and friend of Tyndale, who was burned at Smithfield in 1533.

Squerries Court, to the south, is a William and Mary building of red brick: the home of the Warde family, friends of the Wolfes. Here James Wolfe was handed his first commission. It and its gardens are sometimes open to the public.

(For Chartwell see Crockham Hill.)

Westgate-on-Sea. *See* Margate.

West Langdon. *See* East Langdon.

Westwell 13 is a quiet and pretty village in a fold of the hills north of Ashford. The church, standing back behind chestnut trees, looks plain but is an excellent example of the Early English style, with a triple chancel arch and vaulted chancel, and it has some beautifully carved choir stalls. There is also an effective Jesse window in the East End, recomposed of thirteenth-century glass in 1960. Dotted about behind lanes and trees are attractive private houses and farms.

West Wickham 1, on the Surrey border, south-west of Bromley, is a quintessential middle-class suburb of bright mainly new villas and estates, with trees, grass verges, well-kept gardens, and rows upon rows of little houses of the '20s, usually mock Tudor, or contemporary, serviceable but architecturally negligible. The roads are wide. There is Langley Park golf course to the north, Hayes Common to the east, and green fields to the south. The church, away on high ground from the new shopping centre, is a restored fifteenth-century building with its original lych-gate, and

below and opposite: 18th-century monuments at WALDERSHARE

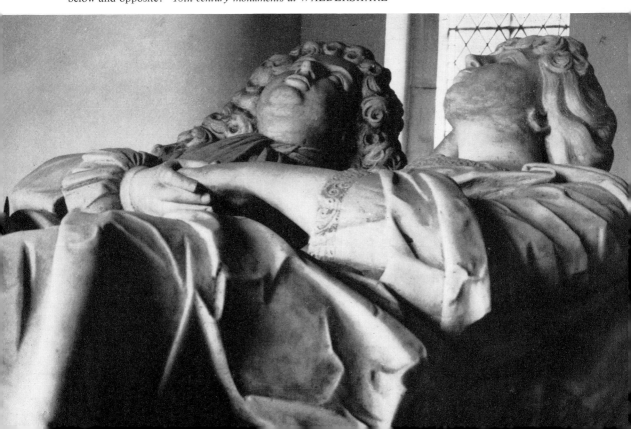

To the Memory of Lady Arabella Watson
6.th Daughter of Lewis Earl of Rockingham
by Kath: Daughter of Geo Earl of Feversham
Born 15 March 1693 Married 1 July
Deceased 6 September

General Wolfe, Quebec House, WESTERHAM

some Flemish glass in the north chapel. A red-brick turreted house nearby is a school, but was Wickham Court, originally built about 1480 by Sir Henry Heydon, who also rebuilt the church.

Whitfield 15 is a large unsightly development area on the main road from Dover to Sandwich, where various minor roads pour in towards the coast. It has magnificent views. The church and older buildings are tucked away at *Church Whitfield*, now a hamlet to the north-east. The church has Saxon and Norman work, but was virtually rebuilt in 1894.

Whitstable 11 has moments of charm, and the *réclame* of the oysters.

Essentially however it is an extending residential resort with maritime overtones, visually incoherent. Ships call here from Scandinavia and the Low Countries, and being in some degree the port of Canterbury, and near the mouth of the Swale, connecting the Medway with the Thames estuary, it has had some historical importance. This has never been entirely lost, and the present harbour was only completed in 1832. The fishing quarter, south-west of it, has alleys and old houses. Shipmaking on any scale has ended, but there are still yards, and Whitstable-built yachts are famous.

So is the oyster industry, which irrupts into the national press when the waters are blessed at Reeves Bay,

west of the harbour, at the start of the season, early each September. It has a history 2,000 years old, and has survived numerous near-disasters. The private beds, or layings, start about two miles off-shore, and extend to some seven miles out, covering about 5,000 acres. They are dredged by the distinctive yawls of the successors to the Company of Free Fishers and Dredgers.

There is another group of older buildings higher up and inland, round a Victorianized fifteenth-century building, All Saints Church. Otherwise the houses are mainly those which were run up after Whitstable's great event in 1830, when the Canterbury and Whitstable Railway opened the first regular steam service in the country. The railway, and then the roads, brought visitors, seaside residents, and now commuters. They are served by modern shops in the crowded old streets, a marine parade and incessant communications in all directions.

The modern residential extension to the east is *Tankerton*, laid out with full suburban trimmings behind a grassy promenade, with an under-cliff, bungalows and bathing huts. A promontory of shingle, called The Street, stretches curiously out to sea for the distance of a mile. There is a Tankerton Circus inland, with shops, and a Tankerton Castle, formerly Tankerton Tower, for the municipal offices, with some fifteenth-century masonry inside Victorian battlements. A suburb of a suburb, further east, is *Swalecliffe*.

Away to the west, past golf-links, is *Seasalter*, where indeed there was once salt-panning and the mother church of Whitstable. It is low-lying, and was inundated by the high tides of 1953. Rescued, it is an unrelieved strip of caravans, huts and bungalows, very popular.

Wickhambreux 14. A delightful spot south of the Stour and of the Margate-Canterbury road, with a small village green surrounded by some Georgian and timbered houses, and with limes and chestnut trees. Whilst there is nothing of outstanding historic interest, it is perhaps one of the best villages in Kent to remain

WESTWELL Church

typical of the county's beauty before over-population. The much-restored medieval church is dominated inside by an elaborate decoration scheme and a large and colourful east window of 1896, full of lilies and floating angels, in an off-beat pre-Raphaelite style—very convincing looking, but good only in details; signed "opus 1: Arild Rosenkrantz."

Willesborough 13 retains a precarious entity in and just off the Folkestone road, on the outskirts of Ashford, with a pleasant church and farm and a few old houses resolute amongst the industrial and dormitory spread. The church is fifteenth century and has a spire with tiny windows in it. It is "towny" inside, and largely nineteenth century. But it has a fourteenth-century chancel with original glass in two windows—that on the north side pretty complete, with the Virgin and St John the Baptist in a grisaille background. *Sevington* has a spired nave and chancel church among orchards and vegetable fields. Victorianized. Some old glass in a north window.

Sevington, on the southern side of the main road, has its own remote little medieval church, but is equally threatened.

Wilmington 2 is a hilltop suburb of Dartford. Desirable residences, and a church with some old features. Limestone tombs in the churchyard —some moved. Interior over-restored. Much Kempe glass. The best features are the hatchments, Commandment boards and Hanoverian Royal Arms.

Witchling 13 is a small parish on high ground. The church, mostly Victorian (restored by J. Clarke, 1883), stands lonely across a field, far from the few scattered houses. It has a shingled spire with gabled openings in it— picturesque. Flint and stone. Little history, but good views, peace, beechwood and bluebells.

Wingham 14 has declined in status, but retains character. It had a market, a sessions court, and a college of secular canons, founded in 1287. The row of sixteenth-century houses opposite the church were part of it. Now Wingham has heavy traffic through it, but it is still possible to

appreciate the charm of its wide High Street, with houses of all periods from Tudor to contemporary, pleasantly mingling ornamented brick, beams and overhanging. The road is bordered by trees, including copper beeches and Spanish chestnuts.

Trunks of six chestnut trees curiously form the pillars of the church. It has a splendid roof, good stalls, carved stonework and fine monuments. The fourteenth-century tower has a handsome green spire. Because it was a collegiate church, it has rich stalls with carved misericords. The monuments are of the seventeenth century. One has recumbent figures under a canopy (in the vestry); another, in the north chapel (Oxenden), is of black-and-white marble—a decorated obelisk on a plinth that has black bulls' heads at the corners: quite remarkable. Another has small, freestanding cherub-like angels. A severe Nonconformist chapel, nobly dated 1835, dominates bungalows in a side street.

Wingmore 14 was long a tiny hamlet in the valley of the Nailburn stream. Now it has the railway, is on the road from Canterbury to Hythe, and has developed into a strip of modern estates and bungalows. It still has a little flint church with a green spire, lurking back amongst a few older and now incongruous cottages.

Wittersham 16. A sizeable ancient village with a number of pleasant old houses and many farms, but expanded and expanding. It is 214 feet up, and the "capital" of the Isle of Oxney. This hump-backed ridge is even now virtually an island when the floods are up, and was once completely so—an oasis of pasture and parkland. It is beautiful, timbered mellow country, with rich contrasts: below it the Rother winding to the sea, and the valleys merging into the marshland.

Wittersham church is Perpendicular, with a high tower and good arches. The tower used to carry an Armada beacon. Inside is some good carving, and a chapel in memory of Alfred Lyttleton (1857–1913) "athlete, lawyer and statesman"—and one of the Souls, and a Victorian aesthete and intellectual who archetypically com-

bined these qualities with an historic drive through the covers.

Womenswold 14. A pleasant if unremarkable little village hidden from the main road, in oak and beech country, seven miles from Canterbury. Red brick cottages and an attractive, oil-lit church which has a thirteenth-century fabric, elegant eighteenth-century wall monuments (two with busts) and attractive and delicate grisaille glass of 1870—the date of restoration.

Woodchurch 16 is a large cheerful village, with weatherboarded cottages, inns and Tudor houses round a wide green. It does its best to ignore undistinguished development towards the bend in the main road from Hythe to Tenterden. The White Mill is an ancient monument, and the church is large and restored, with a spire. It is mainly good thirteenth century, with nave, and piers of Bethersden marble, a Norman font of black marble, a panel of thirteenth-century glass of the death of the Virgin, and a fine Royal Arms dated 1773.

Woodnesborough 15. A straggle on a hilltop near Sandwich. The Trans-Norman church has been much restored. It has an attractive eighteenth-century top to its tower, the ogee cupola of east Kent and a balustrade.

Wootton 14. A remote place in a chalky, flinty, valley with beeches and yews between Dover and Canterbury. The small church, in a well-planted churchyard, is thirteenth-century. It has an old kingpost roof, and an attractive interior.

Wormshill 13. (Some authorities claim "Wodin's Hill".) A secret village on the Downs south of Sittingbourne, near the middle of the county and quite lonely. It is reached through deep lanes fringed with hawthorn and beech. There is a fine brick manor house and a church which is simple inside, in spite of restoration in 1789 and 1901. An early sixteenth-century pulpit and an old timber porch. Good fifteenth-century glass.

WOODNESBOROUGH

Worth 15, above the site of a Roman temple, is a bare but not unattractive village on the edge of the East Kent coalfields, in a loop off the coast road from Deal to Sandwich. The large parish stretches down over the low expanse of the Lydden valley to the sea and the Royal Cinque Ports Golf Links. There is a much re-built church with traces of a Trans-Norman origin, and a scatter of dormitory bungalows. It has been pleasingly whitewashed inside, and has massive arcades, and a few features of interest, including an Elizabethan wall tablet with kneelers.

Wouldham 3. A sad-looking industrial village mainly of nineteenth-century working men's cottages along the east bank of the industrial Medway. It boomed with the cement industry of the 1870s, and declined with the slump of the early 1920s. The scars remain. The grey little church has in the churchyard the tomb of Walter Burke, the purser of H.M.S. *Victory*, in whose arms Nelson died at Trafalgar. Children from the village school lay flowers on the grave each Trafalgar Day. All about are chalk pits and marshes, and a farm to the north has a ruin of indeterminate period called Starkey Castle.

Wrotham ("Root-em") 5. The village is the comparatively still centre of a whirlpool of main roads, of which the greatest is the A2, climbing up to the top of the North Downs, 130 feet high, where cars stop at Wrotham Corner for the most famous vista of the county. The village has a delightful little square, with a church high on one side of it and the red-brick manor house below it on the other. Other houses and shops are handsome and dignified, and there are chestnut trees beside the roads. The church is spacious, with old tiles on the floor, good eighteenth-century monuments on the walls and a hideous Victorian pulpit. Also a thirteenth-century octagonal font, a fourteenth-century chancel screen, a stair turret and good brasses. Outside, under the tower, is a vaulted passage for a processional path round the church, like that at Brading in the Isle of Wight.

Wye 13. An attractive market town, with history, integrity, some good early façades of all periods in the old part near the church, and controlled and sometimes well-designed new buildings on the outskirts. It has beautiful views across the Stour valley to Eastwell Park and is both unspoilt and unselfconscious.

Wye was a royal manor in Saxon times, and after the Conquest belonged to Battle Abbey. Its church was rebuilt in 1447 by its great benefactor John Kempe, a native of the town who became Archbishop of Canterbury. His nave survives, but a new chancel, and the low tower which looks down the wide street in front of it were built, after the steeple had fallen down, in 1701. A good modern restoration was made in 1954, and the oak beams were renewed at that time. The interior is impressive with a high fourteenth-century nave and low eighteenth-century chancel, with reredos and panelling of that date. Collections of tablets and brasses.

Archbishop Kempe also founded a college. In 1892 this became Wye College, the Agricultural School of London University. The present buildings, on the original site to the east of the churchyard, have fifteenth-century traces, but are mainly nineteenth century, with some good contemporary additions. The hall of residence is Withersdene Hall, half a mile to the east, with gardens,

The Pilgrims' Way near WROTHAM

interesting to specialists, which are sometimes open.

To the north is another large estate, that of Olantigh Towers (pronounced "Ollan-ty"). This is an eighteenth-century building on the site of the original home of Archbishop Kempe. Wye was the birthplace in 1640 of the novelist, dramatist and Restoration Mata Hari, Aphra Behn.

Yalding 6 is on the River Beult, where it and the Teise join the navigable Medway. It is the largest hop-growing parish in Kent, and altogether charming. It is much visited,

particularly at week-ends. But exuberance centres round the car park, at a meadow on the river called Yalding Lees, and the village itself remains remarkably unspoilt by crowds. The narrow bridge over the river is fifteenth century, except for the centre span, and the thirteenth-century church tower stands beside it, amongst some cheerful Georgian houses. The whole view downhill to this, from the top of the High Street, is exceptional, with eighteenth-century and earlier façades and roofs making a natural but unplanned entity, and one or two modern houses

conforming in spirit although contemporary in design. A tile-hung building behind the war memorial is called Cleaves. It was originally a free-school, established in 1665. One of its more recent headmasters was the father of the poet Edmund Blunden, himself much influenced by Yalding and its surroundings. This is a Medway village at its best. The church is pleasant inside, but has few notable features. The best is an early seventeenth-century wall monument with two figures kneeling at a *prie-dieu*.

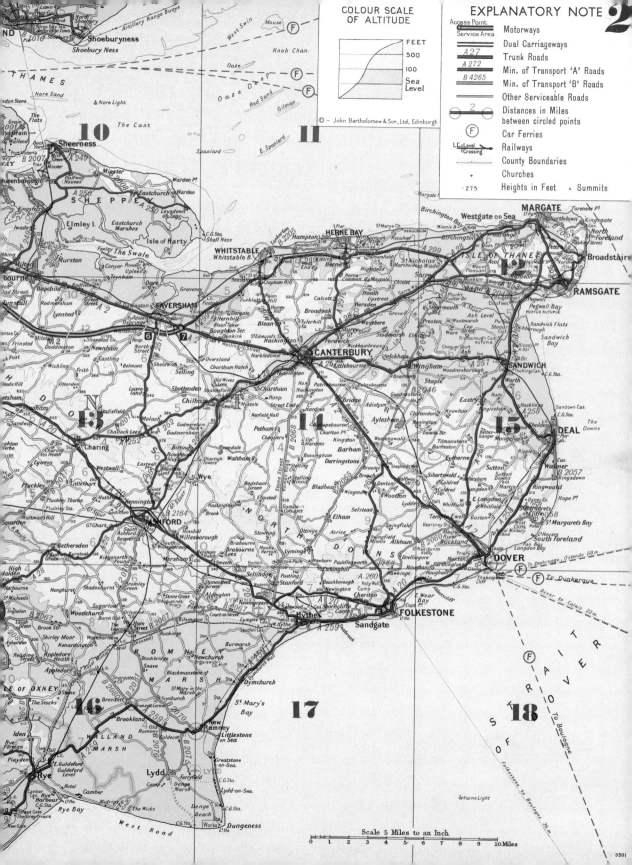

Nineteenth-century churches and restorations

A preliminary list by the Rev. B. F. L. Clarke

r = restoration
reb = a new church, or rebuilding of an old one.

Acol W. L. Sear of Margate 1869
Acrise r A. R. Barker
Adisham r W. White 1870
Aldington r A. W. Blomfield 1875–6
Allington r H. Bensted 1898
Ash (Sandwich) r W. Butterfield 1847–64
Ashford aisles reb 1827, J. Cooper of Canterbury r J. Clarke 1858, nave extended 1860
South Ashford H. G. Austin 1867
Ashurst r B. Ferrey 1861, reredos H. Curzon 1865
Bapchild r E. Christian 1872
Barfreston r R. C. Hussey 1840
Barham tower and spire reb J. Lancefield 1851
Beckenham St George reb W. Gibbs Bartleet 1887–8, finished 1903
   St Barnabas, Alex. R. Stenning and Henry Hall 1878, chancel 1885
   Christchurch, Blashill and Haywood 1876
   Holy Trinity, S. W. Daukes and E. F. C. Clarke 1877, tower 1883
   St James, Elmers End, E. H. Stenning 1884
   St Mary, Shortlands, J. Whichcord jun. 1868 (bombed and reb)
   St Michael, W. H. Hobday 1899
   St Paul, S. W. Daukes 1864
Bekesbourne r W. G. Habershon 1882
Belvedere W. G. Habershon 1861
Benenden r D. Brandon 1861
Betteshanger reb A. Salvin
Bexley r B. Champneys 1882–3
   St John, W. R. Low 1882
Bexley Heath Wm. Knight of Nottingham 1879
Bickley F. Barnes 1864, tower and spire Ernest Newton
Bicknor mostly reb G. F. Bodley 1861
Bidborough r E. Christian 1876–7
Biddenden r J. Clarke 1857
Bilsington r J. Clarke 1882
Birchington r C. N. Beazley 1864–5
Birling Christchurch, H. P. Monkton 1892
Bishopsbourne r G. G. Scott 1871
Borstall C. L. Luck 1878, chancel H. Margetts 1905

Boughton Monchelsea reb (after fire in 1834) Thomas Joy r 1874
Boughton under Blean r J. P. St Aubyn 1871
   St Barnabas, W. M. Fawcett 1896
Boxley r E. Christian 1875
Brabourne r G. G. Scott
Brasted reb A. Waterhouse 1880
Brenchley r J. Clarke 1849
Brents C. Kirk and Son 1881
Broadstairs David Barnes 1828–30 reb J. R. Moore-Smith & H. Colbeck 1929–30
Bromley Holy Trinity, Thomas Hopper 1843
   St John, G. Truefitt 1879
   St Luke, A. Cawston 1886
   St Mark, E. Hellicar 1895
Brompton St Mark, J. P. St Aubyn
Broomfield r G. M. Hills 1879
Buckland r F. R. Wilson 1851, W. Butterfield 1880
Burham E. W. Stephens 1881
Canterbury St Alphege r Carpenter and Ingelow 1888
   St Gregory, G. G. Scott 1852
   Holy Cross r E. P. L. Brock 1895
   St Margaret r G. G. Scott 1850
   St Mildred r W. Butterfield 1861
   St Paul r G. G. Scott 1856
Charing r J. P. St Aubyn 1878
Charlton J. Brooks 1892
Chart, Great r Reginald Blomfield 1894
Chart Sutton (reb Henry Holland jun. 1780–1), altered James Wood and Son 1896–8
Chartham r G. E. Street 1875
Chatham St Mary reb A. W. Blomfield 1896–7 and later Christchurch Inwood & George 1842, new church E. R. Robson 1884
   St John, R. Smirke 1821–2, altered G. M. Hills 1869
   St Paul, A. D. Gough 1853–4
Chelsfield r E. Nash 1857
Cheriton All Souls, E. Christian 1894
Chevening r 1855 and W. D. Caröe 1890–1
Chiddingstone r G. E. Street 1870
   St Luke, J. F. Bentley 1898
Chillenden r G. G. Scott 1871
Chislehurst r B. Ferrey 1849, G. E. Street 1857, Bodley & Garner 1897
   Annunciation, J. Brooks 1870
   Christchurch, Habershon & Pike 1872

Chislet Marsh Side, J. Clarke 1879
Cliffe at Hoo r J. P. St Aubyn 1857, Romaine Walker & Tanner 1884–5
Cobham r G. G. Scott 1860
Coldred r E. P. L. Brock 1890
Collier Street P. C. Hardwick 1848
Cranbrook r W. Slater and E. Christian (chancel) 1863
Cray St Mary, E. Nash 1861–2
[North] Cray reb E. Nash 1851
Crayford r J. Clarke 1861
Crocken Hill E. Nash 1851
Crundale r E. P. L. Brock 1894
Cudham r E. Christian 1891–2
Darenth r W. Burges 1867
Dartford r A. W. Blomfield 1862
Deal St Andrew, Ambrose Poynter 1848–50, aisles and chancel W. White 1867
Dover St Mary reb J. C. Buckler 1843–4
   St Mary in Castro r G. G. Scott 1860–2 and W. Butterfield 1882
   Holy Trinity, W. M. Edmunds 1833–5
   St James, T. T. Bury 1867
Downe r J. Clarke 1872
Dunkirk J. Whichcord 1840
Dunton Green T. Potter of Sevenoaks 1889
Ebony reb S. S. Teulon 1858
Egerton r J. Clarke 1854
Elham r W. Slater 1857 and F. C. Eden
Elmley reb G. E. Street 1853
Erith r W. G. Habershon 1877
   Christchurch, J. P. St Aubyn 1870–1
Ewell, Temple r T. T. Bury 1874
Eythorne r J. P. Seddon 1875
Farleigh, East N aisle 1835 r J. L. Pearson 1891
Farleigh, West r E. Christian 1875
Farningham r E. Christian 1871
Faversham (nave reconstucted George Dance 1754, tower and spire C. Beazley 1799) r G. G. Scott 1853, 1874
Folkestone SS Mary and Eanswyth r R. C. Hussey 1856f
   Christchurch, S. Smirke 1850
   Holy Trinity, E. Christian 1869
   St John Baptist, Rowland Barker 1879, completed 1895
   St Saviour, Somers Clarke & Micklethwaite 1892
   St Peter, R. C. Hussey 1855, enlarged S. S. Stallwood 1870

Fordcombe 1847, altered E. J. Tarver 1883

Four Elms E. T. Hall 1877 (superintended 'from the foundation to the spire' by the Rev Adolphus Klamborowski)

Frindsbury *r* J. L. Pearson 1883

Frinstead *r* G. G. Scott 1870*f*

Frittenden *reb* R. C. Hussey 1847–8

Gillingham *r* A. W. Blomfield 1869
St Barnabas, J. E. K. & J. P. Cutts 1890

Godmersham *r* W. Butterfield 1864

Goodnestone *r* R. C. Hussey 1841

Goudhurst *r* Slater & Carpenter 1868

Gravesend St James, S. W. Daukes 1851
St Luke, W. B. Smith 1889
Milton Christchurch, R. C. Carpenter, completed W. Slater 1854–6, rebuilt 1930–2
Holy Trinity, J. Wilson 1844–5

Greenhithe J. Johnson & G. J. Vulliamy 1855–6

Halden, High *r* G. E. Street 1868

Halling *r* H. Bensted 1887–8

Halstead W. M. Teulon 1880

Halstow, High *r* E. Christian 1887

Ham *r* J. Clarke 1880

Harbledown St Michael, J. P. St Aubyn 1881

Hardres, Upper *r* E. P. L. Brock 1895
Lower *reb* T. Rickman 1832

Hartley *r* J. P. St Aubyn 1860–3

Hartlip *r* R. C. Hussey 1865

Hawkhurst *r* R. C. Carpenter 1853
All Saints, G. G. Scott 1861

Hawkinge *r* J. Clarke 1875

Hayes *r* G. G. Scott & J. O. Scott 1861–2

Headcorn *r* J. Clarke 1855*f*, G. M. Hills 1878

Herne *r* J. H. Hakewill 1850, W. F. Dawson (chancel) 1869, F. Butler (N aisle roof) 1891. reredos Goldie & Child

Herne Bay Christchurch 1841, altered T. Blashill 1876, chancel George & Vaughan 1868
St John, R. P. Day 1897, chancel W. James 1902

Hernhill *r* Newman & Billing 1877–8

Higham St John, E. A. Stephens 1862

Hillborough *reb* J. Clarke 1879

Hoath *r* J. Clarke 1866

Hollingbourne *r* G. G. Scott jun. 1876

Hoo St Mary *r* E. A. Stephens 1882

Horsmonden *r* W. M. Teulon (design is R. A. 1855), T. H. Wyatt 1868
Chapel of Ease, R. Wheeler 1869

Horton Kirby *tower reb* George Smith 1816–17 *r* E. Christian 1863

Hunton *r* E. Christian 1876

Hythe *r* G. E. Street 1876 J. L. Pearson 1886

Ide Hill C. H. Cooke 1865

Ivychurch *r* A. W. Blomfield 1889

Kemsing *r* T. G. Jackson 1870 and 1873, later work J. N. Comper

Kenardington *r* J. P. Seddon 1879

Keston *r* H. Blackwell 1880

Kilndown A. Salvin 1841, altered later first by Roos then R. C. Carpenter (screen, etc.), W. Butterfield (lectern), W. Slater (reredos) etc.

Kingsdown *reb* E. W. Pugin 1865

Knockholt 'thoroughly repaired' Samuel Green 1834

Lamborbey E. Christian 1879

Langdon, East *r* E. P. L. Brock 1892

Langley *reb* W. Butterfield 1855

Langton Green G. G. Scott 1863–4

Leigh *r* G. Devey 1862

Leysdown *reb* R. Wheeler 1874

Lydd *r* J. O. Scott 1887

Lympne *r* J. P. St Aubyn 1878–80

Maidstone All Saints *r* R. C. Carpenter 1850–2, J. L. Pearson 1884*f*
St Peter *r* J Whichcord 1837
Holy Trinity, J. Whichcord 1826–8
St Faith, E. W. Stephens 1871–2, tower finished 1880–1
St James H. Bensted 1869
St Luke, W. H. Seth-Smith 1896–7
St Michael, A. W. Blomfield 1876
St Philip, J. Whichcord 1858

Malling, West (*reb* George Gwilt 1780–2) *reb* J. T. Micklethwaite 1901

Manston W. E. Smith

Margate All Saints, Thomas Andrews 1893–4, tower completed W. D. Caröe 1908
St Paul, R. K. Blessley 1873
St Mary, Northdown, T. Andrews 1893

Markbeech D. Brandon 1852

Matfield Green B. Champneys 1875

Mersham *r* J. P. St Aubyn 1878

Milstead *r* W. Butterfield 1872

Milton (Canterbury) *r* W. L. Grant 1890

Minster (Thanet) *r* Smith & Son of Ramsgate 1863

Minster (Sheppey) *r* E. Christian 1879–81

Mongeham *r* W. Butterfield 1854

Monkton *r* C. N. Beazley 1861

Murston *reb* W. Burges 1873–4

Nettlestead *r* J. Clarke 1856

Newenden *r* G. M. Hills 1858

Newhythe Kendall & Pope 1854

Newington (near Hythe) *r* R. Wheeler 1870

Northbourne *r* J. F. Bentley 1865

Northfleet *r* Brandon & Ritchie 1850–2, E. W. Godwin (chancel) 1862

Offham *r* J. Clarke 1872

Ospringe *r* E. L. Blackburn 1866

Otford *r* G. E. Street 1862

Otham *r* R. Wheeler 1865

Patrixbourne *r* G. G. Scott 1851

Peckham, East *r* J. Clarke 1863
Holy Trinity J. Whichcord & Walker 1841, enlarged R. P. Day 1893

Peckham, West *r* T. F. W. Grant

Pemburg *r* R. Wheeler 1867–8
New Church, E. Christian 1847

Penshurst *r* G. G. Scott 1854–8

Perry Street J. Brooks 1870

Plaistow 1861, enlarged 1880 and 1900, Wadmore & Mallett

Platt J. Whichcord & Walker 1841

Plaxtol (1649) enlarged R. Pearsall 1893

Pluckley St Mary, C. L. Luck 1881

Preston (Faversham) *r* Austin, R. C. Hussey 1853–5, J. Clarke 1866, E. Christian

Preston (Wingham) *r* W. White 1856

Rainham *r* A. D. Gough 1866

Ramsgate Christchurch, G. G. Scott 1846–7
St George H. Helmsley, built under H. E. Kendall 1824–7
Holy Trinity Stevens & Alexander 1844

Ringwould *r* W. White

Ripple *reb* H. Ashpited 1861

River *reb* 1837 *r* Reeve of Folkestone 1872

Riverhead D. Burton 1831, chancel A. W. Blomfield 1882–3

Rochester St Bartholomew *r* G. G. Scott
St Margaret *reb* Samuel Sidden & Son 1824–5
St Nicholas *r* A. D. Gough 1861
St Peter E. Christian 1859

Rodmersham *r* Morris & Stallwood 1875–7

Rosherville H. E. Rose 1851–3

Rusthall H. I. Stevens 1850
St Peter in Thanet *r* J. Clarke 1859

Sandgate G. S. Repton 1822, rebuilt later

Sandhurst *r* R. H. Carpenter 1876

Sandwich St Clement *r* J. Clarke 1865
St Bartholomew G. G. Scott 1878, completed after his death

Seal Chart C. H. Howell 1867–8, enlarged F. W. Hunt 1887–8

Seasalter Old church converted into a chapel by Hezekiah Marshall of Canterbury
New church, Henry Jones 1844

Sevenoaks St Nicholas, surveyed Henry Rose 1810, Carr chosen as surveyor 1811, Sharp appointed 1812. Cockerell later employed as architect, work finished 1814. Clerestory and roof date from this time

St Mary, Kippington, J. M. Hooker 1878–80

St John, Morphew and Green 1850, N aisle E. Christian, chancel J. T. Lee

Sevenoaks Weald J. Carter 1820, chancel T. G. Jackson

Sheerness St Mary Dockyard Chapel, G. L. Taylor 1828, burned 1881 and *reb* C. E. Bernays

Holy Trinity, G. L. Taylor 1835–6

St Paul R. Wheeler 1872

Sheldwich *r* E. Christian and J. P. St Aubyn 1888

Shipbourne *reb* Mann & Saunders 1881

Shoreham *r* H. Woodyer 1864

Shorne *r* T. H. Wyatt 1875

Sibertswold *reb* B. Ferrey 1867

Sidcup St John, Wollaston 1844, *reb* G. H. Fellowes Prynne.

Christchurch, A. Rowland Barker 1887

Sittingbourne St Michael (burned 1762, new roof by George Dance) *r* R. H. Carpenter 1873

Holy Trinity R. C. Hussey 1867

Snargate *r* C. T. Whitley of Dover 1871

Snodland *r* A. W. Blomfield 1869–70

Speldhurst *reb* J. O. Scott 1870–1, tower 1879

Stalisfield *r* H. Bensted 1900

Stanford *reb* E. & W. H. Nash 1879

Stone *r* G. E. Street 1860–1

Stowting *r* R. C. Carpenter 1845, aisle W. Slater 1856

St Nicholas *reb* R. Smirke 1812

Strood St Mary, A. W. Blomfield 1868–9

Sundridge *r* G. E. Street 1850 and T. G. Jackson

Sutton *r* A. Ashpitel 1862

Sutton Valence *reb* William Ashendon 1828 *r* 1875 G. M. Hills

Swalcliffe *reb* R. Wheeler 1876

Swanley St Mary, D. Newman 1901–2

St Paul, E. Christian 1860

Swanscombe *r* J. M. Bignell 1873 and 1902

All Saints, Norman Shaw 1894

Tenterden *r* G. M. Hills

St Michael, G. M. Hills 1864

Thannington *r* W. Butterfield 1847, J. Cowell 1882

Tonbridge SS Peter & Paul *r* G. G. Scott 1858, E. Christian 1879

Tudeley *r* J. F. Wadmore & A. J. Baker 1885

Tunbridge Wells St Barnabas, J. E. K. & J. P. Cutts 1887

Christchurch, Robert Palmer Brown 1838

Holy Trinity, D. Burton 1827–9

St John, A. D. Gough 1857–8, enlarged 1870–1

St Peter, E. E. Cronk 1875

Hildenborough E. Christian 1843

Southborough St Peter, D. Burton 1830, altered E. Christian 1883

St Thomas, F. H. Pownall 1860

Tovil J. Whichcord 1839

Ulcombe *r* Slater & Carpenter 1864, completed 1872

Underriver G. G. Scott 1870

Upchurch *r* A. W. Blomfield 1876

Walmer St Mary, A. W. Bomfield 1888

St Saviour, J. Johnson 1848

Wateringbury *r* J. Whichcord 1824, J. Clarke 1856, W. O. Milne 1883–4

Westbere *r* E. P. L. Brock 1885

Westerham *r* S. S. Teulon 1852, T. E. C. Streatfeild 1882

Westgate St James, C. N. Beazley 1872–3

St Saviour, C. N. Beazley 1883–4

Westmarsh G. Russell French 1841

Westwell *r* E. Christian 1884

Whitstable *r* Charles Barry jun. 1875–6

Wickambreaux *r* R. Nevill 1876

East Wickham *r* G. P. G. Hills 1897

West Wickham *r* J. Whichcord, organ chamber J. D. Sedding 1890

Willesborough *r* J. L. Pearson 1868

Wilmington *r* W. Gibbs Bartleet 1881

Wingham *r* B. Ferrey 1874

Witchling *r* J. Clarke 1883

Wittersham *r* R. C. Carpenter

Wooton *r* R. J. Withers 1877

Wormshill *r* J. Clarke 1879–80

Wrotham *r* Newman & Billing

Yalding *r* M. Bulmer 1862

INDEX

173

Terry, Ellen, *see* Smallhythe

Thackeray, *see* p. 29 and Tunbridge Wells

Thames, *see* p. 10, Erith, Gravesend, Greenhithe, Herne Bay, Higham, Minster (in Sheppey) and Whitstable

Thanet, *see* pp. 10, 12 and Margate

Thomas, Edward, *see* Sevenoaksweald

Thorndike, Russell, *see* Dymchurch

Thornhurst, Sir Thomas, *see* Canterbury

Thurlow, Lord Chancellor, *see* Canterbury

Tilmanstone colliery, *see* Eythorne

Tonbridge School, *see* Tonbridge

Tovil, *see* Maidstone

Town Malling, *see* West Malling

Tradescent, John, *see* Meopham

Trafalgar Day, *see* Wouldham

Trevithick, R., *see* Dartford

Trinity House, *see* Deal, Shadoxhurst and Reculver

Trotwood, Betsy, *see* Broadstairs

Truefitt, G., *see* Bromley

Trust, National, *see* Chiddingstone, Cobham, Crockham Hill, Goudhurst, Ide Hill, Loose, Otham, West Peckham, Petts Wood, Plaxtol, Sevenoaks, Smallhythe, Sundridge, Sutton-at-Hone, Toys Hill, Trottiscliffe and Westerham

"Tudor Way", *see* Petts Wood

Tufton family, *see* Rainham

Tufton, Sir John, *see* Hothfield

Tunbridge Ware, *see* Tunbridge Wells

Tunbridge Wells, *see* p. 29

Turton, John, *see* Brasted

Twisden family, *see* East Malling

Twysden family, *see* East Peckham

Tyler, Wat, *see* p. 19, Bearsted, Dartford and Maidstone

Tyrwhitt-Drake, Sir Gerard, *see* Aylesford

Undercliffe, the, *see* Folkestone

Union Mill, *see* Cranbrook

Uphill, *see* Hawkinge

Upper Hardres, *see* p. 29

Upper Toes, *see* Bobbing

Upton, *see* Bexleyheath

Valenc, William de, *see* Sutton Valence

Vallance, Aymer, *see* Otham

Van Ghent, *see* Chatham

Vane, Sir Harry, *see* Plaxtol and Shipbourne

Victoria, Queen, *see* Broadstairs, Brook, Maidstone and Tunbridge Wells

Victory, H.M.S., *see* Wouldham

Viking Bay, *see* Broadstairs

Vikings, *see* p. 16

Virginians, The, see Tunbridge Wells

Vortigern, *see* Aylesford and Crayford

Waldershare, *see* Northbourne

Walker, Leonard, *see* Lydd

Waller, Sir Richard, *see* Groombridge

Walmer, *see* p. 25

Walmer Castle, *see* Hythe

Walpole, Horace, *see* Ickham, Linton, Mereworth, Sundridge and Tonbridge

Walpole, Sir Hugh, *see* Canterbury

Walter, Archbishop, *see* Canterbury

Wansum, River, *see* p. 12, Richborough Castle and St Nicholas-at-Wade

Warde family, *see* Westerham

Wardes, *see* Otham

Warham, Archbishop, *see* Canterbury and Sevenoaks

Warner, John, *see* Bromley

Warren, C. Henry, *see* Mereworth

Wars of the Roses, *see* Sandwich

Warwick, Earl of, *see* Sandwich

Wastell, John, *see* Canterbury

Water House, *see* Shoreham

Waterloo Tower, *see* Birchington

Watling Street, *see* pp. 14, 16, 29, Canterbury, Cobham, Crayford, Dartford, Faversham, Norton, Patrixbourne, Richborough Castle and Rochester

Watts Charity, *see* Rochester

Watts, Richard, *see* Rochester

Wayfield, *see* Walderslade

Weald, the, *see* pp. 10, 12, 16, 29, Chiddingstone, Cowden, Cranbrook, Crockham Hill, Goudhurst, Hawkhurst, High Halden, Horsmonden, Lamberhurst, Penge, Sandhurst, Sevenoaks, Staplehurst, Thurnham, Toys Hill, Tunbridge Wells and Ulcombe

Wealden clay, *see* Bethersden

Wealden Lake, *see* Maidstone

weatherboarding, *see* p. 29

Webb, Captain, *see* Dover

Webb, Philip, *see* Bexleyheath

Weekes, *see* Canterbury

Weldon, Sir Ralph, *see* Swanscombe

Welles, John, *see* Sutton Valance

Wellington, Duke of, *see* Walmer

Wells, H. G., *see* p. 29, Hythe, Postling and Sandgate

Westbrook, *see* Lydd

West Cliffe, *see* St Margaret's at Cliffe

Westenhanger, *see* Stanford

West Farleigh, *see* Teston

Westgate-on-Sea, *see* Margate

Westlake, *see* Birchington

Westminster Abbey, *see* Penshurst, Stone and Trottiscliffe

Westmorland, Earl of, *see* Mereworth

Westward Ho!, see Upchurch

Westwell, *see* p. 29

Wetherill, John, *see* Tunbridge Wells

Whatman, James, *see* Boxley

Wheeler, R., *see* Horsmonden

Wheler, Rev Granville, *see* Otterden

Whichcord, J., *see* East Peckham

Whichcord and Walker, *see* Platt

White Hart, the, *see* Brasted

White Mill, the, *see* Woodchurch

Whittington, Dick, *see* Sevenoaks

Wickham Court, *see* West Wickham

Wight, Isle of, *see* Brook

Wigmore, *see* Rainham

Wilberforce, William, *see* Teston

Wildernesse, The, *see* Seal

Wilds, Aman Henry, *see* Tunbridge Wells

Willement, Thomas, *see* Faversham and Kilndown

William I, *see* p. 16, Canterbury and Rochester

William II, *see* Tonbridge

William III, *see* Birchington

William IV, *see* Penge

William of Perth, *see* Rochester

William the Englishman, *see* Canterbury

William of Sens, *see* Canterbury

Winchelsea, Archbishop, *see* Otford

Withersdene Hall, *see* Wye

Woden's Field, *see* p. 16 and Wormshill

Wolfe, General, *see* Westerham

Wolsey, Cardinal, *see* Belvedere and Lydd

Woodchurch, *see* p. 29

Wootton, *see* Denton

Wotton family, *see* Boughton Malherbe

Wotton, Dean Nicholas, *see* Canterbury

Wren, *see* Groombridge

Wyatt, James, *see* Cobham and Ickham

Wyatt, Sir Thomas, *see* p. 19, Allington, Cooling and Maidstone

Wye, *see* p. 16

Wye College, *see* Wye

Wye Valley, *see* p. 10

Wye's crown, *see* Brook

Yalding Lees, *see* Yalding

Yantlet Creek, *see* Grain

Yardhurst, *see* Great Chart

Yevele, Henry, *see* Canterbury

York, Duke of, *see* Tunbridge Wells

Yotes Court, *see* West Peckham